The ATOMIC BOMB

The ATOMIC BOMB

Voices from HIROSHIMA and NAGASAKI

Editors: Kyoko & Mark Selden

An East Gate Book

M. E. Sharpe, Inc.
Armonk, New York
London, England

An East Gate Book

Available in the United Kingdom and Europe from M. E. Sharpe, Publishers, 3 Henrietta Street, London WC2E 8LU.

Library of Congress Cataloging-in-Publication Data

The Atomic bomb : voices from Hiroshima and Nagasaki / editors, Kyoko and Mark Selden.
      p.   cm.
  ISBN 0-87332-556-7
   1. Hiroshima-shi (Japan)—History—Bombardment, 1945.
  2. Nagasaki-shi (Japan)—History—Bombardment, 1945. 3. Atomic bomb victims—Japan. 4. World War, 1939–1945—Personal narratives, Japanese. 5. Atomic bomb—Blast effect—Literary collections. 6. Japanese literature—20th century—Translations into English. 7. English literature—Translations from Japanese. I. Selden, Kyoko. II. Selden, Mark
  D767.25.H6A87   1989
  940.54′25—dc20   89-36635
                                                CIP

Printed in the United States of America

BB 10 9 8 7 6 5 4 3 2 1

CONTENTS

Photo Essay

Citizens' Memoirs

Pictures by Atomic Bomb Survivors

Children's Voices

FOREWORD

Robert Jay Lifton

During a recent, early fall visit to Hiroshima, I walked through the Peace Park and found it to be a very gentle place. Couples strolled leisurely, young mothers and fathers pushed baby carriages, children ran about, and there was much feeding of pigeons. To be sure, some people stopped at the Cenotaph to leave flowers and pray, and one had only to enter the Atomic Bomb Museum to be jarred into grotesque nuclear truth. But in the park itself, there was indeed peace, and the atmosphere could be said to have been pastoral, even bucolic.

While experiencing, like others, the pleasantness of the scene, I felt myself to be a bit troubled by it. Was *that* the way to memorialize the atomic bomb and its victims? The problem is that the atomic bomb defies memorialization. There is no adequate way of representing an event of that magnitude to future generations. Perhaps the Peace Park, including the museum and its many monuments, does so as well as could be expected.

The world is insufficiently aware of the terrible value of Hiroshima and Nagasaki. As the two cities in which atomic weapons have been used on human populations, they alone can convey to us certain human truths. These truths serve us well, even though we are aware of how ''tiny'' the explosive power of the weapon used on each city is in comparison to our present nuclear stockpiles. And that value is well captured in this volume, focusing as it does on specific, individual voices from both cities.

I have made it a principle to refer to such voices whenever I write or speak about nuclear threat. I do so precisely because they are ignored by the overwhelming body of discourse on the subject. That discourse tends to focus on "scenarios" of nuclear attack and response, on "nuclear exchanges," on "throw-weights" of particular missiles, on "hard-target kill capability." The discourse, that is, is almost exclusively about *weapons*. That is true even when all is subsumed to the ostensibly peaceful goals of "deterrence." And the seemingly innocuous phrase "should deterrence fail" is usually put forward to represent—that is, cover over—the virtually unimaginable human suffering that would result from the use of the weaponry.

That suffering, in nuance and complexity, is expressed by the voices in this book. Although I have read hundreds of accounts of the experience and many short stories, novels, and poems, the voices in this book moved me profoundly and greatly expanded my knowledge of those two dreadful events. To really listen to them—to absorb them in ways that deeply affect one's view of the world and actions in it—is the beginning of nuclear wisdom.

ACKNOWLEDGMENTS

John Dower, Hayashi Kyoko, Richard Minear, and Tsukui Nobuko shared their extensive knowledge of the atomic bomb and its literature and art. Bill and Nancy Doub, Rebecca Jennison, Victor Koschmann, and especially Brett de Bary and Sato Hiroaki helped to improve the translations. Helen Redding and staff members of the Peace Resource Collection at Wilmington College introduced us to important works in the atomic bomb literature. Herbert Bix, Noam Chomsky, John Dower, Edward Friedman, Terence Hopkins, Akira Iriye, and Michael Klare provided perceptive comments and suggestions on drafts of the introduction.

Doug Merwin skillfully guided and encouraged this project from its inception. We thank Anita O'Brien for professional editing of the manuscript, Sonja Godfried for cover and graphic design, and Domon Ken for providing the dust jacket photograph.

We have followed East Asian practice in writing surnames first.

INTRODUCTION:
THE UNITED STATES, JAPAN, AND THE ATOMIC BOMB

MARK SELDEN

Two events associated with World War II in the Pacific virtually obliterated the distinction between combatant and noncombatant, that fragile distinction at the heart of international efforts of the last five centuries to regulate the conduct of war and restrict human and environmental destruction. These were:

• The Japanese onslaught against the peoples of China and Southeast Asia as exemplified by the bombing of Shanghai, the rape of Nanking, and the attacks on civilians as in the "three-all policy" (burn all, kill all, destroy all) directed against rural North China.

• The use of air strikes by the major powers to terrorize and destroy cities and their populations, notably in the firebombing of European and Japanese cities and the United States' atomic bombing of Hiroshima and Nagasaki.

The common element linking these events, directing the awesome technological might of modern war against combatant and noncombatant alike, denied the humanity of enemy populations and legitimated their wholesale annihilation.

This essay reflects on the implications of the firebombing and nuclear bombing of Japan with an eye toward assessing their significance for war and peace in our times. It considers the historical context and weighs the human cost of U.S. destruction of Japanese cities and the wholesale killing of noncombatants in the context of the international conflicts of the era. It seeks to bridge the gulf separating studies of global strategy and international conflict on the one hand, and those that chronicle the travail of the victims of war on the other. In particular, it presents a view from inside the inferno as a means of illuminating the significance of the first, and thus far only, nuclear war in an era of total war in which the capacity to annihilate whole populations is extended to the capacity to terminate human life on planet earth.

Fire Bombs, Atomic Bombs, and the Road to Total War

The Allied bombing of Dresden, an undefended city with no significant war industry, remains the single best known and most widely condemned example of firebombing and the deliberate annihilation of civilian populations in the history of war. Dresden carried to its inexorable conclusion the escalation of urban bombing by both sides in Europe. Dresden also marked the transition in air strategy from precision bombing to area bombing, that is, from striking at strategic targets to the deliberate destruction of cities and killing of their residents. On February 13, 1945, 1,400 British aircraft followed by 1,350 U.S. bombers destroyed Dresden and unleashed a fire storm visible 200 miles away. The American writer Kurt Vonnegut, then a young POW, recalled: "They burnt the whole damn town down. . . . Every day we walked into the city and dug into basements and shelters to get the corpses out, as a sanitary measure. When we went into them, a typical shelter, an ordinary basement usually, looked like a streetcar full of people who'd simultaneously had heart failure. Just people sitting there in their chairs, all dead." The destruction of Dresden, killing 35,000 Germans, was the prelude to the wave of American B-29 firebomb and napalm attacks that sowed destruction across virtually every major Japanese city and exacted a heavy toll in human life in the spring and summer of 1945.

The Firebombing of Japan

U.S. Air Force planners first explored the possibilities and techniques of firebombing the densely populated cities of a prospective

Japanese enemy at the suggestion of General Jimmy Doolittle in the 1930s. Even before Pearl Harbor, General George Marshall contemplated "general incendiary attacks to burn up the wood and paper structures of the densely populated Japanese cities." Throughout most of World War II, however, U.S. Army Air Force doctrine, if not always its practice, emphasized strategic bombing of military targets as the most efficient road to victory.

In late 1944, the failure of strategic bombing attacks to incapacitate Japanese industry (much of it earlier dispersed to small workshops) or to force surrender led to the appointment of General Curtis LeMay as commander of the 21st Air Force Headquarters. LeMay pioneered and promoted the firebombing and napalming of defenseless populations, first in the cities of Japan and in subsequent decades in city and countryside in Korea and Vietnam. The blunt-speaking LeMay, for thirty years the most visible spokesman for the strategy of setting cities to the torch, was but a link in a chain of command that sanctioned terror bombing extending upward through the Joint Chiefs of Staff to the president.

On February 25, 1945, two weeks after firebombing Dresden, U.S. bombers in a "test raid" destroyed a one-square-mile area of snow-covered Tokyo. Robert Guillain, a French journalist in Tokyo, described the raid:

> Falling endlessly in the absolutely still afternoon air, the flakes smothered the throbbing of the B–29s in a plume of white, muffling the shrouded whine of the bombs. Suddenly, the slowly descending snow was lit up by a mysterious inner light—huge, invisible fires that I judged to be near my neighborhood. The half-light veiling the city gradually took on a luminous yellow tint shot with a wondrous pink gold that pulsated weirdly, fading slowly, then flaring anew. At last, in the total silence that returned at the end of the day, everything bathed in a final raspberry-colored glow that flickered and dwindled, disappearing in the snow-filled air behind a curtain of bluish twilight.

The full fury of U.S. firebombing was unleashed on Tokyo on the night of March 9–10, 1945. Abandoning high altitude daylight raids, LeMay sent 334 B–29s flying low over Tokyo from bases in Guam, Saipan, and Tinian. Their mission: to reduce the city to rubble with jellied gasoline and napalm. Whipped by fierce winds, the flames leaped across Tokyo like wildfire, generating firestorms so turbulent that the giant superfortresses were tossed hundreds of feet in the air and then sucked groundward.

In contrast with Vonnegut's cool "wax museum" recollection and Guillain's lyrical description, accounts from inside the inferno that engulfed Tokyo chronicle scenes of utter carnage. Police cameraman Ishikawa Koyo described the streets of Tokyo as "rivers of fire. Everywhere one could see flaming pieces of furniture exploding in the heat, while the people themselves blazed like matchsticks" as their wood and paper homes exploded in flames. "Under the wind and the gigantic breath of the fire, immense incandescent vortices rose in a number of places, swirling, flattening, sucking whole blocks of houses into their maelstrom of fire." Dr. Kubota Shigenori, head of a military rescue unit, recalled that "In the black Sumida River countless bodies were floating, clothed bodies, naked bodies, all as black as charcoal. It was unreal. These were dead people, but you couldn't tell whether they were men or women. You couldn't even tell if the objects floating by were arms and legs or pieces of burnt wood."

Fleeing the flames, thousands plunged in desperation into the freezing waters of rivers, canals, and Tokyo Bay:

> A woman spent the night knee-deep in the bay, holding onto a piling with her three-year-old son clinging to her back; by morning several of the people around her were dead of burns, shock, fatigue and hypothermia. Thousands submerged themselves in stagnant, foul-smelling canals with their mouths just above the surface, but many died from smoke inhalation, anoxia, or carbon monoxide poisoning, or were boiled to death when the fire storm heated the water. Others, huddling in canals connected to the Sumida River, drowned when the tide came in. In the Hongo and Asakusa districts people jammed onto steel bridges. As the metal became unbearably hot, those who clung to the rails started to let go, falling off in waves and were carried away by the waters below. Huge crowds lined the gardens and parks

along the Sumida, and as the masses behind them pushed toward the river, walls of screaming people fell in and vanished.

Father Flaujac, a French cleric, compared the firebombing to the Tokyo earthquake twenty-two years earlier:

> In September 1923, during the great earthquake, I saw Tokyo burning for 5 days. I saw in Honjo a heap of 33,000 corpses of people who burned or suffocated at the beginning of the bombardment. . . . After the first quake there were 20-odd centers of fire, enough to destroy the capital. How could the conflagration be stopped when incendiary bombs in the dozens of thousands now dropped over the four corners of the district and with Japanese houses which are only match boxes? . . . In 1923 the fire spread on the ground. At the time of the bombings the fire fell from the sky. Where could one take refuge? In the shelters where I was sure to suffocate? Where could one fly? The fire was everywhere. It was impossible to find refuge in such a furnace, and besides, an order was given to stay and put out the fires. Yes, an inferno was created by the war and the wind made it even more wicked.

Nature reinforced man's handiwork in the form of *akakaze*, the red wind which swept with hurricane force across the Tokyo plain.

The U.S. Strategic Bombing Survey provided a technical description of the firestorm and its effects on the city:

> The chief characteristic of the conflagration . . . was the presence of a fire front, an extended wall of fire moving to leeward, preceded by a mass of pre-heated, turbid, burning vapors. The pillar was in a much more turbulent state than that of [a usual] fire storm, and being usually closer to the ground, it produced more flame and heat, and less smoke. . . . The 28-mile-per-hour wind, measured a mile from the fire, increased to an estimated 55 miles at the perimeter, and probably more within. An extended fire swept over 15 square miles in 6 hours. . . . The area of the fire was nearly 100 percent burned; no structure or its contents escaped damage.

The survey concluded—plausibly, but only for events prior to the summer of 1945—that "probably more persons lost their lives by fire at Tokyo in a 6-hour period than at any time in the history of man." People died from extreme heat as the winds fanned temperatures to 1,000 degrees centigrade, from oxygen deficiency, from carbon monoxide asphyxiation, or from being trampled beneath the feet of stampeding crowds.

How many died that night in what flight commander General Thomas Power termed "the greatest single disaster incurred by any enemy in military history"? The Strategic Bombing Survey provided precise figures for what can only be the crudest estimates: in that single raid on Tokyo, 87,793 people died, 40,918 were injured, and 1,009,005 people lost their homes. Richard Rhodes, estimating the dead at more than 100,000 men, women, and children, suggests that probably a million more were injured and another million were left homeless. The Tokyo fire department estimated 97,000 killed and 125,000 wounded. In sum, vast areas of Tokyo lay in ruins, more than one million refugees fled, approximately 100,000 people died, and many more were injured.

Following the raid, General LeMay explained that he wanted Tokyo "burned down—wiped right off the map" to "shorten the war." Tokyo did burn, far beyond LeMay's hopes and expectations. But the war ground on. In the following months, U.S. firebombing destroyed substantial areas of virtually every important Japanese city, killing tens of thousands and driving many more to rural and mountain areas. By July 1945, in attacks involving 6,960 B–29 sorties and 41,592 tons of bombs, U.S. planes had bombed sixty of Japan's largest cities, driven eight million citizens from their communities, and destroyed millions of homes. LeMay's bombers were rapidly running out of targets to strike.*

In July 1945, U.S. planes blanketed Japanese cities with an "Appeal to the People." "As you know," it read, "America, which stands for humanity, does not wish to injure the innocent people, so

---

*In 1964 the Japanese government awarded General LeMay the First Class Order of the Rising Sun for his contribution to the postwar development of the Japanese Air Force.

you had better evacuate these cities.'' Half the leafleted cities were firebombed within days of the warning, bringing home to their residents the absolute impunity of U.S. bombers to counterattack by Japanese batteries and fighter planes. Despite the pounding of defenseless cities, the destruction of important industrial concentrations, and the virtual paralysis of Japanese air and naval forces, the war continued.

Throughout 1945, American planners deliberately spared Kyoto, the ancient imperial capital, and four other cities from firebombing. Hiroshima, Kokura, Niigata, and Nagasaki were reserved by the Atomic Bomb Target Selection Committee to display the awesome power of the atom to Japan and the world.

A few U.S. military men raised questions about the efficacy of the area bombing of Japanese cities in the spring and summer of 1945, but no significant discussion of the ethics or the political ramifications of civilian bombing took place either in policy councils or in the public domain. In routinizing the uses of air power for the extermination of urban populations, firebombing constituted the critical background to the atomic bombing of Hiroshima and Nagasaki. Despite fleeting discussions about demonstrating the power of the bomb at an uninhabited test site, discussions which took place largely outside the corridors of power, the road to the atomic bombing of Hiroshima and Nagasaki was essentially devoid of consideration of the ethical implications of its use.

The Atomic Bombing of Hiroshima and Nagasaki

With the successful atomic test at Los Alamos on July 16, 1945, and with Soviet troops scheduled to enter the war on August 15, the United States raced to deliver the final blow against Japan. At 8:15 a.m. on August 6, the *Enola Gay* dropped the first atomic bomb over Hiroshima, whose population of approximately 350,000 included 43,000 troops. President Truman's official release proclaimed, ''It is an atomic bomb. The force from which the sun draws its power has been loosed against those who brought war to the Far East.'' The *New York Daily News* headlined the story:

BARE SECRET WEAPON
'ATOM'
BOMB
JAPAN
Most Destructive
Force in Universe

The *New York Times* banner headline proclaimed:

FIRST ATOMIC BOMB DROPPED ON JAPAN;
MISSILE IS EQUAL TO 20,000 TONS OF TNT;
TRUMAN WARNS FOE OF 'RAIN OF RUIN'

Three days later, on August 9, a second atomic bomb was dropped on the 270,000 people of Nagasaki.

The uranium weapon known as Little Boy exploded 1,850 feet in the air above Hiroshima with a force estimated at the equivalent of 12.5 kilotons of TNT. The plutonium Fat Man exploded over Nagasaki with a force of 22 kilotons, equivalent to the power packed by 4,000 B–29s carrying conventional bombs. Physicist Shohno Naomi offers a precise description of the Hiroshima blast:

> At the moment of the explosion, a fireball with a temperature of several million degrees centigrade and an atmospheric pressure of several hundred thousand bars was formed at the burst point. The fireball rapidly expanded to a sphere with a maximum radius of about 230 meters, emitted particularly strong thermal rays until three seconds after the explosion, and continued to shine for about ten seconds. Because of the thermal rays, the temperature of the hypocenter is thought to have risen to 3,000–4,000 degrees centigrade— far higher than the temperature at which iron melts, 1,550 degrees centigrade.

The destructive power of the bomb was not restricted to its heat.

> The strong expansive power of the fireball produced what is known as a shock wave followed by a high-speed wind. . . . The pressure from the shock wave at Hiroshima was extremely destruc-

tive. . . . The wind velocity of the blast at the hypocenter was about 440 meters per second. . . .

Buildings were smashed to pieces and incinerated by the blast and thermal rays, and it was the great quantities of dust from the destroyed buildings, carried by the winds, that cast the city into pitch-darkness just after the bombing.

Atomic Holocaust:
The View From the Ground

"The hour was early, the morning still, warm and beautiful. Shimmering leaves, reflecting sunlight from a cloudless sky, made a pleasant contrast with shadows in my garden," Hachiya Michihiko, director of the Hiroshima Communications Hospital, recorded in his diary of the early morning of August 6.

A student clearing firebreaks recalled her teacher saying, "Oh, there's a B!" and, looking skyward, "felt a tremendous flash of lightning. In an instant we were blinded and everything was just a frenzy of delirium."

A female junior college student recalled the instant of the explosion. "I felt as though I had been struck on the back with something like a big hammer, and thrown into boiling oil. . . . I seem to have been blown a good way to the north, and I felt as though the directions were all changed around."

The force of the blast and the heat of the thermal flash tore away the clothing and peeled away the skin from many of the victims. A young sociologist described "a park nearby covered with dead bodies waiting to be cremated. . . . The most impressive thing I saw was some girls, very young girls, not only with their clothes torn off but with their skin peeled off as well. . . . My immediate thought was that this was like the hell I had always read about."

Hiroshima was in flames. A girl of five at the time of the bombing recalled: "Black smoke was billowing up and we could hear the sound of big things exploding. . . . Those dreadful streets. The fires were burning. There was a strange smell all over. Blue-green balls of fire were drifting around. I had a terrible lonely feeling that everybody else in the world was dead and only we were still alive."

A history professor looked down at the city from Hijiyama hill to find "that Hiroshima had disappeared . . . that experience looking down and finding nothing left of Hiroshima—was so shocking that I simply can't express what I felt. . . . Hiroshima didn't exist—that was mainly what I saw—Hiroshima just didn't exist."

Hiroaki Ichikawa, five years old, was trapped under his house but was able to wriggle free. Fleeing the city, at Hijiyama Bridge he saw "naked people with their burnt skin hanging from them like rags. We saw others covered with blood, being carried to safer places on trucks."

Twenty-year-old Shibayama Hiroshi entered Hiroshima on foot from his suburban workplace within hours of the bombing. Crossing the Kyobashi River he encountered a scene reminiscent of "a painting of hell."

> Floating there were scores of dead bodies, faces swollen to twice their normal size and trouser-encased legs stiff as logs. The upper half of one body was burned black and the lower half swollen and waterlogged. The sight chilled us to the bone. . . . It began to rain. Black stains spotted shirts. The multicolored smoke generated at the time of the blast had become a cloud of dirty brown and black hanging like a pall over the city. It was a demonic ceiling, a malediction.

Returning to the city the next day he encountered a sight he would never forget:

> a man, his face burned and his blue clothes in shreds, riding along apathetically with what looked like black wood fastened to his bicycle with coarse straw rope. As he approached, we saw that what we had taken for wood was a stiff, blackened corpse, probably the remains of a loved one. The man himself seemed crazed. All the inhabitants of Hiroshima appeared deranged.

Okabe Kosaku, a young soldier, entered Hiroshima on the afternoon following the bombing to find a burnt-out wasteland. "Burned into my memory is the sight of a young mother, probably in her twenties, a baby on her back and a three- or four-year-old child clasped tightly in her arms. Caught against a girder of the bridge, her body bobbed idly in the gentle current.'' Approaching Hiroshima station, he observed that

> Houses had been shattered and their inhabitants buried in a welter of tiles and plaster, their naked bodies covered in ashes. Here and there an arm or a leg protruded. Other bodies lay strewn about, their stomachs torn open and their entrails pouring into the ashes. . . . The expressions on the dead faces as they gazed emptily into space were more contorted and agonized than those of the fierce gate-guardian deities of Japanese temples.

Sato Kiyoko, a third grader, entered a darkened Hiroshima at night two weeks after the bombing in search of her mother. ''No life disturbed the dead streets,'' she later wrote.

> What was more frightening than anything else was the sight, in the moonlight, of the skeleton of a burned-out streetcar with its load of fire-blackened passengers. One corpse was still clinging to a strap. I could see trails of silvery phosphorus weaving all about, for all the world like the spirits of the dead in my storybooks.

Survivor accounts of the agony and destruction of terror bombing are among the most important and neglected documents of modern war and the nuclear era.

In both Hiroshima and Nagasaki, 50 percent of all those located within 1.2 kilometers (three-quarters of a mile) of the hypocenter died on the day of the explosion, and 80–100 percent of those exposed at this distance eventually died from wounds or radiation inflicted by the bomb. Within five months, the atomic bomb claimed the lives of 140,000 of Hiroshima's 350,000 people and 70,000 of 270,000 people in Nagasaki. Many more subsequently died from bomb-related injuries. In Nagasaki, the victims included more than 8,500 of the city's 12,000 Roman Catholics whose residences clustered near the great cathedral close to ground zero, and a high percentage of the city's 10,000 Korean workers, many of whom had been forcibly brought to Japan to work under virtual slave labor conditions.

On March 9–10, in the worst single firebombing disaster, 100,000 people, 10 percent of Tokyo's one million, died. In Hiroshima, 34 percent of those exposed to the bomb at 1–2 kilometers died within three months. A study conducted in Hiroshima one year after the bombing revealed that 118,661 people, or 37 percent of the civilian population of 320,613, were killed, 3,677 were missing, and 79,130 were injured.

Richard Rhodes plausibly estimates that within five years, Hiroshima's atomic bomb-related deaths numbered nearly 200,000 and Nagasaki's 74,000. No single attack in the annals of warfare exacted so heavy a cumulative toll in human lives as the atomic bombing of Hiroshima. Bomb-related deaths have continued at lower levels in subsequent years down to the present. Hundreds of thousands of others have suffered "death in life," in Robert Lifton's evocative phrase. The victims included not only those who felt the direct effects of blast and fire but tens of thousands of others, including fetuses in utero, who were exposed to residual radiation days after the bombing.

One measure of the destruction of the firebombing and atomic bombing is the comparison with U.S. wartime casualties. The U.S. Armed Forces lost 292,000 troops and very few civilians in all theaters during all of World War II, that is, a fraction of the noncombatants killed in the bombing of Japanese cities in the spring and summer of 1945.

Michael Sherry has reflected on the qualities that distinguished the Tokyo firebombing from the experience of the atomic bomb. Tokyo

> was a process of destruction, not a simple act. As the American bombers poured gasoline and chemicals into the inferno, the observer could see the destruction take place and watch the thing come alive, becoming some living, grotesque organism, ever changing in its shape, dimensions, colors and directions. . . . In Hiroshima and Nagasaki, most victims did not know what hit them, confronting personal extinction first; the survivors only later suffered the shock of communal annihilation as they crawled out of their wreckage and met the parade of the damned.

This unfathomable quality of the atomic experience, together with the vastly greater power unleashed, however puny by the megadeath standards of today, and the agonizing physical and emotional toll exacted in the course of subsequent decades, distinguish the atomic bombing from earlier forms of holocaust.

The Decision to Drop the Bomb

The atomic bombing of Japan, and indeed much of the firebombing that preceded it, were directed against a nation that was militarily defeated in all but name yet spurned surrender: isolated and without allies following the defeat of Germany; in full retreat across Asia and the Pacific; its cities and much of its industry in ruins or starved of raw materials; its civilian morale at low ebb; its navy and air force paralyzed; and its armies desperately short of food and supplies, though still largely intact. By spring 1945 Japan lacked the capacity to wage aggressive war beyond its borders against the U.S. and its allies. Soviet troop mobilization to attack Japan in Manchuria on August 15 increased the desperation of the situation. Nevertheless, the Japanese military had not lost its capacity to inflict substantial damage on forces invading the home islands. Halting and inconclusive efforts by Japanese leaders to negotiate acceptable surrender terms assuring the person of the emperor and the continuity of the imperial system through Soviet and Swiss mediation throughout 1945 came to nought. The war continued.

How are we to understand the U.S. decision to drop the atomic bomb? Four mutually reinforcing factors lay behind the action:
* wartime goals that required Japan's unconditional surrender;
* the belief, subtly reinforced by racist stereotypes, that the behavior of Japanese forces, from attacks on Chinese cities in 1937 through Pearl Harbor to the Bataan death march and the rape of Manila in 1945, nullified any humanitarian consideration for the Japanese people;
* the conviction that the atomic bomb would save the lives of numerous American soldiers by obviating a costly invasion of Japan which would otherwise be required to secure surrender;
* the leaders' commitment to establish American primacy and to

check Soviet advance at the outset of a postwar era that would be
shaped by Soviet-American conflict.

The Good War and Unconditional Surrender

"There never has been—there never can be—successful compro-
mise between good and evil. Only total victory can reward the
champions of tolerance, and decency, and faith," Franklin Roosevelt told the U.S. Congress one month after Pearl Harbor. From the
outset, U.S. leaders defined the war in manichean terms of unmiti-
gated good versus evil that required unconditional surrender, and
never questioned the legitimacy of the U.S. mission. In July 1945 at
Potsdam, Truman's decision to overrule suggestions by Secretary of
War Henry Stimson and Under Secretary of State Joseph Grew to
soften the unconditional surrender provisions precluded an armi-
stice prior to dropping the atomic bomb. "The bombs," Richard
Rhodes has observed, "were authorized not because [the Japanese]
refused to surrender but because they refused to surrender uncondi-
tionally."

The evidence suggests that had the United States softened the
language of unconditional surrender—indeed, had it employed the
very language that secured Japan's surrender *after* the Hiroshima
and Nagasaki bombings—surrender could probably have been
achieved without the atomic bomb or an invasion. The cruelest irony
lies in the fact that after dropping the bomb on Hiroshima and
Nagasaki, the United States did soften its unconditional surrender
provisions with respect to the emperor. Emperor Hirohito not only
retained his life, but he continued to occupy the throne for more than
forty years as U.S. occupying forces assured the existence of the
imperial system while transforming Japan into an "imperial democ-
racy."

Viewing the end of the war from the perspective of the responsibility of the Japanese leadership, the price of holding out to secure
guarantees for the person and institution of the emperor—the single
issue blocking surrender prior to dropping the bomb—was the loss
of more than 250,000 lives in Hiroshima and Nagasaki, the estimated 300,000 out of a total of 1.3 million Japanese prisoners who

never returned from detention in the Soviet Union and are presumed to have died, and 81,000 Japanese soldiers who died overseas after surrender but before they could be repatriated.

Japanese Atrocities

By 1945, U.S. officials had closely studied examples of Japanese treachery, brutality, and fanaticism which became staples of U.S. war propaganda: from the Nanking Massacre, when marauding Japanese troops killed several hundred thousand Chinese, to Pearl Harbor, when 3,000 U.S. military personnel (but few noncombatants) were killed, to the Bataan Death March, when thousands of American and Filipino prisoners died or were killed en route to a prison camp, to kamikaze suicide missions in 1944 and 1945. Many U.S. military and civilian leaders concluded from examples of such barbarous and fanatical behavior by the military that the Japanese people had forfeited all right to be treated like human beings. Air Force General Haywood Hansell recalled the "universal feeling" that Japanese were "subhuman." And Air Force Commanding General Henry Arnold believed that Japanese brutality and atrocities were so immoral as to justify American retribution from firebombs to the atomic bomb. Canadian Prime Minister MacKenzie King privately expressed relief that the bomb was dropped on an Asian people and not on "the white races of Europe." Most important, as John Dower has brilliantly shown, American leaders, who had carefully distinguished throughout the war between Nazi leaders and the German people, made no such distinction between Japan's leaders and the Japanese people. These judgments—with their racist overtones, embodied in four years of U.S. and Allied wartime propaganda presenting the Japanese as barbarous, subhuman creatures, madmen, and yellow vermin—precluded any morally grounded hesitation about dropping the bomb.

The conclusion that racist assumptions shaped patterns of U.S. bombing in Asia emerges out of comparison with bombing patterns in the European theatre. Noting the "agonized handwringing" by Allied leaders prior to bombing European cities and its absence in the Asian theatre, Michael Sherry concludes that "a different set of standards applied not only to the enemy population, but to conquered friendly people as well." This difference was similarly manifest in the decision to intern Japanese-Americans but not German-Americans for the duration of the war. In short, U.S. bombing of Japan exemplified "the lower value Americans put on Asian lives. . . ."

Several of the major participants in World War II developed self-justifying ideologies framed in significant part in racist comparisons. The centrality of racial, and racist, elements in these ideologies differed substantially, leading the Nazis, for example, to pursue a deliberate course of racial genocide culminating in the annihilation of six million European Jews. Precisely because the United States was hardly alone in acting on racist impulses in the Pacific War, it remains essential to understand the part played by constructed communal hatreds in countering moral misgivings about premeditated mass murder of entire populations, whether by gas chambers, poison gas, or air power.

In focusing on American firebombing and nuclear strikes, we do not minimize the savagery of the Japanese military and the imperial state in its conquest and rule of China and much of Northeast and Southeast Asia, nor their direct responsibility for the loss of more than 2.5 million Japanese military and civilian lives in World War II and, still less, the many more deaths inflicted on Asian victims of Japanese aggression. The Japanese army's rape of Nanking, the use of poison gas and bacteriological warfare against Chinese troops and civilians, and the savage repression of resistance movements in colonial and semicolonial areas from Korea to the Philippines to China were all elements integral to the subjugation of Asian peoples. Japan's aggressive war of conquest in China and Southeast Asia, like the U.S. air war against Japan, eradicated the distinction between combatant and noncombatant. Interestingly, Japanese racist ideology was more sharply honed toward the "inferior" peoples of Asia than toward the Western powers who constituted the major rivals for empire. In juxtaposing and comparing Japanese killing of noncombatants in colonial wars in Asia and U.S. firebombing and atomic bombing of Japan, our focus is on the indiscriminate killing in both instances.

The Ethics of the Bomb

American disregard for the distinction between the Japanese imperial-military state and the ruled civilian population, comprising predominantly women, children, and the elderly, and the deep confidence of American leaders in the justice of their own conduct and mission produced one of the great tragedies of the twentieth century in the final months of the war. This antinomy of high U.S. moral purpose and savagery is well brought out in the Truman diaries. In a private diary on the events leading up to the atomic bombing, discovered some years after his death, Truman underlined the distinction between strategic and civilian targets, but in a most curious fashion:

> I have told the Sec. of War, Mr. Stimson, to use it so that military objectives and soldiers and sailors are the target and not women and children. Even if the Japs are savages, ruthless, merciless and fanatic, we as the leader of the world for the common welfare cannot drop this terrible bomb on the old capital or the new.

On Stimson's prompting, Truman spared the ancient capital of Kyoto. But U.S. firebombing had long since destroyed the new capital of Tokyo and sixty other Japanese cities. And it was precisely the women and children of Hiroshima and Nagasaki who bore the brunt of atomic attack.

For U.S. policymakers, the destruction of most Japanese cities and the extermination of large numbers of their residents in the spring and summer of 1945 eased the transition to nuclear holocaust by removing moral constraints against noncombatant bombing. "We scorched and boiled and baked to death more people in Tokyo on that night of March 9–10 than went up in vapor at Hiroshima and Nagasaki combined," General LeMay later lashed out at critics of the atomic bombing of Hiroshima and Nagasaki. The best evidence available today indicates that LeMay's numbers were incorrect. Death totals at Hiroshima and Nagasaki, long underestimated in standard American accounts, substantially surpassed those in Tokyo. But LeMay did capture graphically the central element of continuity that lay behind the new phase in air warfare, which negated all distinction between combatant and noncombatant, and which exacted so heavy a toll in human life prior to dropping the atomic bomb. The great majority of those killed and maimed by the atomic bombings of Hiroshima and Nagasaki, like the victims of earlier firebombings, were women, children, and the elderly.

A few high-ranking U.S. officials voiced doubts about the atomic attacks on Hiroshima and Nagasaki in the months and years after the bombing. Admiral William Leahy, Chief of Staff under Roosevelt and Truman, ruminated that it would "take us back in cruelty toward noncombatants to the days of Genghis Khan. It will be a form of pillage and rape of a society done impersonally by one state against another whereas in the Dark Ages it was a result of individual greed and vandalism." In his diary, David Lilienthal, chairman of the Atomic Energy Commission, reflected on both the firebombing and the atomic bombing:

> Then we burned Tokyo, not just military targets, but set out to wipe out the place, indiscriminately. The atomic bomb is the last word in this direction. All ethical limitations of warfare are gone, not because the means of destruction are more cruel or painful or otherwise hideous in their effect upon combatants, but because there are no individual combatants. The fences are gone. And it was we, the civilized, who have pushed standardless conduct to its ultimate.

Perhaps the most trenchant contemporary critique of the American moral position on the bomb and the scales of justice in the war was voiced by the Indian jurist Radhabinhod Pal, the lone dissenting voice at the Tokyo War Crimes Tribunal, who balked at accepting the uniqueness of Japanese war crimes. Recalling Kaiser Wilhelm II's account of his duty to bring World War I to a swift end— "everything must be put to fire and sword; men, women and children and old men must be slaughtered and not a tree or house be left standing"—Pal observed:

> this policy of indiscriminate murder to shorten the war was considered to be a crime. In the Pacific war under our consideration, if there was anything approaching what is indicated in the above letter

of the German Emperor, it is the decision coming from the Allied powers to use the bomb. Future generations will judge this dire decision. . . . [I]f any indiscriminate destruction of civilian life and property is still illegal in warfare, then, in the Pacific War, this decision to use the atom bomb is the only near approach to the directives of the German Emperor during the first World War and of the Nazi leaders during the second World War.

Pal concluded that a victor who destroyed noncombatant populations with weapons ranging from firebombs to atomic bombs had no moral claim unilaterally to brand its enemy as a desecrator of the laws of war.

One final critique of the nuclear bombing, which the U.S. government effectively suppressed for twenty-five years, bears mention. On August 11, 1945, the Japanese government filed an official protest over the atomic bombing to the U.S. State Department through the Swiss Legation in Tokyo, observing that

combatant and noncombatant men and women, old and young, are massacred without discrimination by the atmospheric pressure of the explosion, as well as by the radiating heat which result therefrom. Consequently there is involved a bomb having the most cruel effects humanity has ever known. . . . The bombs in question, used by the Americans, by their cruelty and by their terrorizing effects, surpass by far gas or any other arm, the use of which is prohibited.

Japanese protests against U.S. desecration of international principles of war paired the use of the atomic bomb with the earlier firebombing, which massacred

old people, women and children, destroying and burning down Shinto and Buddhist temples, schools, hospitals, living quarters, etc. . . . They now use this new bomb, having an uncontrollable and cruel effect much greater than any other arms or projectiles ever used to date. This constitutes a new crime against humanity and civilization.

It is tempting to view Japanese charges of U.S. atrocities as no more than the pot calling the kettle black, particularly because Japanese leaders in the half century since 1931 have shown no greater willingness to accept responsibility or apologize for crimes committed against other Asian peoples than have their American counterparts. Nevertheless, the Japanese protest correctly pointed to U.S. violations of internationally accepted principles of war with respect to the wholesale destruction of populations.

In the United States, as in Japan, the dominant scholarly and official interpreters of World War II and other wars have generally ignored the dark side of their own nation's behavior and hewed to celebratory themes. Louis Morton is perhaps representative of mainstream American writing in this respect: ''In the late summer and autumn of 1945 the American people had every reason to rejoice. . . . Unprecedented evil had been overcome by the greatest display of force ever marshaled in the cause of human freedom.'' Our analysis suggests the necessity to reexamine the scales of justice in World War II, in particular to draw insight from the experiences of its victims.

A Means to Save Lives

The conventional justification for the atomic bombing is that the only alternative capable of securing Japan's surrender was Allied invasion, which would necessarily result in massive U.S. casualties and, inevitably, far greater Japanese casualties. The most influential text is Truman's 1955 *Memoirs*, which states that the atomic bomb probably saved half a million U.S. lives—anticipated casualties in an Allied invasion of Japan planned for November. Stimson subsequently talked of saving one million U.S. casualties, and Churchill of saving one million American and half that number of British lives.

The heavy casualties incurred on both sides in Japan's defense of Pacific islands in 1944–45 provided U.S. planners ample reasons for caution in planning an invasion of Japan. Between March 1944 and April 1945, 13,742 Americans died battling in the Pacific while killing approximately 310,000 Japanese, a ''kill ratio'' of 24:1, indicative of the overwhelming supremacy of U.S. firepower and particularly the near monopoly of power at sea and in the air. In the battle for Okinawa from April to June 1945, 13,000 U.S. troops died and nearly 36,000 were wounded while an estimated 70,000 Japanese troops and 150,000 Okinawan civilians—one-third of the island's total population—lost their lives.

Nevertheless, retrospective accounts by Truman, LeMay, Stimson, Churchill, and other U.S. and British leaders claiming that the atomic bomb saved half a million or more Allied lives are grossly inflated. Declassified files reveal that U.S. military planners at the time worked with estimates in the range of 20,000 to 46,000 American lives as the projected cost of landing in Kyushu. Most important, given the destruction of Japan's naval and air power, and the Soviet decision to enter the war, there is strong reason to believe that without the atomic bomb Japan's surrender could have been secured well before the planned invasion.

U.S.-Soviet Rivalry

Revisionist historians have long argued that the United States dropped the atomic bombs not to defeat Japan but forcefully to project U.S. primacy in the already brewing Soviet-American conflict, which has, of course, organized the postwar international order. Their analyses of planning for the postwar world, from 1942 forward, underscore official designation of the Soviet Union as the primary threat to U.S. supremacy in world affairs. We have seen that by the spring of 1945 a crippled Japan was no longer a significant military rival to the United States, whose strength had expanded greatly through the war effort while all rivals and potential rivals suffered heavy damage. Nevertheless, while the U.S. military had destroyed Japan's capacity to fight aggressive war beyond her borders, devastated major cities, and blocked access to critical materials, it had neither secured Japan's surrender nor broken the will to fight of the Japanese military.

There seems no reason to choose between analyses that view the bomb as a weapon to force Japan's surrender and those that stress its value as a weapon to intimidate the Soviet Union and establish U.S. hegemony. In summer 1945 both were high priorities for U.S. policy makers, and both were amply served by dropping the atomic bomb. The atomic bomb thus simultaneously punctuated the end of World War II, including Japanese subordination to the United States, and provided the opening salvo in U.S.-Soviet conflict.

From the perspective of establishing American supremacy, the atomic bomb served a triple purpose: It contributed to a swift end to the war on U.S. terms; it forestalled a possible Soviet invasion of Japan, leaving the United States free to shape unilaterally Japan's postwar course under the Occupation; and it sent an electrifying signal to the world, particularly to the Soviet leadership, of nuclear power and American readiness to deploy it ruthlessly in the service of its global ends.

Atomic Censorship

The ethico-political issues surrounding the bomb did not end with the destruction of Hiroshima and Nagasaki. One long hidden dimension of the nuclear politics of the 1940s concerns U.S. information suppression. A pattern of censorship of information about the bomb is discernible from day one of the nuclear era with the barring of reporters from Hiroshima and Nagasaki and an American blackout on much basic information about the bomb, including information vital to treatment of its victims.

The Australian Wilfred Burchett was the first and only reporter to break the American monopoly on information about the bomb by circumventing U.S. censorship procedures and arriving by train in Hiroshima within days of the bomb. Burchett's story, pounded out "sitting on a chunk of rubble that had escaped pulverization at the very center of the explosion," ran in the London *Daily Express* on September 5 under the headline "THE ATOMIC PLAGUE." "Hiroshima does not look like a bombed city," he wrote. "It looks as if a monster steamroller has passed over it and squashed it out of existence." Burchett described people "dying from the uncanny after-effects of the bomb." What he had discovered, and what General Leslie Groves, head of the Manhatten Project, and other U.S. military officials scornfully dismissed as Japanese propaganda, was that people were dying not merely from the heat and blast but also from residual radiation that affected those who entered the city after the bombing.

This official position denying the effects of radiation was loyally supported by such eminent writers as the *New York Times*' science editor William Laurence. Laurence, who subsequently won a Pulitzer Prize for his atomic reporting, doubled as a news manager for the War Department. He continued to write for the the *Times* as an ostensibly independent journalist while reiterating official denials that the bombs had released dangerous radiation.

Among the first actions of the U.S. Occupation was denunciation of the censorship mechanisms imposed by Japan's wartime government. The constitution that U.S. Occupation authorities presented to Japan proclaimed that "No censorship shall be maintained, nor shall the secrecy of any means of communication be violated." But Occupation authorities immediately established their own Civil Censorship Detachment to carry out precisely these tasks. Concealment and disinformation about the effects of the bomb ranked high among its priorities.

Throughout the Occupation, Japanese newspapers functioned under a secret system of precensorship, with atomic reporting closely monitored by U.S. censors. The U.S. authorities encouraged Japanese scientists to conduct research on the effects of the bomb then appropriated the results and barred publication not only of scientific papers, articles, and books, but also of reportage, short stories, or even poetry describing the atomic bombing and its effects.

Beginning with day one of the nuclear era, Americans and Europeans were deluged with powerful images of the bomb: From graphic photographs and accounts featured in newspapers and *Life* magazine, to John Hersey's *Hiroshima*, to films and cartoons as well as school texts, atomic war quickly made its way into American popular consciousness. By contrast, because of the U.S. information blackout, most Japanese, with the important exception of the residents of Hiroshima and Nagasaki, encountered the atomic bomb experience for the "first time" in the final years of the Occupation, and particularly following the end of the Occupation in 1951. This consciousness of atomic war, coming to Japan belatedly at a time when U.S. conflict with the Soviet Union and China directly threatened to engulf Japan through enlargement of the Korean War, shaped the character and perspectives of both the Japanese peace movement and rightwing nationalists seeking to exploit the image of Japan as a victim of World War II.

In one celebrated censorship case, Nagai Takashi, a Christian physician, was not permitted to publish *The Bells of Nagasaki*, a personal account of the bombing, until 1949. Nagai won his four-year legal battle only after accepting the demeaning condition that the volume also include an account by another author of the Japanese sacking of Manila. America's censors, with the stroke of a pen, had unwittingly—and unerringly—equated the atrocities of the bomb with Japanese atrocities in the Philippines. The killing of noncombatants on all sides constitutes the ultimate tragedy of the Second World War, a tragedy which links Japanese atrocities against Asian peoples and American terror bombing of Japan, culminating in the atomic bombing of Hiroshima and Nagasaki.

Nor was U.S. censorship restricted to Japanese writers. While John Hersey's *Hiroshima* was an immediate best seller in the U.S., Occupation authorities blocked publication of a Japanese translation until 1949.

The U.S. government systematically collected—indeed, monopolized—information on the effects of the bomb through the Atomic Bomb Casualty Commission (ABCC) but prohibited Japanese scientists and physicians from publishing their research results on the effects of the bomb. Secrecy and censorship impeded Japanese research and the dissemination of information vital to the treatment of victims of the bomb. The top secret label affixed to all Japanese manuscripts detailing the effects of the atomic bomb was not removed until 1949. Moreover, rather than making research findings available to Japanese physicians or providing assistance in treatment, the ABCC remained exclusively an information-gathering agency, even to the extent of shipping the results of autopsies to the United States and denying Japanese medical authorities access to information germane to the treatment of atomic diseases. Not until 1973 were the photographs of the bombing and its victims, scientific data, and autopsy specimens returned to Japan.

The Legacy of Atomic War

Annihilation of Asian peoples in the course of suppressing resistance to the expanding frontiers of Japanese colonial rule, and American firebombing and atomic bombing of Japanese cities, for all their differences, represent two faces of the pattern of total war that carried the killing of noncombatants to new heights during World War II. It is this legacy that threatens the survival of humanity in the atomic era.

The writings that constitute the heart of this book are a poignant statement of the meaning of war at the dawn of the nuclear era. These memoirs, poems, and novellas, as well as the drawings and photographs, convey the agony and terror of the bomb as seared into the consciousness of those victims who survived to record their experiences, including leading artists and writers as well as citizens from all walks of life. The records of the nuclear experience included here are not confined to the "nuclear moment" of August 1945. They chronicle the experiences of survivors in Hiroshima and Nagasaki—their suffering, their psychological, social, and physical traumas, the substance of their daily lives, as well as some of their hopes and dreams—from August 6 and August 9, 1945, to the present.

"Before 1945," Michael Sherry has observed, "it had been possible to see in air war the potential for global destruction, but survivors of Hamburg or Tokyo rarely connected the extinction of their cities with the fate of the species. For atomic bomb victims, that connection became indissoluble." These voices from Nagasaki and Hiroshima merit careful listening.

References

Alperovitz, Gar, *Atomic Diplomacy* (New York: Simon and Schuster, 1965 [1985 edition with a new introduction]).

Bernstein, Barton, *The Atomic Bomb: The Critical Issues* (Boston: Little, Brown, 1976).

Braw, Monica, *The Atomic Bomb Suppressed. American Censorship in Japan 1945–1949*, Lund Studies in International History 23 (Lund, Sweden: University of Lund).

Burchett, Wilfred, *Shadows of Hiroshima* (London: Verso, 1983).

Churchill, Winston, *The Second World War*, vol. 6, *Triumph and Tragedy* (Boston: Houghton Mifflin, 1953).

Committee for the Compilation of Materials on Damage Caused by the Atomic Bombs in Hiroshima and Nagasaki, *Hiroshima and Nagasaki. The Physical, Medical, and Social Effects of the Atomic Bombings*, trans. Eisei Ishikawa and David Swain (New York: Basic Books, 1981).

Dower, John, "Rethinking World War II in Asia," *Reviews in American History* (June 1984): 155–69.

————. *War Without Mercy* (New York: Pantheon Books, 1986).

Flaujac, Father, "Tokyo Under Bombardment, 1941–1945," *Bethanie Institute Bulletin*, no. 5, trans. in General Headquarters Far East Command, Military Intelligence Section, *War in and Around the Pacific*, vol. 12, *Defense of the Homeland and End of the War*, ed. Donald Detwiler and Charles Burdick (New York: Garland, 1980).

Grew, Joseph, *Turbulent Era: A Diplomatic Record of Forty Years* (Boston: Houghton Mifflin, 1953).

Groves, Leslie, *Now It Can Be Told* (New York: Harper, 1964).

Guillain, Robert, *I Saw Tokyo Burning: An Eyewitness Narrative from Pearl Harbor to Hiroshima*, trans. William Byron (Garden City, N.Y.: Doubleday, 1981).

Kato, Masuo, *The Lost War: A Japanese Reporter's Inside Story* (New York: Knopf, 1946).

Kolko, Gabriel, *The Politics of War* (New York: Random House, 1968).

Leahy, William, *I Was There: The Personal Story of the Chief of Staff to Presidents Roosevelt and Truman Based on His Notes and Diaries Made at the Time* (New York: Whittlesey House, 1950).

Lilienthal, David, *The Journals of David E. Lilienthal*, vol. 3, *Atomic Energy Years* (New York: Harper and Row, 1965).

Rhodes, Robert, *The Making of the Atomic Bomb* (New York: Simon and Schuster, 1986).

Schaffer, Ronald, *Wings of Judgment. American Bombing in World War II* (New York: Oxford University Press, 1985).

Sherry, Michael, *The Rise of American Air Power. The Creation of Armageddon* (New Haven: Yale University Press, 1987).

Sherwin, Martin, *A World Destroyed* (New York: Knopf, 1975).

Shohno, Naomi, *The Legacy of Hiroshima. Its Past, Our Future* (Tokyo: Kosei, 1986).

Stimson, Henry, "The Decision to Use the Atomic Bomb," *Harper's Magazine* (February 1947).

Thorne, Christopher, *Allies of a Kind: The United States, Britain, and the War Against Japan, 1941–1945* (Oxford: Oxford University Press, 1978).

Truman, Harry, *Memoirs*, vol. 1, *Year of Decisions* (Garden City, N.Y.: Doubleday, 1955).

U.S. Strategic Bomb Survey Reports, Pacific War: no. 3, *The Effects of Atomic Bombs on Hiroshima and Nagasaki*; no. 13, *The Effects of Atomic Bombs on Health and Medical Services in Hiroshima and Nagasaki*; no. 60, *The Effects of Air Attack on the City of Hiroshima*; no. 93, *The Effects of the Atomic Bomb on Hiroshima, Japan* (Washington, D.C.: Government Printing Office, 1945–1947).

Weart, Spencer, *Nuclear Fear: A History of Images* (Cambridge: Harvard University Press, 1988).

Wyden, Peter, *Day One. Before Hiroshima and After* (New York: Simon and Schuster, 1984).

The ATOMIC BOMB

NOVELLAS

AUGUST 6

Agawa Hiroyuki

The Father's Note

The second anniversary of those who died from the atomic bomb approaches. Memories of the nightmare are gradually fading. I would like to record my family's experiences at that time.

My family was then six people: my parents, myself, my wife, and a son and daughter. I was fifty-four. Of these, only my father died, in circumstances which my wife will describe later; the other five survived, having gone through different experiences in different places. My son, however, did not directly encounter the bomb, as you will see when you read his note.

Until then I had worked at xx section in the Hiroshima City Government. On August 6, I went to City Hall somewhat earlier than usual, entered xx section on the southeast side of the third floor, and, facing east at my desk in the center of the room, was making a chart needed in my work. Then, suddenly, I heard a strange sound which had great depth. It sounded like "packkoon." As I looked to my left (north), puzzled, my eyes caught a white, egg-shell-color light, and I thought, oh no, a direct hit above our heads; instantly I felt as though the entire ferro-concrete City Hall swayed, and I lost consciousness.

I do not know how many minutes I was unconscious; anyway,

after a while I became aware, as if in a dream, of my own groaning
and of thick smoke, and while thinking and thinking that something
was wrong, I came to my senses. I felt as if I was bathing in grease.
Looking at myself I found that blood was streaming all over my
body. The bleeding was worst around the left wrist and head; blood
was also flowing from the shoulders to the chest. I looked around the
room, my eyes wide open. Until just a moment ago I was sure there
had been six people, but now I was the only one left, and, as if toy
boxes were turned over and pushed to one side of the room, chairs,
desks and document shelves were blown off to the side in a great
mess. I, too, had been blown there. Smoke streamed in through the
door. Collecting myself, I rose. Since my legs were somewhat
wobbly, I went out to the hallway holding onto something. I heard
low groans from different directions; I looked around, however, to
find the building apparently intact. Concerned about my bike, which
I had left in the janitor's room with important registration papers
strapped to it, I started down the stairs.

On the way down, a woman of about forty (so I thought but she
might have been younger) was dead, her mouth, like a wolf's, torn
from ear to ear and both eyeballs blown out. It hardly looked like a
human face. When I went down to the second floor, I saw several
more such people. My feet refusing to move, I stopped and looked
down at the courtyard from a second floor window. In the courtyard
below, thick yellow smoke was hanging at human height, and above
it was a mass of jet black smoke. From the public hall next door a
rather thin stream of smoke was approaching. When I saw this, for
the first time I felt that some new weapon might have been used.

Then, too, I saw an odd sight through the smoke. Many office
girls were walking in a circle in the courtyard, raising their hands as
they would in a Bon dance. Half of them were barefooted, and they
were all calling: "Mother, please come." "Mother, why aren't you
coming?"

Their voices were sad screams that resembled sobbing, in an
indescribably pitiful, disagreeable tone. The moment someone di-
verged, the odd Bon dance circle went out of shape in that direction.
And, while becoming now circular and now oblong, it was going
round and round in the same way. They seemed like human beings

who had lost all reason. Although in retrospect all might have been able to flee if someone reliable had skillfully guided them, beneath my eyes about ten fell one after another.

I no longer cared about my bike. I ran from the south stairs in the center to the streetcar road. My legs became firmer, though probably only from terror. On the street, electric poles lay on one side like fallen incense sticks. A horse-drawn wagon carrying metal pipes had tumbled and lay on its side, both horse and man having died instantly. I started to walk a little northward, but, frightened by high-voltage electric sparks, I retreated and passed through the west gate of the College of Arts and Sciences in the direction of the Red Cross Hospital. On the campus, where there were as yet no flames, I saw five or six men, probably teachers, talking with few words as though all spirit had gone out of them.

I was worried about my home in Hakushima, but at that point what worried me even more was what had happened to my daughter, who should have been working at the Postal Savings Bureau right near where I was. Passing before the Red Cross Hospital, I looked up at the reddish building. She worked there every day due to student labor mobilization. That morning, she should have left home slightly later than I. With painful thoughts, I paced up and down in front of the building. Injured people flowed into this wide street from different places and all walked toward Ujina. There was also a naked woman who, although not wounded, ran barefooted muttering something unintelligible, her hair in disarray. I grabbed many people to inquire, but none knew about the Savings Bureau. After a while an old man told me, "At the Savings Bureau, they dragged seriously injured people down to the basement."

Approaching the basement entrance, I saw two guard-like men with pickaxes barking, "We'll kill anyone who goes in here." Since my nerves were on edge, however, I tried to break in, paying no attention. One of them blocked me, brandishing his pickaxe: "How dare you break in here?"

"What? Kill me if you like. My precious daughter was drafted for forced labor service: What's wrong about her parent entering to search at such a time? Go ahead, kill me if you can," I yelled loudly. I must have glared at him with a terribly threatening expression.

Cowed, the man put down his pickaxe and let me pass.

Compared with the tumult outside, the basement was gloomy and subdued. I heard low groans here and there.

"Kazuko, Kazuko," I called my daughter's name, my voice resounding in the basement. I walked around, peering at one face after another of the seriously wounded people. Among them were a few young women. Once, I stepped on something soft and limp and jumped back startled. It was a human hand. It belonged to a lean man of about thirty, seemingly already dead.

"Ojisan, ojisan" (sir, sir), a boy called in a low voice, holding out both hands as though asking for help.

"Keep up your spirits. Someone will come soon."

Holding his hands, I think I said something like this. I myself could do nothing for him. I just went outside. I could not find my daughter. Although I went outside, I could not give her up. While gauging the flames visible in all directions near and far and the possibilities of escape, I wandered this way and that, hatless under the scorching sun, until I think it was about eleven. No matter who I asked, no one responded in earnest. Finally giving up, I started to flee, following the lines of people. When I came as far as the Miyuki Bridge and looked from our neighborhood toward Ushita, I saw smoke rising from the shadows of the Ushita mountains. The mountains seemed to have caught fire.

From this point on, my memory is somewhat hazy.

Where was it?—I seem to think it was on the river bank.

I ran through something like an army dump and a split second later fire from across the street licked the whole building.

Around Danbara, everyone I saw told me about what lay ahead. I was trying somehow to reach home.

"It's no use. Even if you went further, you'd just be burnt to death. Every place is a sea of fire," some said, while others said, "The fire isn't as bad as you think. Cheer up."

Then, somewhere, four trucks, I think of the army, were busily working at moving seriously injured people. I was urged to get on. When I asked their destination, I was told that they were taking the injured to Kaita-ichi and Ujina. It was the wrong direction, so I continued to walk on.

When I put together what various people had said, it seemed that I could get to Ushita if I bypassed Hiroshima Station, went through Iwahana, and crossed Nakayama Pass beyond the east parade ground, so I set out intending to do that. If I reached Ushita, I could return to Hakushima, or, even if I failed, I thought I would be able to get some information about my family. When passing Onaga, where the damage was relatively light, someone said, "Sir, you are bleeding heavily. I don't know how far you're going, but why don't you stay here for the night?"

Although I felt grateful, I declined that offer, too.

Soon I came to the pass. By then I keenly felt the pain from my wounds, and my legs were heavy as though there were metal rods in them; it wasn't easy to climb the trail at the pass.

I looked back, resting on the roots of a tree. The entire city was engulfed in black smoke, and although it was still early, the feel of evening dusk hung everywhere, the sun only faintly visible. Beneath my eyes, only the flames on Hiroshima Station were bright red.

Passing seriously injured people lying on both sides of the pass, I walked a little and rested, rested and climbed again. When finally I could no longer walk, I crawled to a hut I happened to find. Peering inside, I saw several soldiers, who invited me in. Among the soldiers was an army captain, who looked like a doctor, accompanied by a woman of about thirty-four or thirty-five. He prepared strong sugar water to revive me. After I drank two cups, my body was suddenly invigorated and I felt elated. I also received from him two green tomatoes and nibbled at them. He gave me no treatment; probably he had nothing to treat my wounds with.

I rose after staying there a while, thanked them, and started to walk again. Now and then I met people coming from the opposite direction. I was the only one walking toward Ushita. A young man passing by tried to stop me: "Don't be a fool, ojisan. Why are you going there? Everyone's fleeing from there. Don't be a fool."

But I shook him off, too. The sugar water had only revived me momentarily: fatigue permeated my entire body. I was walking, half-awake, half-asleep, thinking that the house was no longer there and both my parents and my wife had died. In time big sparks started to fly toward me one after another, and at that point I met another person, a woman of about fifty, appearing from the opposite direction. From this old woman I heard that Ushita had not burnt, that Hakushima was slow in catching fire, and that many Hakushima people survived, having fled to Ushita. While listening, I felt my legs become light and fell on the grass, losing consciousness.

The Daughter's Story

A fourth-year student at the Second Prefectural Girls' School of Hiroshima, I had been mobilized to work at the Savings Bureau. On the morning of the 6th the alarm sounded, so I waited for the all clear and then left home. When I came to the Hakushima terminal, a streetcar was just about to leave. It wasn't that we had a special promise, but since I always met my friend Yasuko there and went to work with her on the same streetcar, I hesitated a little when I didn't see her, wondering if I should wait for another car. However, I was somewhat late that day and, moreover, the car was conveniently bound for Dentetsu Station (a car bound for Dentetsu Station spared me the trouble of changing at Hatcho-bori), so I made up my mind and got on. Around the time when the streetcar passed Kamiya, I recalled that I had left at school the book *How to Grow Vegetables at Home* which I had promised to lend to the section head a few days earlier. Again I hesitated whether to go to the bank or stay on as far as school to get the book. I decided to go to school first. Besides the book, there was something I wanted to see Teacher S about. I hesitated twice; I don't know what would have happened to me had I acted differently on even one of these two occasions.

Past the Red Cross Hospital, past the Savings Bureau, when the streetcar ran a little further, a terrible blue light flashed, spreading as far as I could see. Instantly I thought that the streetcar had had an accident, and I reflected: what a mistake, after all I shouldn't have taken this car. In fact, of course, it was just the opposite: although the details are unknown, Yasuko seems to have come from the Hakushima terminal to Hatcho-bori on the next car, and while waiting to transfer there she was hit by that light and, seriously wounded, just managed to run home. She died the next day. Well, the car I rode stopped right away and its passengers noisily got off.

As I, too, got off and stood on the street, the world was all dark, visited at that moment by an eerie hush. Forgetting myself, I shouted loudly, "I can't see, I can't see."

The hush, however, lasted just for a second, and soon howls rose everywhere. Voices calling for help, cries complaining of pain, groans—while I was wondering what could have happened, little by little the darkness wore off and changed to a dawn-like color around me. As I looked in that light, those wearing army caps were intact only under their caps; the rest of their facial skin had peeled off in big pieces like loquat peels and was hanging from cheeks and necks. The skin on their hands had also come off. Many people dangled both hands in front of their chests ghostlike, everyone in the same way, the skin hanging. They aimlessly paced this way and that. Their faces and arms where the skin had slid off looked pink. This pink was truly chilling, and, although my father says it is better to avoid exaggeration, I really thought this was hell. I myself seemed without injury of any kind. That day my outfit was navy blue work pants, a half-sleeve gym shirt, and on my feet a pair of clogs. How I had escaped wounds anywhere on my body puzzles me even now. When I noticed, I had only one clog on. I had left the other in the streetcar. When I looked at people wandering left and right, at least everyone had clogs on both feet. Suddenly embarrassed, I thought of going back to the streetcar for my other clog. Putting a foot on the step, I found that the floor of the car had collapsed, and it was in such a mess that I could not get in. I seem to remember that the car was burning, but it may just be that it had broken down. Giving up the clog, I started to run.

After that, I don't remember how I ran, or what road I took. I think I probably didn't pass the Savings Bureau. I remember standing helplessly for a while in front of City Hall, worried about my father. Since my body was fine, many people called out to me "help me, help me." This made me feel helpless. A bloody man lying on the road called for help; an old woman also called, only her hands and face visible beneath a flattened zinc roof. Each time I fled, pretending to close my eyes and covering my ears. I met people coming from the opposite direction spreading rumors that the bridge ahead had burnt down and that oil had been poured into the river, turning it into a river of fire. I wondered what I should do; but such rumors were all lies. When I came to the bridge, an army officer was talking loudly with someone in a boat moored to the bank. Since the boat started drifting upstream propelled by the wind the moment he tried to untie the cord, he seemed preoccupied with doing something about it. Someone questioned the officer: "Sir, what on earth happened today?"

The officer, a young man with the rank of lieutenant, answered, "It seems that the enemy dropped air torpedoes."

Since my brother was in the navy, I had heard that air torpedoes were dropped from airplanes against enemy ships; I thought the answer strange, but thinking at that moment that he might be right, I started to run again. When I had run for quite a while, a young man a little over twenty called to me, "Say, wait a second."

When I stopped, he said, "It's dangerous to cross the bridge the way you are. Let me give you this."

He took off his army sock and handed it to me. I realized that I was running with one clog on. Then, for the first time, I clearly knew where I was. I was about to cross Yokogawa Bridge. There, I dusted dirt off the foot without a clog, wore the sock the young man offered me, and crossed the bridge as he pulled my hand. Although a little blood somehow smudged the foot without a clog, I wasn't injured much. From then on I walked with him. A while later, a man of about fifty years old also joined, and the three of us ran side by side.

Soon after we three got together, it suddenly started to rain hard. The rain was as black as heavy oil, and my clothes became wet black. When I took a careful look, they were—since when I didn't know—spotted with blood here and there. It was not my blood; I think injured people's blood splattered. The young man said, "Let's go, let's go. Whether rain falls or spears fall, it's all the same now."

Besides, there was no place for sheltering against the rain. We three kept on walking, drenched. The man about fifty also said, "Anyway it's better to get out and away from Hiroshima as quickly as possible." Somehow unable to mention that my house was in

Hakushima, I followed the two men like someone without will. The fiftyish man, we learned, had been fishing near Misasa Bridge. When he chanced to look up, he saw three round shining objects fall side by side, and he barely had time to wonder about them before he was blown to the center of the river by the boom. His partially dry clothes became wet again in the rain. His left arm was badly injured.

We had walked along the right bank of the Ota River quite a distance from Hiroshima City when the rain stopped. Since there happened to be a boat on the river bank, I decided to ask the boatman to ferry me to the opposite bank so I could go home, and I parted with the two men. The opposite bank was the northern limit of Ushita. This time I headed south and reached the house of my friend Miss Kimura. I meant to leave after a little rest to look for my parents and grandparents, but I was forced to stay. "Right now fire seems to be raging in Hakushima, so we can't let you go; wait a little longer," they said. After all I stayed at my friend's house for the night. About that time, people in the neighborhood were panicking, saying that the air raid alarm had gone off again.

That night I slept poorly due to fear and worry. Early the following morning I tried to find the ruins of my house in Hakushima. The town was completely burnt, but I found my mother and grandmother absentmindedly sitting with neighbors in a field near the river. Recognizing me, mother rose reeling and said, "Oh, Kazu-chan."

Unable to say anything, I went down with a thump on my knees as though in prayer. Soon my father returned with terrible injuries. Although I learned that my grandfather had died, I was not at all sad then. Much later, when a shed was built and we had a monk recite sutras, then for the first time I cried aloud.

As I have written earlier, I was uninjured, but a little later the so-called atomic disease symptoms appeared: spots broke out here and there on my skin, my body felt dull, I had a fever, I lost appetite. For a long time I commuted to the hospital with my father and mother. When I was tested, the number of white cells had gone down to the 1,900s. I learned that the normal figure is about 7,000. At one point I thought I was dying, but since late fall I gradually recovered, and now I am fine.

The Son's Note

Although I had a memo, I have lost it; and, since it has already been two years, I'm afraid my numbers, etc., may often be inaccurate. I will write relying on memory.

I was an ensign out of the student reserve, serving in a so-called airborne unit. I was stationed in Yokosuka in the Swallow Corps, which was planning a "reverse landing" on Saipan using the Renzan, the navy's prized four-engine attack plane. On August 6, I had gone to Atsugi for liaison work.

I had just finished lunch in the gun room at Atsugi. The officer on duty, a first lieutenant from the Naval Academy, entered the room and read aloud the following telegram. There may be a few memory errors about this telegram, too. It originated from Kure Naval Station.

0800 SMALL NUMBER OF ENEMY PLANES INVADED SKY OVER HIROSHIMA, NEW TYPE BOMB APPARENTLY EMPLOYED. DAMAGE. SHATTERED BUILDINGS 200,000. HIROSHIMA CITY TOTALED. AT PRESENT IN FLAMES. DEAD AND INJURED UNKNOWN

The young first lieutenant on duty read this stammeringly, looking abnormally agitated and ashen pale. Several minutes later, a senior staff officer ordered warrant officers and up to report to the wardroom. We rose and left the room. Immediately about fifty warrant and commissioned officers gathered in the wardroom. After a glance at the turnout, the senior staff officer opened his mouth. The content of his talk was largely the same as the telegram. Four or five officers arrived late. Then, surveying all those present, the senior staff officer said, "Are any of you from Hiroshima City?"

Two raised their hands: a chief warrant officer by the name of Otsuki and myself. Chief warrant officer Otsuki was a pilot from the navy's pilot training school. The senior staff officer said, "Fine," and, turning toward the chief aviation officer by his side, asked: "Officer, is any plane ready for flight?"

There was a Type 1 land-based attack plane prepared for flight to

Mihoro, Hokkaido. This is a fat, round, twin-engine plane shaped like a cigar, whose photographs we often saw during the war in the newspapers. We two were ordered to fly this plane to Hiroshima to survey the situation. At once we dashed out of the wardroom, changed into flight suits, and in several minutes we were on board. The information was still to be withheld from enlisted men, which is why just we two went on the plane. I think the Atsugi departure time was about 12:25.

Soon we saw Mt. Fuji on our right. Our altitude was approximately 2,000 meters. Officer Otsuki held the control stick, and, although I could not operate a plane, I sat with him in the cockpit. Past Hamana Lake, over the Suzuka mountains, we took the plane south of Osaka City, above Awaji Island, and then flew along the sea line of Chugoku region. Our average speed was probably around 200 knots per hour. We approached Kure keeping an altitude of approximately 3,000 meters, after which we headed northwest for Hiroshima. We could already recognize black smoke from above Kure (or it might have been earlier than that); as we approached somewhat nearer the island, Muko-Ujina looked as though it was floating by itself. Other than that, the entire city was enclosed in black smoke. At first the smoke seemed to be streaming westward to around Itsuka-ichi. According to what we discovered later, however, the wind at high altitudes was southeastern, and therefore the smoke was streaming northwest, much farther than we had thought. We reached the sky above Hiroshima City at exactly 15:00.

"Since we may be shot at by our own forces, let's circle around once at this altitude," Officer Otsuki barked. I nodded. So we headed west from the south side and circled around once at 3,000 meters, but there was no sign of firing. At 3,000 meters, our plane seemed to be flying near the upper end of the black smoke. We saw many pieces of scorched paper floating in the air. As we often observe in a normal small fire, things like these pieces of paper fly higher than smoke.

"Anti-aircraft battery positions seem to be totaled," said Officer Otsuki. We brought the plane down to 1,500 meters. Mt. Chausu northwest of the city was invisible, covered by black smoke, while Mt. Gosasau on the northeast was clearly visible. As we dropped to

1,500 meters, the plane also became engulfed in blackish gray smoke. A little smoke came inside the plane. After circling around at 1,500, we boldly descended to 400 meters from above Mt. Gosa-sau. Chief Warrant Officer Otsuki repeatedly indicated his concern about his house in Yokogawa. I too worried about my house in Hakushima. We went above the northern part of the city, flying, we assumed, over the line connecting Hakushima and Yokokawa, that is, along the San'yo Main Line; however, with smoke all around us, by our sides, above, and below, we could see absolutely nothing. It was a totally blind flight, but I felt no fear because we both knew the map of Hiroshima by heart. As we headed southwest and came over the sea, the smoke disappeared. Circling left, we started going back. I felt numb. Officer Otsuki said, "Well, we got hit, didn't we." "We did, didn't we," I also said. Climbing, Otsuki said as though to himself, "My wife's dead, too."

After the war I returned home, discharged from Yokosuka. Since I have not heard about Otsuki's whereabouts, I don't know whether his wife died. My sister says that an alarm went off just as she escaped to Ushita. After the bombing, alarms were totally erratic that day: I hear that there were even civil guards who, taking thunder for an airplane, noisily rang bells and called "Air raid! air raid!" Therefore, although I cannot be confident, I imagine that at least one alarm sounded when our plane was spotted.

The Mother's Story

After sending off my husband and daughter, I finished washing the dishes in the kitchen, glanced through the newspaper, rose, leaned against the pillar in the corridor, and, while standing, was about to put on my tabi. Then, unexpectedly, there was a yellowish purple-tinted flash. At that instant the deep green leaves of the trees grow-ing thickly in the yard turned white. It was an unpleasant color suggestive of the end of the world. Puzzled, I looked right, then back left as the house shook, and I was hurled down, red dirt falling on me. I'm dying, I thought, falling. A bomb seems to have made a direct hit on our house, but the ground is supposed to shake when a bomb strikes, and it didn't happen; strange in the first place that there was no big noise—just this much crossed my mind. Then suddenly the red dirt stopped falling and it became quiet. Well, perhaps I'm safe, I thought, and I looked around trying to be as calm as possible. I lay in the corridor almost flat on my stomach, pillars above me and on my sides. It was as if I was made to fit into a triangular frame of wood. The front and back were blocked off by gas pipes and other things I could not identify. I had no idea what they were, and I could not slip out of the frame. Before my eyes was an odd iron sheet. I tried touching it, though nervously: I couldn't tell what it was. Some time later, I figured out that it was the iron board in back of the sewing machine.

"Grandmother, grandmother, are you all right?" I asked my mother-in-law. From the direction of the dining room, a pessimistic voice came: "Are you all right, Yumi? I'm a total mess."

When I told her that I couldn't move either, instead of speaking to me, my mother-in-law started to call for help repeatedly in a shrill voice.

"It's better not to shout so much, you'll just get tired. In a while civil guards will come for us," I comforted her. Never did I dream that all Hiroshima had become what it was. From grandfather I had no reply although I called to him. When falling down, I think I heard a voice: "Namu Amidha-butsu, namu Amidha-butsu."

The praise of the Buddha thus repeated twice may have been my father-in-law's last words. A man of faith, he must have been saying prayers that morning as usual, seated before the family shrine. After everything that was to be done was done, grandfather's half-charred body came out of the ruins of the house.

In a while, encouraged by the Morikawas whose voices I heard somewhere behind our house, I loudly called for help. They came to look for us, saying, "Where are you, where?" It was encouraging that fire did not yet seem to have started. As I was under the fallen roof the Morikawas apparently had a hard time locating me, but after a while they found me and said, "Ah, there you are."

"We might have to break through the roof," I heard the couple talking above my head. I called to them again from underneath and, telling them that my mother-in-law was around the dining room, asked them to help her out first. The Morikawas went off in that direction, and soon, as they apparently tried to move her, I heard mother scream: "It hurts, it hurts, it hurts."

All that while I was wriggling, hoping to extricate myself. Just as it began to look as if I could free my body a little, I stretched my legs with all my might, and in so doing, a piece of glass badly pierced the back of the left big toe. As I groped around again, the gas pipe that had blocked me moved with a jerk, and in one unexpected motion I was able to pop out. I felt relieved but not particularly happy. Picking up a housecoat which happened to be there and two of the scattered sewing machine bobbins, I went out to the street. In retrospect, why I picked up such things is hard to tell. Then I saw the Morikawas and was told that I also had a slight wound on my face. Touching it, I realized it was bloody.

"Get a saw, a saw," said Mr. Morikawa. I hurried to the second floor in back, which had not collapsed, to get a saw. On the way up I thought, what a place for a picture, seeing on the floor the photograph of my husband's younger brother who had died about five years earlier, but I just went upstairs. In the four-and-a-half-mat upstairs room were many pumpkins which had rolled in from the clothes-drying veranda where we had been growing them. Getting the saw out of the overturned tool box, I went downstairs and set to rescuing grandmother with the Morikawas. Many pillars leaned on her as if about to trap her small body. She seemed to have been hit somewhere, for, the moment we forced a little, she screamed, "It hurts, it hurts."

So the work was not easy, but after cutting through five pillars, we were finally able to get her out. It probably took half an hour or so. The three of us sawed by turns. Since we had to saw in various postures, I picked up a piece of cloth I happened to see on the ground, and with it brushed away powdered glass where we had to kneel or put our hands. Although there were as yet no flames, everyone we saw had a bloody face, and the Morikawas also had a fair number of injuries on their shoulders and legs. Looking toward the embankment, I saw many blood-covered people fleeing toward Ushita. As though by agreement, they all tottered forward alike with no clothes on their upper bodies, their chests all black, their hands dangling in front of their chests as we do when imitating a ghost.

Seeing this, I thought that the Hakushima area must have been quite badly hit.

"I wonder if my husband knows that this area was hit like this. He's got to come home quickly," I said.

In a while, since the blood on my face dried and stretched the skin, I suggested to my mother-in-law that we go to the river to wash. As for my father-in-law, there was no response although we called his name together, nor was there a sign of him anywhere although we searched. Thinking we should not go empty-handed, however, I started to pull the rice can. Since it was obstructed by something and hard to release, I asked a man who happened to be passing to get it out. Beans were scattered all over the place. It was a pity to leave them, so I picked them up with my hands and put them in the rice can; mud from the walls and glass powder also went in. After that I opened the ice box and took out half a pound of sugar and a can of Lipton tea. Along with these I picked up a pot, rice bowls and chopsticks, put all of them in the rice can, and went out holding it by the handles. My mother-in-law was shuffling around in the broken down storeroom. "Grandmother, what are you doing?" I asked.

"Well, I have no idea what I should take." As she answered, I saw her putting two hatchets in a big flower basket, and busily cramming charcoal over them.

"My, what odd things." Surprised, I urged her to leave. Since we were both bare-footed, we put on straw sandals and headed for the river. We met Mrs. Sakuma. Her upper body was completely bare and her chest was smeared with blood. Between the breasts there was a diagonal tear, flesh showing in the gash.

"My, what happened to you?" I asked. Even in this condition she was rather steady.

"As if I had any idea!" she answered, disappearing somewhere. As the hatchets were heavy, we decided to come back for them later and, placing them against the ditch under the embankment, climbed the embankment. Then my mother-in-law and I went through by the side of the Kagawas' to the river. The shore was already full of people: we saw a neighbor here and a neighbor there, but there were many strangers. I washed the blood off my face with river water.

About an hour had passed since the bombing when the air raid alarm went off. Although usually I was calm, this time it sounded so eerie that I decided not to go back for the hatchets and other things, like clogs and matches, that occurred to me. In the south, flames were visible here and there. As they gradually started to rage, the sky became heavy with clouds, and we could no longer clearly see the fire. In the north, the Ushita mountains in flames looked beautiful. Realizing that the damage extended over quite a wide area, I started to feel anxious about my husband and daughter. On the shore were many young men in tattered clothes who looked like beggars. Since they were so oddly downcast as though they had lost their souls, it was a while before I realized they were soldiers. On asking, I learned that they had fled the two regiments. Not only these soldiers but the many people on the shore were in a state of shock: they hardly talked, and their movements were sluggish.

Someone was limping back toward us using a big umbrella for a walking stick, having scooped water in a bucket at the edge of the river. It was Mrs. Kagawa. On her invitation, the two of us moved to the hut on the Kagawas' farm. This hut beneath the slope had been spared. The farm was between the embankment and the river: the cowpeas and cucumber leaves had all blown away leaving no trace; only pumpkins were on the ground. We gathered as many as possible and carried them into the hut. On the loquat tree, the leaves facing south were all scorched. Big burdock leaves remained here and there. Toward the south was the San'yo Line railroad bridge: a freight train had stopped with the last ten or so cars still on the bridge. In time, it started to burn. It was just smouldering, without flaring up. Now and then the fire became strong and flames would jump to the next car. Thus, one car after another burnt. A shower started. Although I often hear people say that black rain fell, I didn't think it black. About that time, the Morikawas came to the hut. Both my mother-in-law and I thanked them for what they had done and, with Mrs. Kagawa's support, suggested that they join us in this hut. Mr. Morikawa stopped us: "There's no time for that. The Tanimoto family on the embankment are trapped under the house. Since the flames are getting close, let me ask whoever has energy to come and help."

He was pale. In response, I rose, along with three or four people who were nearby, and ran to the Tanimotos'. Ran, I wrote, but in my case, all I could do was hobble on the heel of the left foot with the glass. Mrs. Tanimoto's husband and her oldest daughter were calling for help from under the house, holding out just their hands. We could also see their faces. The other members of the family could not be seen; better that way, on looking back. Lintels and walls having fallen in piles, nothing could be done by the seven or eight people who had gathered with small saws. We only held their hands, stretched for help, to encourage them, or uselessly tried to pull them. Those who had gathered also had injuries, big and small, on their legs and hands, so that it was hard to do anything that required real exertion. The two people under the house seemed to be badly injured, but they were fully conscious. The fire reached next door. Flames were licking the eaves of the Tanimoto house. Of those who came to the rescue, one ran, two ran, and in the end only the Morikawas and I were left. There was a terrible, rumbling noise of something burning down. Frightened by this, we three exchanged glances. Without a word, our thoughts were the same. The hot air started to blow against us till it almost scorched our hair. Uselessly stretching just their hands like monkeys in the zoo, and having stopped crying and screaming, Mr. Tanimoto and his daughter were ruefully looking at us. I put my saw in Mr. Tanimoto's hand, joined my hands in prayer toward the two with my eyes closed, and ran away covering my face. The Morikawas followed. Returning to the hut, I could not watch the Tanimoto house burn.

I developed a fever. My body was unbearably heavy. Spreading a straw charcoal sack on the ground in front of the hut, I lay down and for a long time kept thinking absent-mindedly about many things. My heart was overcast from worrying about my husband and daughter.

When someone said, "I wonder what time it is now," I peered at my wristwatch for the first time. Although there was a crack in the glass, it was working regularly. The hands pointed at 3:10. Seeing the time, we all suddenly realized our hunger. However, no one else had brought rice. I opened my rice container and washed some rice in the pot with river water. Preparing a makeshift cooking stove with rocks and bricks, I boiled the rice and also pumpkins. When they were ready, I made the rice into balls and distributed one to each person around me, and as for pumpkins I passed the pot around to eat from. While walking about giving out rice balls, I saw two middle school boys, swollen with blisters from the fire, lying under a mandarin orange tree near the center of the field. Their faces were both swollen round, their eyes narrow as though blinded. One of them said in a feeble voice, "Obasan (ma'am), please give me water."

"When you are badly wounded, I hear you can't have water; I wish I could give you some, but I must ask you to be patient," I comforted him, recalling what I had often heard. On the orange tree were many small and hard green oranges. I wished there were some fruit I could offer, but there was none. The sun hung like a demon in the middle of the sky, reddish black in the center, dimly yellow around the edge. Twilight hues drifted around us. About the time the actual evening by the clock approached, people from afar began to appear in twos and threes looking for their relatives. Since they told us about the dreadful damage in the city, I started to think that it might be all over now with my husband and daughter. People also left us with rumors such as that the enemy had used a new weapon today or that it had been death rays. With the pumpkins in the pot, I went back to the blistered students. As I asked, "How about some pumpkin?" one of them faintly shook his head while the boy who had asked for water said, "Please."

The boy who had shaken his head no longer seemed to have the strength to talk. The other one, too, merely took a mouthful and weakly spat it while it was still in his mouth.

"This is in place of water, try it," I said, dropping cooked pumpkin juice into the mouths of the two boys. The one who could speak complained repeatedly of cold: "Obasan, I'm cold, please, I'm cold."

So I went back to the hut, got out a straw jacket and a charcoal sack, and put them over the boys. In the hut someone talked about how cold one got after being burned. Under the fig tree, too, I heard, a similarly blistered middle school boy lay, a first-year student who had come from Miyajima for labor service. Around six o'clock, his older brother who was about twenty came looking for him, and we all felt happy about the find as though it were our own.

In time night came. Swallowing the many cruel sights I had seen in a single day, their much too intense impressions, and the unbearable thoughts of my husband and daughter, I lay once more on the charcoal sack. The middle school student under the fig tree kept complaining of cold while being firmly held by his big brother. The others, too, lay here and there, each in a different posture. From the dark, only low groans were heard. There was not one single mosquito. Mosquitoes did not come out for three or four days after that; sometime later when I watched children digging for bait for fishing, earthworms were nowhere to be found. Even insects and worms must have all been killed at one point. Houses along the embankment had all burnt long ago, leaving red embers. From about the time the Tanimoto house caught fire, I had tried to keep my eyes away from the fire; I now found that no trace was left of our house, either, on the other side of the embankment.

An uneasy night was over. As I climbed the embankment to take a look, what had been Hiroshima City twenty-four hours earlier was a surprisingly wide wasteland. In the morning, we had humble morning chores even on a day like this. The young man from Miyajima walked over as my mother-in-law and I were washing chopsticks and pots, so I inquired.

"Yes, he passed away at eleven last night," he said. And, carrying his little brother's body to the side of our hut, he said that he was going home to inform his parents. After repeatedly asking that the body be kept as it was until his parents came and not handed over to soldiers even if they came, he headed back for Miyajima. The two middle school students under the orange tree, too, were already cold.

Soon my daughter returned, looking vacant. Within fifteen minutes after that, my husband also came home. I could say nothing; watching the two of them, only tears trickled down.

The following day, soldiers started to clear away the dead bodies, carrying them one by one on stretchers to the river bed. We tried to keep the body of the middle school student who was left in our care, but the soldiers said that there was no way they could leave it. After negotiating for a while, we finally handed him over when they promised to make sure that he would be separated from the rest on the river bed. Soon the boy's parents came from Miyajima.

It was on the ninth or tenth. When I happened to look at the river bed while being treated for the wound in my foot at the first aid station set up at the side of the farm, about twenty soldiers standing in formation near the edge of the water were presenting arms. Beyond them I saw a fire burning, and smoke rising. They were burning the bodies collected on the river bed. Forty-eight bodies, I hear, were burnt there at that time.

The Father's Postscript

The above is a composite record of that day by my wife, children, and myself. On rereading it, I cannot help feeling exasperated: unless we add much, much more, we will not really convey to the reader the events of the day. Indeed, our experiences were such that one who did not see that day could never imagine them however he tried.

From around the time my external wounds finally healed in November, I started to be afflicted by diarrhea of unknown cause. I visited every doctor I could find and tried every possible treatment, such as taking plum puree I obtained from someone in Kyoto, a traditional family medicine in Wakayama. Around the time the year changed, however, it only grew worse and worse. My stomach grumbled like a musical band, and everything passed through even though I felt no pain and enjoyed meals. For this reason I became nearly skin and bones and wondered whether I would die of this diarrhea after having luckily survived. Hearing around that time of Dr. T who had come from Tokyo for research, I visited him and found as many as eleven patients with the same symptoms as mine squeezing into his office. Told that this was a kind of atomic disease, I followed his directions to take as much bone marrow as possible: preparing myself to enter into a life like that of a wild dog, I bit into all the bones I saw, whether sardine or chicken. Perhaps it had some effect, for a year later the tenacious diarrhea finally stopped, and my body began to recover daily. Later, I had a chance to see Dr. T's research notes. According to the beginning portion of his notes, the estimated Hiroshima City population at the time of the bombing was 230,000 to 260,000; the dead excluding soldiers were 59,000 to 64,000 in mid-December that year; and the number of the dead decreased in the manner of a geometric progression from the day of the bombing, 50 percent dying during the first six days, and 99 percent during the first forty days. The bombing occurred at 8:15 a.m. on August 6, 1945 (the 20th year of Showa).

TWO GRAVE MARKERS

Hayashi Kyoko

Clusters of pale yellow acacia flowers sway in the early summer breeze. The wisteria-like clusters call to mind flocks of butterflies.

Wakako sits in the roots of the trees. Her hair is in braids. By her side is a baby. The baby wears a rose-colored baby dress and her small hands are open; she is dead.

Just like a doll—so sweet, Tsune thought.

Ants swarm around her lips, and maggots crawl in and out of her tear ducts.

Her cheeks are still pink, and the baby smiles as if she were tickled. At a gentle touch of the finger tips, some of her skin peels off.

Grease runs from the baby who has started to melt, making just that part of the earth glisten, dark with moisture. The clusters of flowers shine lustrously, absorbing juice from the baby's flesh.

The wind blows. The baby's fine hair trembles.

Every day the baby melts and returns to the earth, emanating fragrance and nourishing the heavy clusters of acacia blossoms.

Tsune often has the same dream. She likes the tenderly plump Wakako she sees in her dream. She likes the dead face of the baby who is an exact image of Wakako.

On the outskirts of N City, there is a small mountain with a hollow on its northern slope carved out by the blast of the explosion. The southern slope, which faced the target area of the atomic bomb, is charred in dark and light stripes, which retain traces of the arrows of radiation which shot out in all directions. Turning its back on the shifting sun, the hollow is in dark shade and utters a low groan in the wind that blows upward. In August when the atomic bomb was dropped, a few dozen girl students died on this slope.

All that remained were several brittle pieces of bone which crumbled easily like dry sugar cakes when they were picked up.

In the mountain wind that started to blow that day, the bones rolled down the slope with a dry rustling sound.

They made a little mound in the hollow.

After a month, a grave marker of unpainted, white wood appeared in the hollow. It belonged to Yoko, who had died at the age of fourteen. As though to surround it, other white wooden grave markers were erected one by one. They were for the girl students rumored to have been on the mountain.

As the days pass the few dozen grave markers which crowd the narrow hollow incline slightly in the blowing wind, sighing, each with a different voice.

Wakako's tomb is there, too. She was a close friend of Yoko's.

It was in the morning four days after the bombing of Nagasaki that Wakako returned to the village of orange groves where her mother lived. Wakako's mother saw her standing, her face expressionless and reeling in the green light of the orange mountain that rose high over the inlet. Holding an orange branch in her two hands, Wakako's mother said syllable by syllable, as if verifying something: "Wa-ka-ko, it's you."

Many faces appeared through the brush of the orange mountain. They were the faces of villagers. Looking past the faces of men with sturdy cheekbones, Wakako sought her mother's face in the thicket from which the voice had come.

"Otsune-san, quick, quick. It's the real Waka-san," Obatchan (aunt), the oldest of the villagers, pushed Tsune forward.

Wakako's village was 180 kilometers from N City. It was a small village past several tunnels on the train from N.

With its four hundred and fifty inhabitants in seventy houses, the village bordered on a small inlet connected to O Bay. Wakako's father was the village master. The orange mountain rose right up from the steep shore of the inlet, leaving this a hilly village with hardly any flat land. They say N City is full of dead bodies, it's completely destroyed, and not even a cat is alive—rumors reached the village on the evening of the day of the bombing.

That night, as her husband had fastened his gaiters tight around his calves and set out for N City to search for Wakako, Tsune had handed him a purple crepe scarf used for special occasions and said: ''Please bring her home, if just her bones. She was a slender child, so if you see slender bones, they are probably hers.'' Rumor after rumor arrived, and all concerned the destruction of the city which used to love merrymaking, with the biggest or second biggest Shinto festival in Japan: due to a single strange bomb, it had become a totally soundless city.

Had Wakako alone survived?—no, this hardly seemed possible. Besides, that day while she had been supervising village workers in the orange groves, Tsune saw the huge, tornado-like column of fire from the atomic bomb dropped on N City. In that column of fire which shot up into the vast sky, a slender girl like Wakako would burn more easily than a mayfly thrown into a gas flame.

Tsune had given up on Wakako.

Yet, without so much as a scar, Wakako was standing before her eyes. Seeing Wakako before her, part of Tsune still wondered if this was, in Obatchan's words, the real Wakako.

The news of Wakako's safety spread from thicket to thicket of the orange groves. Waka-san has come home? Is it true? Men asked in loud voices. It is true, Tsune answered, smiles breaking out all over her face. She's not injured, is she? Is Yo-chan with her? While they questioned her, Tsune scrutinized Wakako from the thicket, then answered cheerfully, her voice equally loud: It looks like there are no injuries; Yo-chan . . . isn't with her.

Wakako was exhausted. The unrestrained voices of the villagers making a fuss over her return, the brightness of the unpretentious sun, as transparent as paraffin, the firm green of oranges—everything in the village was so healthy it disturbed her.

"I'll steam rice and red beans right away so we can celebrate with everyone. All right Wakako?"

Her finger tips still red from crushing the insects which sucked sap from the orange trees, Tsune held Wakako's hands. They were cold.

As she had often done when Wakako was small, Tsune pressed her lips against her daughter's forehead to see if she had fever.

She felt slow heat from Wakako's forehead, which seemed to retain heat deep within.

"Do you have any wounds?" Tsune knit her brows checking Wakako's body with both hands.

"Otsune-san," Obatchan called, and cautioned her in a suppressed voice, "the bomb this time's different: everyone died, with or without wounds. The earlier the better. Have the doctor examine her."

"I will. Wakako, let's ask old doctor Tanaka to take a look. He can cure any wound."

Wakako shook her head like a small child. She wanted to go home as soon as possible to the house under the thick thatched roof, where a cool wind from the sea blew in. Having spent three days and three nights on the hot soil of the burnt fields, she longed for the big, grainy pillars at home which felt cool to touch.

Wakako started to walk down the mountain trail away from the doctor's place.

"You want to go home? Then let's go home quickly, Wakako," Tsune said.

When they got home, she would wipe her daughter's entire body with water from the well in the yard. With pure water pumped from the depths of the earth, she would wipe away the horrible poison of the bomb. Tsune remembered that when Wakako was born she had given her baby her first bath in the same well water.

It was an early morning in August, and when Tsune bathed Wakako on the veranda, she yelled with a robust, almost convulsive voice, eyes tightly closed from the shock of the first sunlight— Tsune recalled this as she followed Wakako, determined never to let her die. They were followed by Obatchan and the noisy train of villagers who had thrown away their work.

Shige, Obatchan's grandchild, in a Kintaro bib which she rarely wore, walked next to Wakako, asking, "Was it scary, Waka-chan, was the flash scary?" Wakako softly shook her head as Shige repeated the question with shining eyes.

Scary? Or not scary? Shige pursued, not knowing which Wakako had meant. When asked this way, Wakako herself was not sure which was right. Although Shige seemed to think it roughly the same kind of scare as when thunder hit, the horror was so great that it defied Wakako's comprehension.

Not even a single wound, Waka-san is really lucky; the gods protected her—the villagers made as much noise as if it were a festival night as they headed for Wakako's house on the hilltop.

A few rice paddies lay between one mountain and another. The villagers walked cheerfully, single file, along a narrow footpath.

Green grass was abundant in the village. It grew everywhere along the narrow paths between the rice paddies, steaming in the summer light and giving off a damp smell. The grass smell, moist and shapeless, was the same as the faint odor of scorched bodies carried by the wind over the burnt field.

"Mother, I smell the bomb," Wakako said, covering her nose. Obatchan, who was now walking side by side with Wakako along the narrow path, responded: "It's the sagebrush. Don't you like their nice smell? You are too sensitive, Waka-san." She laughed as if she breathed the laughter through her toothless mouth, "Ho-h-ho."

"Waka-chan escaped death, so she'll live long," a man holding Shige's hand called to Tsune in a loud voice from behind her. "Thanks to you all, yes. I want her to live as long as Obatchan," Tsune said, bowing; but even as she spoke, she was anxious about Wakako's bloodless face.

When Wakako finally reached home, she laid her tired body on the wooden floor near the entrance.

The floor polished with rice bran cooled her feverish body. Although she had not a single scar, both her arms and legs felt as heavy as if she were dragging the earth; her head was like a heavy weight she could not support. Yielding the burden of her head to the floor, Wakako opened her lips lightly. That made her feel better, since it eased the tension around her jaw.

Obatchan bent to look at Wakako, saying, "You're beautiful, Waka-san. Like a wax doll." Tsune, too, watched Wakako's pale, translucent skin and had to think, even of her own child, that she was beautiful. However, this was a beauty she had not detected in the healthy looking Wakako who had said "I'll be back" and left with Yoko four days ago. If this beauty was something she had brought home from N City, didn't it signify death, as the rumors maintained?

"Wakako, are you feeling poor? Excuse yourself and sleep a little," Tsune said.

"Yes, yes, that's best. Yo-chan will come home eventually. She survived, didn't she, Waka-san?" Obatchan turned her gummy eyes to Wakako.

Wakako's lips convulsed lightly as she looked at her mother. "Yes?" Tsune looked into Wakako's eyes which seemed to be supplicating, but Wakako looked down without answering.

The villagers who had gathered at the entrance, too, watched her mouth, waiting for her answer.

"Please let her rest; she's tired," Tsune greeted the villagers, propping Wakako up by the shoulders. Observing Wakako's expression, she wondered what could have happened to her daughter's friendship with Yoko.

"Obatchan's asking you something. Be pleasant and tell her what you know," Tsune chided Wakako, as she hung a mosquito net in a room facing the sea. Any little detail would help. Yoko and Wakako were among the students mobilized to work at the same factory. Since they even belonged to the same work area, Wakako couldn't get away with simply saying she didn't know what happened to Yoko. However, the inexpressible horror of the "new model" bomb had already come home to the villagers. It would be all right for her to answer that she couldn't tell because she had been overwhelmed by fear. One word about Yoko would have given Obatchan and others peace of mind.

"Yo-chan . . . is dead, is that it?"

Wakako said nothing, and pulled the summer futon all the way up over her face. She had nothing to tell Tsune or Obatchan and the others who could say such things as "Tell her what you know," or "The gods protected you."

"That's just the smell of sagebrush," the others laughed carelessly about the wild plant along the path, without any misgivings. The four days Wakako had spent in N City were worlds away from that simplicity.

"Sleep a little," Tsune stroked Wakako's hair, and Wakako closed her eyes unresisting.

The scenes of N City where she had been until several hours ago came back before her closed eyes. Wakako did not think that what she had done to Yoko in the mountain where they took refuge was wrong. However, if she faithfully described to the villagers what had happened, they would probably condemn her as heartless. How could anyone who had not been there then understand? Even for those who were there, as time passed, the extraordinary ball of fire would fade away, leaving behind nothing but judgments on the results. When all the conditions that had brought about the facts grew dim, and only the facts remained, what would Wakako do?

Just a moment ago, Wakako had encountered Yoshi, Yoko's mother. She was wearing her black monpe,* and said she was going to look for her daughter. Wakako told her it appeared that Yo-chan had run off into the mountains.

Appeared—no, Wakako knew it for a fact. "Did she run away by herself? She is alive, isn't she?"

Seeing the tears fill Yoshi's eyes, Wakako nodded unequivocally. The tears in the eyes of many of the people she had seen in the burnt fields dripped in strands, sticky like a sea turtle's tears.

Yoshi's tears were clear and shiny. Watching her, Wakako, too, felt as though tears were welling up. Yet she lied to Yoshi. The two of them, Wakako and the wounded Yoko, had run to the mountain on the outskirts of N city. In that mountain Yoko had died.

"I've brought bleached cotton just in case she has big burns. Did she have burns?" Evading the eyes of Yoshi who asked question after question, Wakako shook her head: I don't know.

---

*Work pants with or without a matching top.

On the day the bomb fell, it was fair in N City. And it was hot. The factory where Wakako and Yoko had been mobilized was a big armory located on the outskirts of N City.

Rumor had it that the factory was producing torpedoes. Yet no one had even once seen a finished torpedo. Japan had run out of materials, the workers said. They whistled blithely and added, "We're going to lose."

Wakako and others who had been mobilized to work there had nothing to do but stand around and chat in a corner of the factory.

A sharp-eyed worker, who also had nothing to do, would find the girls talking and report them. The chief, who prided himself in having lost an arm in the China Incident, called out, "Polish the windows—ready, go!" Their mobilized life meant daily window polishing.

Each of the few glass windows in the factory always sparkled.

The chief, who rarely skipped a day, was absent that day. Wakako and Yoko were chatting with each other, their backs against the large, polished windows.

Yoko in her navy blue and white monpe slacks stood with her back to the widest window in the factory. This single piece of glass, in which their chief took great pride, was said to be three millimeters thick.

The glass window, drinking up the summer sun, shone on Wakako's cheeks. Since Wakako was very sensitive to light, she found the sun too dazzling. As she sheltered herself in the shade of the concrete pillar beside her, something white seemed to float in one corner of the window.

A cloud? Wakako asked. It looks like a parachute, said a young man who passed by carrying a grease can and making a heavy rapping noise with his cedar clogs.

The factory clock, which lost exactly one minute per hour, struck eleven o'clock. The one-armed chief was a man of precision: every morning on his arrival he corrected the clock. It remained slow that day.

"It's almost lunch. I'm having rice and omelette." Yoko was fond of sweet omelette.

As if too impatient to wait till noon, she picked up her lunch box from the desk and smiled, smelling it from outside the wrap.

At the same time as Wakako saw Yoko's white eyeteeth, something white tilted diagonally across the glass window and shook violently back and forth, with the sun as an axis.

In that instant, a purple light seemed pasted across the whole space of the window. Up until that moment, Wakako had thought of light as something that ran with sharp, shooting needles like those on a metal plant holder for flower arrangement, and disappeared immediately. The lightning that had struck over the orange mountain when she was five years old had a pointed shape, creating a jagged streak drawing a track of light exactly like the ones in comics. Lightning that she had seen shoot out across the sea, too, was like that. This light outside the window was different, however. It extended all over the sky so slowly and even tenaciously, that the eyes could follow its spread. Because its mass was felt to be tangible, this light was different from the energy without thickness that Wakako, until now, had thought of as "light."

The window glass shattered, and simultaneously the light outside the window broke, blowing against the shoulders and back of Yoko, who turned her face down.

As glass splinters shot against the floor like arrows from a blowpipe, spiral metal fragments scattered across the floor whirled upwards. A black crack ran through a square beam as it fell from the ceiling.

Wakako grasped precisely what transpired in that instant. Everything was fluid, like pictures in a revolving lantern rapidly flowing across the surface of the eyeball.

Was it reality that was actually assaulting Wakako, or was it an event in a dream? In a vagueness that defied comprehension, she heard a light, scratchy noise made by the glass that landed on Yoko's back and cut into the skin.

It was the same sound made by the colorful blizzard in the autumn sun at the school athletic meet, when the huge paper ball split and released small pieces of paper which danced with a dry noise.

"Last, again? You're no good, Wakako." Yoko, who always got a red ribbon for first place, reproached Wakako for being a slow runner.

The same proud face loomed up amidst the rain of glass splinters. It became contorted in a way Wakako had rarely seen, and it cried: Help! Looking at the cave-like darkness of Yoko's mouth, Wakako echoed her cry, in exactly the same tone of voice.

Wakako lay under the debris of the crushed factory.

Fire seemed to have broken out: she saw flames at her feet. "Help me! Isn't anyone going to help me?"—a man crawled out of the debris grabbing at any pieces of concrete that his hands could touch.

In front of his hands there was a tiny space. Smoke blew in from the space, moving the air around Wakako. It was the only space through which escape was possible.

Wakako pulled the man's leg with all her might and begged him to help her. The hairy shin of the man who wore wooden clogs kicked her shoulder. Wakako did not let go even then.

The man took off his sturdy, home-made clog, and hit her slender shoulder with it. Her bone creaked.

The hairy shin disappeared from sight with the quickness of a squirrel. Realizing that no one would help her, Wakako started to pull down, as the man had done, whatever debris she could lay hands on. When she came to, she was standing outside the building.

Around her was a sea of fire. The wind was hot, occasionally scorching her hair. Amidst wind that made a noise like the rumbling of the earth and flames that encircled clouds of smoke, a human shape appeared.

It was a girl with long hair, probably a student. Wakako started to run after her.

Wakako did not remember from what part of the crushed factory she had crawled out. However, as she had slipped free, someone had grasped her ankle. She remembered five damp fingers clinging stubbornly to her ankle as she tried to make her escape.

Like the man, Wakako too kicked that hand with the heel of one of her sneakers. Reluctantly, one by one, the long, damp-skinned fingers released Wakako's ankle and fell into the flaming debris.

They felt like the fingers of Yoko, whose little finger Wakako had intertwined with her own in a symbolic act of friendship.

I heard that a missionary school student tried to help a nun who was crushed under the church. When she ran toward the building, the nun chided the girl and said, Don't come, it's all right, run away quickly. The nun's robe caught fire . . . and the girl ran away crying, they say. Pity, how she must have felt. A young girl, not too many years behind her—

In the next room Obatchan was talking.

Wasn't she wonderful, that nun?—Tsune sniffed. A faint smile floated on Wakako's pale cheeks.

That story is a fake—Wakako mumbled to herself. Obatchan's story was an embellished fabrication, not the truth. As in the tale of Urashima Taro, in which the young fisherman becomes an old man in a whiff of white smoke, N City was instantly transformed into a city of the dead in one flash of light that day. Those who lived had just barely managed to save their lives. Who would have deliberately run back to help others? There could not possibly have been time to worry about others.

The girl student who fled home probably fabricated the story when recounting her experiences to her parents, the image of the nun she had forsaken haunting her eyes. It must be that she wanted to believe in her own good will. The made-up story moved Obatchan, brought tears to Tsune's eyes, and would do the same to many other well meaning people.

As the days pass, the lie will penetrate the girl's body and she herself will begin to believe it. For the first time, then, she will be liberated from the nun.

Just as she unconsciously lied to Yoshi, some day Wakako, too, might tell Obatchan and Tsune about Yoko, conveniently coloring the truth.

She wished the day would come soon.

While rejecting Obatchan's story as a lie, part of Wakako thought that perhaps it was how it was meant to be.

When she saw the painful expression on Yoko's contorted face amidst the falling glass, a glint of cruel satisfaction, although just for a second, crossed her mind.

Wakako no longer understood herself. She wondered if something that remained unaffected by any circumstance whatsoever might not lie deep in the human mind.

"Obatchan is worrying about Yo-chan's safety," Tsune said in a soft voice, opening a screen door.

"If she's really worrying, Obatchan can go find her. She's not going, is she? In that case, be quiet." At the time of the explosion, Obatchan probably just watched, sipping tea, and said, How frightening, what can that fireball be?

"Nobody is blaming you, Wakako. You look so grim." The sudden barb in Wakako's voice was incomprehensible to Tsune.

Trying not to lose sight of the long haired student, Wakako, the slow runner, ran with all her might. From time to time, the girl reeled, engulfed in flames. Each time this happened, her back shone in colors that changed like a chameleon's shell. In red flames it turned red; in flickering blue flames that burned horses and men, it shone coldly.

As she ran, Wakako wondered vaguely why a human back shone. Again and again she fell, stumbling over dead bodies. The bodies, which had just breathed their last, were still soft and the flesh had an elasticity which was resilient to Wakako's touch.

Wakako was afraid of dead bodies. The tender flesh that pressed against her chest, and its smell, turned her stomach. She burped with a foolish noise, and vomited on the spot.

After a while she was exposed to too many deaths to feel fear any more. She also became used to the tenderness of the bodies' flesh.

Her toes learned to distinguish, on the basis of the softness of the flesh, male from female, young from old bodies.

A young woman, with thick bouncy flesh between the bone and soft skin, number 16; a man, old, with hard bones and thin flesh, number 9—unconsciously she counted with her fingers as she ran. She felt no sympathy.

However, when what she had thought was a corpse woke from the impact of her stumble and looked up, his eyes narrow slits, saying, "Give me medicine," Wakako caught her breath in horror. A human being who was clearly dying, or ninety percent dead, still wanted medicine—that attachment to life frightened her. Wakako ran on, avoiding those who appeared to be still alive.

The sunlight shone on the chameleon back of the girl running ahead of her, making slight rifts in the smoke.

Wakako found herself at the foot of the mountain which had been designated a refuge.

If anything happens, be sure to assemble at the mountain.

As usual, this was the instruction their teacher had given to Wakako and the others on the morning of the bombing. If only she could get to the mountain she could see her teacher and her friends. That thought had sustained Wakako as she ran desperately through the fire.

The gently sloping mountain, which had been covered with green cedars, was burning and smoke rose everywhere. Some of Wakako's classmates were supposed to have been working at the mountain.

Since the side cave which Wakako and others had used as an air raid shelter had simply been dug into the earth without reinforcement, mountain water had dripped from its ceiling and covered the floor to about knee level. According to the instructions they had received, a team of girls should have been scooping up buckets of water and passing them outside the cave. Outside, students from other schools were supposed to be cutting grass.

If they were still alive, at least one would call her name.

Wakako tried skirting the foot of the mountain. When she had gone about half way around, she found a small brook about two meters wide.

A cluster of water cress still grew in the running water, creating an impression of coolness that seemed incongruous with the burnt surface of the mountain. Wakako felt like drinking water. Stripped of clothing which had burnt, and covered with blood, many people were drinking, thrusting their heads in the water of the brook. They lay on their stomachs and drank, their faces touching the surface of the water and their legs stretched apart.

There was a kind of intimacy about this scene of river and people, as if the running water were a giant centipede and the people its legs. Wakako's throat was dry.

Finding a tiny space, she started to drink, lying on her stomach like the others.

The water was tepid and smelled strongly of moss. The weight of the water spread throughout her empty stomach which had missed lunch. As she was absorbed in the act of drinking, she felt the finger tip of the man next to her on her cheek. When she brushed it away, the man with crew cut hair flipped upside down as simply as the shutter carrying the poisoned Oiwa in the kabuki story, and fell into the water.*

The man's eyes were open, and he was dead.

The river was shallow. It flowed in ripples over the man's wide open eyeballs. He seemed about forty, probably the head of a family with wife and children. He was no more than an object which created a slight variation to the flow of the water.

Wakako took another look at the stream.

It seemed unchanged from when she had seen it earlier that morning, flowing calmly through a field scorched by the atomic blast. At the moment of the explosion, the water seethed as if it were boiling, and the surface, bubbling up in foam, rose twenty or thirty centimeters. But that was just for a second; the flowing water before her eyes had returned to the tranquility of the early morning.

Wakako recalled:

It was when she was in grade school. For a year or so, she lived in a city on the Chinese continent.

It was an English style city where red brick houses stood side by side. A river flowed through the city, full, literally full, of yellow water. The amount and depth of water in that river were unfathomable.

Wakako had been fond of this river, and often walked along it with the amah who worked for them.

On early summer mornings, little boats called sampans and shaped like rabbits with ears erect floated along the river as though they were sleeping.

Putt, putt, putt came the sound of a steam boat from the upper

---

*In *Tokaido Yotsuya Kaidan* by Tsuruya Nanboku (1755–1829), Oiwa is poisoned by her husband. He ties the bodies of Oiwa and a young man on each side of a shutter and lets it float in the river. Her ghost, her face deformed from poisoning, haunts him to death.

river. It was the water police patrol boat. It made the rounds of the river every morning.

Wakako would count—one, two, three—pointing at the back of the boat with her forefinger. She was counting the number of drowned bodies tied to the stern.

Tied together in a row with a fat rope, the bodies kicked up water heroically as they were towed along. One stretched his arms to heaven, crying for help. Another had one leg still raised, with which he had violently kicked the water trying to rise to the surface. Each body assumed a different posture as the boat tugged them behind it. They seemed to ride on the waves with their heads and swollen bellies.

Amah, which of those men do you like?—Wakako would ask. The amah always ignored her question: Miss, they aren't men, they are baggage because they're dead.

Those corpses, because they had lost the repugnant fleshiness of living human beings, were a nature poem which added colors to the yellow flow. The sight of those limbs beating the water in an effort to regain life only added a special touch to the landscape, making the river itself look that much more peaceful. It was a natural scene within which the dead were now returning to mother earth.

In comparison, the dead bodies strewn before Wakako's eyes in the burnt field suggested no peace associated with a return to nature.

Wakako, is that you?—a girl called to her. It's me, Yoko, the voice approached from behind with the sound of dragging feet. Yoko's monpe were torn from the knees down, revealing flesh which had been scraped away in several places as though with a spoon. Her wounded legs faltering, the girl fell. Her back glistened as she lay on her side. Her blouse had burned up in the flash, and glass splinters stuck in her bare back. Around the root of each splinter, powdery thin pieces, mosaic-like, formed a spiral. Each time she breathed, the tips of the fine pieces trembled. No doubt from the pain, she held her body tense, stifling her breath.

Could this be the same Yoko?—the same Yoko who, in the prime of her innocent and inviolable youth, had raised her lunch box and rather proudly announced that she had rice and omelette?

"Look what shape I'm in—" Yoko spoke in the Nagasaki dialect which was forbidden at school, showing Wakako her wounds. "I see that you didn't get any wounds," Yoko said as she rose slowly.

It looks like I didn't—as Wakako tried to give an ambiguous answer, Yoko turned just her head toward her without moving her body and said, "I wish I could give you half of my wounds."

Although they had been standing in the same place, Yoko was badly wounded, while not even a piece of glass stuck to Wakako's body. Apparently, it had been a stroke of luck that Wakako had sought shelter from the light behind a large pillar a second before the explosion.

Wakako had been saved by chance, but Yoko seemed unhappy about it.

Yoko was better looking than Wakako. She was also brighter.

It was only in social status that Wakako surpassed her because her father was the village master. However, Yoko's family was richer.

In the mountains, too, the sun shone longer on the oranges belonging to Yoko's family. They had a glossier, deeper color and were sweeter than those of Wakako's family.

Yoko was superior in every respect. Yet at the moment that decided life or death, luck had favored Wakako. If ever the villagers reached an impasse or became embarrassed when they had to choose between the two, the referee's fan would be raised to the one whose family status had been higher since before the children's births. In the same way chance made Wakako the winner.

The two sat silently, holding their knees, at the edge of the brook. Four or five hours had passed since the bombing. In less than an hour, the sun would sink behind the mountain, and the first night after the explosion would come to N City.

"Why don't we run to some place where there are people," Wakako stood up. I'm tired of running, Yoko said in a low voice. Seeing that Wakako remained standing, Yoko looked up and said: You want to run away, don't you? It's all right if you go alone.

"We'll go together," Wakako started to say, but she held the words back.

So after all those white fingers had belonged to Yoko. The long fingers which Wakako had kicked heartlessly were Yoko's.

Yet Yoko had not even referred to this when she suggested that
Wakako run away by herself. She had done so in her typically cruel,
indirect manner.

Yet at the time Wakako had been unable to think of anything else
to do. Yoko herself would not have had the impulse to help another.

All she could do was save herself. In fact, hadn't Yoko run ahead
of Wakako—and faster than Wakako?

Yes, that chameleon back had been Yoko's. Wakako had run after
her back. If this were so, Yoko had escaped from the crushed
building one step ahead of Wakako.

It made sense that Wakako, sheltered behind the fat, square pillar
proved lucky as far as the flash of light was concerned, but for that
very reason she had been more deeply buried under rubble. Although Yoko had been burned, she must have escaped from the
building more easily.

Then the white hand could not have been Yoko's. Wakako must
have kicked someone else's hand. In either case, it was true that she
had left a human being surrounded by flames. But that was another
matter.

Wakako felt the lump in her chest subside.

"If we're running at all, it's got to be both of us together,"
Wakako stroked Yoko's hair, which was wet with blood. Yoko had
started to doze off, perhaps due to her wounds.

"Let's go near the fire," Wakako said. Yoko stood up without
ado, leaning on the hand Wakako held out.

I'm cold . . . , Yoko trembled, firmly clasping Wakako's hand as
tightly as if she were a little child.

The sea, the sky, and the sloping trail on the ridge of the mountains—everything glowed in the evening sun.

"Red dragonflies, so many of them," Shige's voice came from
the trail.

"Do you want some?" said the voice of a village man. Shige
nodded. Two days had passed since Wakako's return. She was
watching red dragonflies swarming between the yard and the mountain pass.

Their diaphanous silver wings trembling, the red dragonflies flew toward the yard of Wakako's house.

The man wore only his underwear and had a wet towel around his neck. Apparently he had just taken a bath. B–29's almost never visited this village of orange groves deep in the mountains.

Even though they had heard about the disaster in N City, the villagers seemed oblivious to the war as they basked in the evening glow which dyed the sea red.

Shige, too, wore only her underwear.

"Shige, bring the throw-net."

"What are you going to do with it?" Shige, who had just turned four, ran down from the pass, her little round bottom bouncing, and returned dragging the fish net behind her.

Shige was a plucky child who would run all along the small river and the footpaths between the paddies never wearing more than underpants.

"There," Shige handed the man the net she had been holding to her chest and nodded, sticking out her tummy and clasping her hands behind her back. "I see, you're going to catch dragonflies, right?"

"No clothes again? Girls have to wear something," the man poked her navel as he took the net. Shige laughed, showing her white teeth, and asked,

"That's really a fish net, isn't it?"

"Fish and dragonflies are all the same," the man took a step forward and struck a pose against the sky, using his left hand to hold the net closed and his right hand to pull it.

"What are you doing with the net, uncle?"

"Just watch. There!" he drew a fan-shaped arc across the vault of the sky.

The thin threads of the net wafted toward the evening sun, opened slowly, trapped some dragonflies in its meshes, and came floating down.

The red dragonflies' silver wings danced inside the net like small fish.

"They'll get hurt if they bump against the lead weights, won't they, uncle?" Shige asked worriedly.

"No, they won't. They won't get hurt. Now catch them quickly."

Shige sprang to the net like a grasshopper.

Catching sight of the red dragonflies trembling in the net, their thin bodies strong as piano cords, Wakako felt she could not bear watching as their lives were extinguished. She closed her eyes.

Yoko was dead—Yoshi's voice was heard, mingled with Shige's shouts.

Wakako seemed to fall asleep for several minutes. The sunset had faded, leaving both the room and the yard in gloom. Shige was still releasing red dragonflies trapped in the net.

Most had become so weak that they hovered close to the ground, lost balance in their wings, and fell

"I would like to see the buddha* and offer my prayers." It seemed that Obatchan was still in the next room. Wakako heard her feet shuffling across the tatami. The buddha? Wakako sat up on her mat.

Was Yoko's body in this house? Her breath hushed, Wakako listened to the sounds in the next room. Why had they carried Yoko to Wakako's house on the hilltop? Yoko's house was at the bottom of the hill.

What could Yoshi mean by this? Had she heard in N City anything about Wakako and Yoko?

"Please don't look, Obatchan. The only reason I brought her up the hill was because I thought Waka-chan must be concerned about Yoko. Yoko, too, would love to have a glimpse of Waka-chan. Besides, Yoko hasn't changed a bit. I found her dead looking exactly the same as the girl you've always known."

"Really? How fortunate. . . . She was a beautiful girl. How beautiful she must be now that she has become a buddha. Yoshi-san, please let me take one look."

"No." Yoshi paused and then said steadily: "She was dead, eaten by maggots. I wound strips of bleached cotton cloth around her and carried her home carefully so they wouldn't unwrap. So I don't want to show her to you."

"Yo-chan eaten by maggots. . . . How painful, Yoshi-san. But I'm sure it wasn't just Yo-chan. I hear all the bodies in N City were that way."

---

*A dead person or his soul is referred to as "buddha" (*hotokesama*).

Tsune reproached Obatchan for speaking so bluntly, without regard for the feelings of whoever might be listening. Then she said to Yoko's mother, "Thank you for the trouble you've taken, Yoshi-san. I'll wake Wakako right away." Tsune quietly opened a sliding door. Wakako saw that the light was on in the adjacent room. Yoshi's face was pale under the cylindrical light, draped with black cloth as a precaution against air raids. Her hair was tightly combed with a bun in back. The front portions of her monpe collar were pulled tight over one another, while the narrow strip of white kimono undergarment showing around her neck lent a sword-like focus to her expression.

Despite her day-long search for Yoko through the burnt fields, Yoshi's white collar appeared even whiter than before in Wakako's eyes.

Yoko's body lay on a shutter, under a white cloth, just beyond the circumference of the cylinder of light.

Wakako impulsively turned her face down on her bedding.

"Please, Yoshi-san, let me see the buddha just for a second. Think of it as an old woman's duty," Obatchan said to Yoshi. I feel such pity for Yo-chan. Only Waka-san survived. I wish there was some way both of them could have lived. I wouldn't have minded taking her place, old woman that I am—As she approached the place where Yoko lay on the shutter, Obatchan looked in at Wakako who was under the mosquito net.

Obatchan was so agitated by Yoko's death she was weeping. In this village, at most one or two people died every ten years. Death was not only a rare occurrence but one limited to old people. Her playmates of long ago had died one by one, leaving Obatchan alone. Now it was her turn: it was inevitable that she would die some time in the near future. Obatchan was frightened of her own death. Yet while she had been waiting for death to come, maybe today, maybe tomorrow, the fourteen-year-old Yoko had died.

Even though she was saddened by the girl's death, Obatchan appeared to derive peace of mind from this death which had upset the natural order: her own turn might, just might, come much, much later.

Perhaps even the sorrow that brought tears to her eyes was a sham. At least Wakako thought so.

As a matter of fact, Obatchan had tarried in their home ever since Wakako had run home from N City that morning. While repeating again and again that Waka-san was lucky indeed, she accurately detected that the paleness of Wakako's skin was abnormal: When will Wakako die? Wakako's death didn't seem so far off.

The villagers had welcomed Wakako's escape with festive merrymaking. The more familiar faces were around, the better her journey toward death would be, as well.

"Yoko was in the hollow of the mountain, just as Waka-chan said. She was dead, all by herself, holding her knees."

Yoko's body was stiff. The white cloth over the board bulged around it as if it were a wine keg.

"Just as Waka-san said? So she knew, after all? Some say they saw them running away to the mountain together," Obatchan said to Wakako, looking in from behind the sliding door.

"Who said so?" Tsune questioned her in a tense voice.

Could that have been yesterday, after all?—Obatchan dodged Tsune's question, either because she was being evasive or because she had truly forgotten—no, it feels like it was this morning.

"Did you hear the same story, Yoshi-san?" Tsune asked. Without answering her, Yoko's mother said:

"When I held her up, a maggot on her back fell on my lap . . . and squirmed like a baby, just the way Yoko used to." She stroked Yoko's stiffened body through the white cloth. Obatchan said: Maggots are maggots, Yoshi-san. Don't lose your senses; they say the war's going to go on for a long time.

Who could have seen them? Wakako tried to picture the day's scenes in her mind. The only live person she had encountered was the man she stumbled over when running.

He, too, was half dead. He had asked for medicine, yet, without waiting for her answer, had closed his eyes. Even if he might have been from this village, he probably died before nightfall. Besides, Wakako was alone when she passed him.

The only other person was Yoko. But Yoko was already dead by then, so she could have told neither Yoshi nor Obatchan. No one could know.

Wakako grew weaker as the days passed. Each day her skin grew paler and more transparent, until the purple capillary vessels were visible under her eyes.

Wakako, her mother would call, but she would only turn her head wearily, without speaking. Old doctor Tanaka came to examine her, but his advice was always the same: Try giving her some fresh fruit.

Stretching arms which had been reduced to nothing but bones on her summer comforter, Wakako just stared at the ceiling.

Is there something on the ceiling? When Tsune questioned the child who was gazing and gazing, she answered: The ceiling—you see, its wood grain looks like Yoko.

When half a month or so passed, Tsune found a small, red spot on Wakako's arm. It was a tiny dot like a mosquito bite or a flea bite.

When Tsune scratched at it without thinking with the tip of her finger nail, it was crushed and a downy hair with a ball of pus at its root came off. Taking a careful look, she found similar red spots scattered here and there on both of Wakako's arms. Careful not to be noticed by Wakako, Tsune scratched another dot by way of experiment.

Like a weed with a rotten root, the hair came off easily, attached to a drop of infected fat.

The new model bomb that had been dropped on N City caused the open wounds and pores of human beings who had returned alive to the village to rot, sending them to certain death.

At present there is no treatment that would prevent their death, said old doctor Tanaka. He had given up.

Tsune could only watch Wakako dying day by day. Flies gathered, attracted by the odor of the infected skin. Tsune chased away the swarming flies.

She regretted that she could do nothing else.

Faithful to their promise to their teacher, the two girls had climbed the mountain the following morning. Although the fire had been extinguished, purple smoke rose from the charred trees and a strange heat enveloped the mountain. Yoko seemed to be suffering from the wounds on her back: every now and then she would stop and sigh, "How they hurt."

On the mountain slope, which had been smooth just the day before, Wakako found a hollow of freshly exposed soil.

The hollow faced north, away from the target of the bombing, and its soil was moist. With her back against the wall of the hollow to cool her skin, Wakako sat and embraced her knees.

Yoko sat by her side, her back not touching the wall but close enough so that her skin felt the cold air of the earth. Since the night before the two had rested in the same posture, holding their knees. It was the curled posture of the fetus in the mother's womb, floating without the least resistance in the protecting water.

The mountain was quiet. Wind blew through the hollow. They heard a sound of something tumbling down the slope.

It was a small noise, perhaps of a nut. Or could it be the teacher, or a classmate? A wounded human being only made a whimper.

Wakako strained her ears. The sound stopped when the object hit the earth with a little thud, and the mountain reverted to silence.

"I feel as if something were pecking at my back," Yoko complained of the pain, grimacing with cheeks that had turned the color of the earth.

The splinters of glass were more deeply buried in her flesh than they had been the day before. Even a splinter of wood hurts when it digs into the skin. If one single piece of glass could be pulled out, the pain would be reduced by just that much.

A splinter sticking into the middle of Yoko's back seemed at least four or five centimeters long. Trying not to touch the other splinters, Wakako swiftly pulled it out. With a scream, Yoko pushed Wakako. Knocked off balance, Wakako inadvertently grabbed the middle of Yoko's back.

Yoko gasped and hunched over even more. At that instant something fell from her back. It was a maggot.

The maggot, with blood in every section of its fat body, stretched and contracted its way up the mountain of glass, fell off, and quickly found a nearby wound, which it dug into, squeezing itself into a tight, narrow shape.

Maggots which could easily be crushed under a finger were lapping up blood and eating Yoko.

Only unclean wastes attracted maggots: a manure container beside a footpath on the farm in the village, fish bones in the trash dump, the swollen body of a cat thrown into a water pool, the intestines of a snake flushed out of a bush on to the summer road.

Only worthless things fester with maggots.

"Maggots," Wakako pointed at Yoko's back. "Maggots?" Yoko asked back. "Why me, why do they collect on me?" she queried resentfully.

"They're alive and moving, Yoko."

Even as she said this, horror at the meaning of the words she had never intended to utter made Wakako dizzy.

A fly which had been in the target area had survived miraculously, just as Wakako had, with even its crepe-paper wings intact. That fly must have been the first to smell out Yoko's death from among countless piles of corpses. What a clever fly! Wasting no time, it had procreated in the waste left by the destruction.

The maggots swarming in Yoko's open wounds would soon become flies, and it would be their turn to create new lives. They were devouring Yoko's flesh at great speed as they prepared to bring forth the next generation. They would turn into flies, and then assault Wakako. The succession of life cycles had not a moment to spare. Having even eaten into Yoko's almost haughty prime of youth, they would next attack Wakako.

Just as the drowned bodies in the yellow river had returned to mother earth, the maggot might be a reincarnation of Yoko. A maggot with Yoko's eyes and eyebrows would start to eat Wakako: You're turning into a maggot, too, Wakako.

But Wakako could not grant this favor to Yoko, even if it was Yoko's right, as a best friend, to demand it. She would crush every maggot that attacked her: she was determined to defeat Yoko.

Even if Yoko disappeared from the world because of these actions, it could not be helped.

Supporting her body with her hands from underneath while maintaining a sitting posture, Wakako tried to move away from Yoko without attracting her attention.

Sensing something in the air, Yoko turned her head, her cheek still on her knee, to look at Wakako. A satiated maggot fell from her back. Disoriented by finding itself on the less slippery earth, the maggot moved its gorged belly up and down as it crawled toward Wakako.

As it moved toward her leaving a light trail in the fresh dirt, Wakako, still sitting, crushed it under her heel. Yoko watched in silence.

Yoko's clean eyes, whose brightness Wakako used to envy, had already lost their light.

"Maggots hatch quickly, don't they. I raise maggots, and they become me," she laughed softly.

Her slackened nerves no longer seemed to find the swarming maggots eerie. Suddenly Yoko said, staring at Wakako with dull eyes, "You mustn't kill it. It's me."

Wakako ran down the mountain as fast as she could.

"Don't leave me alone," Yoko shouted. Wakako covered her ears with both hands and raced down the slope.

Wakako did not start to walk slowly until she had reached level ground. The small river flowed brightly, reflecting clouds in the sky.

When she caught sight of the shallow water flowing in a clear stream, Wakako fell to the ground. She lay there looking up at the sky. In the blue sky was the white sun. The sun she had looked up at yesterday from beside the stream trembled like a rotting tomato with too much soft flesh to keep its shape. The sun of the midsummer noon which should have been above her head had sunk to the horizon. Now the sun was utterly calm, its sharp light like a silk needle in one corner of the vast expanse of sky. Wakako could also hear an engine.

It was the metallic sound of a B-29. But no one tried to run for shelter now. Those who were checking dead bodies, anxious about missing close relatives, as well as those wounded who were, so to speak, dressed in tattered rags, just looked languidly up at the sky.

As the noise of the approaching engine grew louder, Wakako closed her eyes. Even if the same light flashed across the sky again, I would not run; I am too tired, Wakako thought.

I'll sleep for a while. . . .

The shadow of the low-flying airplane passed over her.

The burnt field was more crowded than it had been the day before. It was already three days after the bombing, and people from other areas who had heard about the disaster in N City had joined the crowds, looking for family members. They moved to and fro, their noses and mouths covered with towels, carrying canteens and bundles of necessities. Even in this charred field, the morning had its distinctive freshness. Some people were washing their bloodstained faces and rinsing their mouths in water gushing out of a broken water pipe. Wakako felt somewhat stronger.

Along the trail by the stream, many people were climbing toward the mountain top. Wakako, who had taken in nothing but water, joined the line of people on shaky feet.

She wondered how Yoko was doing.

"I wonder where she went to school. What a pity."

Wakako heard some women whispering and peered inside the circle of people. She was standing in front of the hollow where she and Yoko had stayed. The mothers joined their hands in prayer, while their shoulders slackened with relief at the realization that this body was not one of their daughters.

Yoko was dead. Still crouched down and holding her knees, just a few steps further away from the wall of the hollow than she had been yesterday. The stench which had accumulated in the hollow made Wakako nauseous.

"Poor child, flies are collecting on her," a woman brushed away the flies swarming on Yoko's face.

The flies' wings made a hideous noise as they flew away from the hollow.

Watching them fly toward the sun, Wakako thought: Yoko's dead.

"But that has nothing to do with me," she muttered, walking back down the mountain.

Wakako died.

She died one day after the ritual was observed marking the forty-ninth day since Yoko's death. For two or three days before death she had run a fever of approximately 104.

When she opened her eyes between long periods of sleep, the

wood grain in the ceiling smiled at her. Wakako did her best to keep her eyes closed.

When she closed them, Yoko never failed to appear. Many little Yokos, smaller than the span between the joints of a finger, would appear and circle around Wakako's bed. Each wore the same long hair and navy and white monpe Yoko had worn that day.

The Yokos walked in step around Wakako's bed.

Yoko, Wakako would call, but they didn't turn to look at her.

Each and every one of the Yokos walked with back turned to Wakako. No matter which side of the bed they were on, they never showed their faces to Wakako.

Yoko was angry.

It couldn't be helped. There was no other way at that moment, don't you see—Wakako said, but still they didn't look at her.

Walking with precise steps, the circle of Yokos gradually closed in on Wakako.

"Mother," Wakako called Tsune.

"I'm right here," Tsune held Wakako's hands in her warm hands, gently bending toward her: What would you like? Opening her eyes narrowly, Wakako said, Maggots, mother. "Where?" Tsune looked around the room. Wakako pointed at her head with her finger.

"In my head." Tsune grasped Wakako's hands tightly. She was prepared for her child's death.

She had given up hope the day she found the red spots on Wakako's arms.

Tsune had heard that survivors of the bombing died insane. Was it due to the high fever or to that flash of light? The sick person would die babbling incoherently, she had heard. Moreover, almost every single one of the pores in Wakako's arms was beginning to rot, oozing pus. Now her legs had started to be affected. Even though Tsune changed her sheets every day, they immediately became soiled with blood and yellow pus.

"There are no maggots there," Tsune said, her mouth to Wakako's ear. Wakako tucked in her head and giggled as if she had been tickled. "Can't you see? The inside of my head is full of them." Gesturing as she used to as a little girl when confiding a secret,

Wakako said, "I didn't help, you see. So they are rioting." "Who are you saying you didn't help?" Tsune wanted to know what had happened between Wakako and Yoko in N City. If Wakako had abandoned Yoko on the mountain as rumor had it, she wanted to somehow console her so she would feel more at peace. It must have been the sheer will to survive that led Wakako to abandon Yoko and exert her final strength to return to the orange mountain where Tsune lived.

The brief days after the bombing must have been the first time in her life that Wakako lived to the hilt, lovingly attached to her own life. If, during these most precious days of her life, she were to be blamed for not having helped Yoko, it would be too cruel, Tsune thought

Yoshi might know the facts.

Tsune went to her house.

"Is the rumor true? Tell me if you know." Tsune was facing the new memorial tablet standing in the miniature family shrine, hands joined.

"True? That's something Waka-chan should know. I want to hear it from her mouth, too. The only truth I know is that Yoko was dead in the mountain all by herself. That's all," she looked at Tsune, the rosary still in her hands.

"Yoshi-san, you took the trouble to bring Yo-chan over here that day so Wakako could see her. Wakako couldn't have left Yo-chan alone in the mountain, and because you believed that, you brought her, didn't you?"

"—But it was Waka-chan who told me Yoko was in the mountain."

Tsune looked steadily into the gleaming eyes of Yoshi, who so resembled Yoko.

"It's too cruel. I'm sure Wakako heard about it from someone else. The rumor is false. Wakako ran alone, all alone by herself. Think how much stronger she would have felt if she had been with Yo-chan."

This is the truth, Tsune added.

"Then, that must be the truth. Yoko has already died. I can't ask her."

"All sympathy goes to Yo-chan anyway because only Wakako survived. Yo-chan's death has nothing to do with Wakako. All right, Yoshi-san?"

Yoshi had turned her back against Tsune. With joined palms raised toward the memorial tablet, she continued her prayers. Tsune went on, "Please make this very clear to Obatchan and the village people, in your own words. She makes no excuse whatsoever, poor Wakako."

A villager came across Tsune on the road and asked her, as she was quickly passing by, How's Waka-chan doing? Tsune answered in a calm voice, I won't let her die.

Tsune knew Wakako's gentleness. Even if the rumor was true, who could blame her? Even Yoshi who had lost Yoko could not blame her.

It was wrong of Yoshi to resent Wakako. If she was to resent something, let it be the huge, monster ball of fire.

Let her resent the misfortune of her child who was not able to survive.

"There are a lot of Yokos around my bed," delirious with fever, Wakako waved both hands in the air.

"There's nothing to fear, Mother is watching you."

Tsune's voice did not penetrate Wakako's ears. Flies circling around inside Wakako's head buried her mother's words in the whir of their wings.

They were the flies which had lived in her head ever since she stayed in the mountain hollow.

The noise bothered her. How I long for quiet, the sooner the better, Wakako thought.

"Will you kill the flies?"

"Of course, Mother will kill everything that's nasty to you, Wakako."

A faint smile appeared on Wakako's cheeks, which were as somber and bloodless as those of a wax figure.

Taking a deep, audible breath, Wakako died with her mouth open.

Tsune kept looking long at the smile which lingered around Wakako's eyes.

The morning sun near the beginning of autumn shone into the room where Wakako lay, her pale cheeks shadowy where the flesh had sunk. The faint smile pasted on her cheeks took on a dark shade which did not become a young girl who had lived fourteen years and one month. Tsune kept fanning Wakako's body which was starting to become cold. Why Wakako had feared flies so much remained unknown to her mother. Once in her delirium she had said, "Mother, flies have teeth, so they bite me." Tsune could not begin to imagine where those words came from, but she could understand the terror Wakako had suffered from being condemned by something. She did not want to think that it was Yoko.

Obatchan, who had rushed over, said, "How frightening. Waka-san looks so grim. But everything is over now. Yoshi-san, forgive Waka-san." Her last words were addressed to Yoshi, who had arrived after her.

"Wakako has nothing to be forgiven for," Tsune said firmly, "I will have Wakako's grave dug side by side with Yo-chan's in that hollow. They were close friends."

"Then Yoko won't be able to rest in peace," Yoshi said.

"Yoshi-san, don't spread strange rumors. If you do, then it'll be Wakako who won't be able to rest in peace. The children bear no guilt at all. I'd like you to remember that at least," Tsune said clearly.

Wakako's grave marker of fresh wood was erected beside Yoko's in the mountain hollow.

Although her husband opposed it, reminding her of the fine ancestral tomb in the village, Tsune would not hear of anything else: It's proof of Wakako's innocence.

Facing away from the burnt field of N City in the autumn wind, the grave markers of the two girls were surrounded by many grave markers. They stood side by side in the breeze.

Tsune carried orange branches from the village across many hills, and put one, with fruit that was still hard and green, in the flower holder at Wakako's grave. She placed another for Yoko.

Intercepted by the grave markers, the wind that blew into the hollow seemed to be speaking in a slender voice.

What's so interesting? Share it with me, Tsune asked of the two girls' graves.

She thought she was hearing the laughter of Wakako and Yoko.

RESIDUES OF SQUALOR

Ota Yoko

Around the little ramshackle shed, there was a splashing sound of rain. It looked like a torrent.

At midnight, when the world was hushed in sleep, this awful-looking hovel did not stand alone in solitude, for around it hundreds of identical houses stood side by side, and human beings were alive, asleep in those houses. When I thought of this, my mind was, unusually, at peace. Speaking of solitude, the whole cluster of hundreds of houses beaten by the June rain was, I should say, enwrapped in solitude. I felt as though the warm breaths of those asleep reached my skin from neighboring houses not one iota different from the one in which I was sitting. Maybe at least one person was awake in each family, I thought, and like me was engrossed in killing the slugs that were creeping around in the shabby, rain-soaked house.

I peered into the adjacent room. Since I had brought the only electric bulb in the house to the three-mat dining room next to the kitchen, there was only dim light on part of the old pale green mosquito net hung from corner to corner filling the adjacent six-mat room. Between the lighted spot and the shadowy rim, I could see countless slugs creeping. They clung to the skirt of the aged mosquito net and slowly climbed the surface of the net, creeping as slugs do. Filing up at a fixed interval, they silently crept one after another, sticking all over the mosquito net, their molluscan bodies slowly undulating. Every bit of moisture seemed to serve as the slugs' food and air.

Inside the mosquito net, five relatives were sleeping together, almost piled on one another. From the side of the dining room where I sat, closest to me was the face of my younger sister Teiko, asleep. Her face was close to the net, her nose pressing against it. She was a young widow with two-year-old and six-year-old girls. The two girls were sleeping in a disorderly manner, half crouched, near their mother's feet. Perhaps to avoid the electric light, my mother lay facing away from the others so that my eyes only caught sight of an old *kaimaki*, a kimono-like comforter with sleeves, covering her legs. The other sleeper was a female house guest who was not ordinarily here, my younger cousin Hashimoto Miyano, who had come from the country that morning to see me on my return from Tokyo after three years. Not yet having been able to tell me all about the changes in her fate, she seemed to be asleep with her back toward me on the far edge of the space inside the mosquito net crawling with slugs. There seemed no space for me to sleep inside the net. Miyano lay where I usually slept. She seemed to crunch up her body intending to leave some room for me, and there was a slight space between her and the edge of the mosquito net.

A bunch of blood relations was asleep scrunched up under one mosquito net, each shouldering a misfortune that was unthinkable in normal situations; on that net a group of slugs, also unthinkable in normal times, was creeping around. Needless to say, I was aghast at this sight. However, I objected to the method my mother and my sister Teiko used, annoyed by the infestation of the slugs: they prepared salt water in an empty can and, picking them up with throw-away wooden chopsticks, dropped them in. I did not want to kill slugs. I wanted somehow to save their lives. Slugs knew nothing; they were innocent. After the defeat in the war, Japanese typhoons with female foreign names came and devastated various places year after year. In the ruins of H City, which had suffered a unique war disaster, too, torrential rains poured, and typhoons blew. On the ruins of the old parade ground in the city of death which had been reduced to nothing, houses for those whose homes were burnt down were quickly built, leaving the rubble of the destroyed army

buildings which had once stood close together. Not everyone camp-
ing out could get into those shacks. Teiko and her husband barely
managed to get one by winning the black market lottery.

Houses for bombed out people were built all over one corner of
the spacious former parade ground. Exposed to heavy rain and
stormy winds each year during the rainy season, every house crumbled and rotted while slugs bred under the floor. Since this was a
valley, there was no drain for the water. The floorboards, steeped in
mud throughout the year, were starting to rot. Slugs were breeding
there in swarms. My mother and Teiko diligently dropped them in a
can of salt water. I looked in the can. They were half melting, but not
completely melted. Thick and muddy, there was no sign of their
having put up resistance to this sole primitive measure. After once
eyeing this sight, I had begun to suffer from an association. It was
about human beings heaped up in a mound of death, half burnt but
not completely melted, with no energy to show any sign of resistance. They were so alike. I could not think of slugs as mere slugs.

Heartless molluscs to me seemed personifications with hearts,
and I could not bring myself to kill them by sprinkling them with
salt. I made sure that the people in the mosquito net were asleep and
no one saw what I was doing. I had bought DDT during the day. If I
repeatedly and carefully sprinkled DDT all over the room instead of
massacring them with salt, which must be a horrible shock to slugs,
eventually they would give up entering the room, I thought. When I
mentioned DDT, Teiko and and my mother were silent. It was
palpably clear that, cornered into penurious living, they thought salt
was less expensive than DDT. Having touched that chilling reality,
sadness weighed heavily on my heart, but I had to try it while they
were asleep. Peeling the seal of the cylindrical DDT container, I shot
white powder onto the dining room floor. Turning and twisting,
slugs had encroached in groups from the side of the door sill under
the glass doors—there were no wooden rain shutters. The door sills
on the four sides of the room were not even well grooved. They crept
all over the dining room, climbed pillars, and clung to the legs of the
low dining table. Their traces shone, forming many glittering
streaks. Since the slugs were mostly swarming in the slits between
the glass doors and the door sill that led directly to the outside, I

repeatedly sprayed white powder there. The slugs would run away, I thought. I immediately realized my ignorance. While the strong smell of the chemical attacked my eyes and nose, the soft bodies of the slugs on which it was sprinkled slowly melted and flowed.

They could not leap or fly like fleas or mosquitoes; nor were their boneless bodies able to resist the stimulus of the chemical. I felt nauseous. This was what I feared most. On the day the pale white radioactive flash burnt H City as though to toast it, I was in that city, and I saw how human beings were burnt and melted not by flames of fire but by the rays of the homicidal weapon that had fallen from the sky. I had been suffering from the intense shock for six years. It was now June 1951; but for me every moment of the long hours after the war was dark. Trying to escape from that dark affliction, I sometimes took sleeping pills, even during the day, and gave myself injections of antihistamines which were narcotic. I tried drinking but found that it affected the stomach before I could get drunk enough to efface the pain.

I dreamed of escape in death. That very spring, a poet* who had experienced the same thing, and who seemed to have been afflicted by the same pain, killed himself. Instantly, I thought I had fallen one step behind. Now that he had died, I thought, I, also an author, could not follow suit. When I went to his wake, I wanted to question him about the meaning of his death, but the poet who had killed himself was no longer there. Realizing that death meant that he was gone forever, at that moment I thought suicide ugly.

I stopped sprinkling DDT and turned my eyes away from the melting slugs. Still I could no longer tolerate it. Folding a newspaper narrowly, I covered that place. I had to forget the presence of the slugs as quickly as possible. It was because I recalled the groups of humans massacred seven years ago. On the night of my return from Tokyo about ten days ago, my mother bought a little sake for me. I

---

*Hara Tamiki (1905–1951), Hiroshima-born poet and author, was in Hiroshima in 1945, thinking, as did Ota, that it was safer than in Tokyo. Hara's "Summer Flowers" (Natsu no hana, 1947), translated by George Saito with additions by the editor, and "The Lord of Heart's Desire" (Shingan no kuni, 1951) translated by John Bestor, are available in *Atomic Aftermath, Short Stories about Hiroshima and Nagasaki*, ed. Oe Kenzaburo (Shueisha, 1984).

wanted to drink it in one gulp and paralyze some portion of my nerves. I peered toward the mosquito net. Teiko was looking at me, her eyes wide open inside the net.

"What's the time?" Teiko asked. She didn't seem to have noticed that I had sprinkled DDT and melted slugs.

"Twelve-thirty."

"Somehow the smell of a chemical woke me. I wonder what it is."

"I just sprinkled DDT around because there were fleas and mosquitoes. Say, why don't you get up for a minute? Let's drink," I said, without even a smile. I wanted quickly to finish turning the corner of my heart that was filled with dark depression.

"Shall we?" Looking faintly despairing as though in response to my face which suggested despair, Teiko, who hardly ever drank sake, lifted the skirt of the net and came out. She went to the kitchen and started to make a fire in a pitch black earthen hibachi.

"You needn't heat the sake. Let's drink it cold."

"No need to stand on ceremony. Making a fire's nothing."

"It's not ceremony. Sit down quickly."

With sake in a glass bottle and sake cups, Teiko sat at the small dining table facing me. She stretched her arm behind her and took out damp peanuts from the cupboard. Teiko and I lifted our cups of cold sake and, after letting them touch with a click, drank silently.

"Everything's cold, isn't it?" I said.

"These peanuts are too damp. Wait a second." Teiko rose lightheartedly, sliced a cucumber in random shapes, dotted it with salt, and brought it over. The green peel of the cucumber looked refreshing.

"Raining, isn't it?"

"Yes, it rains so much."

"If it rains too badly, the mud'll be washed away and human bones will come out, don't you think?"

"They come out even if it doesn't rain."

"Even after decades, if someone digs in the ruins of the parade ground, human bones'll still come out, won't they?"

"You don't have to wait decades. Even now, when we dig around here to make a vegetable garden, lots of things like *bijoh* come out besides bones. Slates and eating utensils, too.''

I didn't immediately grasp the meaning of *bijoh*.

''The buckle for soldiers' *obigawa* leather belts. They called *obigawa* 'taikaku,' giving it a Japanized Chinese reading. Military terms are all disgusting, aren't they?''

''Lots of *bijoh* of *taikaku* come out? What I'm saying is that not now but decades from now, lots of them will still be unearthed— *bijoh* and eating utensils.''

''Even after hundreds of years, I'm sure human bones and soldiers' *bijoh* and eating utensils will come out.''

These words conveyed the numbers of soldiers and other humans who died inside and outside the military buildings that were in this parade ground. Tetsuji, younger brother to me and older brother to Teiko, met instant death on August 6 six years ago at the site of the First Unit, the present housing site for those who were bombed out, without even having his bones identified. As we drank cold sake, however, neither Teiko nor I said a word about this. We did not want to wake the wailing that had sunk to the bottom of our hearts. Even among blood relatives, people refrained from talking about their grief and shed unbearable tears, perhaps in bed, when the world was quietly asleep. Soichi, Teiko's husband, had been called at one point during the war to the military hospital that was on this parade ground. It was adjacent to the First Unit where Tetsuji died instantly. Since Soichi was in the army in Kyushu on August 6, the day of the atomic bomb, he did not die in combat. Soon after the war he suddenly died of tuberculosis. Sometimes I connected his death with war, and I had the illusion that his was a kind of death in action. While entertaining this illusion, I thought it was no illusion, and the deaths of Tetsuji and Soichi were imprinted in my heart, as two deaths in combat, heterogeneous yet overlapping.

''Oh no, I'm getting itchy,'' Teiko said, her face red from not even two cups of sake, suddenly starting to scratch a corner of her lip with her right hand. Right at the edge of her mouth a deep cut forming an x-shaped keloid mark pulled in an ugly manner. At the time of the bomb, she was cut in more than thirty places all over her body by glass splinters which flew at her like knives. From the center of the x-shaped cut in the lip, water and medicine that she put into her mouth poured out. My mother and I had said it was good that Teiko was already married. However, now that Soichi was dead, what we said invoked the contrary psychological response in us.

"It's bad to drink sake, isn't it? Oh, it itches."

"Shall I give you a shot for hives?" I meant the antihistamine which I habitually used to sleep.

"I don't want a shot. Must you give yourself those shots? Poisonous to the health, no?"

"Control poison with poison. I can't live straight, can I?"

I was a little drunk. The procession of slugs creeping around came vaguely into sight. Teiko went out to the kitchen and drank gulps of water.

"Does it still itch?"

"It's a little better now."

Teiko saw that I was somewhat more cheerful. As though waiting for a chance to tell me about it, she suddenly started in a soft tone, "Mr. Kurata, you know."

"Mr. Kurata?" I thought. It was no longer possible that my heart leaped at that name. Yet the name seemed to penetrate gently into my chest.

"Huh?" I said to my sister, who was more than ten years younger. I was expectant.

"About a month before you came this time, Big Sister Mitsue saw him at the street car stop in Misasa."

"So he's alive."

There was a lie in this. I had heard it rumored that he had survived August 6.

"Yes, she said that he was dressed up as much as before. He knew that you went back to Tokyo after the war and are writing, but wondered if you were fine. He asked the same thing twice. Then he also asked about mother, and said he felt sorry for mother about you, now that his children are getting big, especially his daughter being in the prime of maidenhood, the time for her to marry drawing near—I hear he was on the verge of tears. Big Sister Mitsue said she felt sorry."

My younger sister Mitsue, older than Teiko, who married into the Misasa Shrine, was now a mother of five children. From her childhood till about the time she married, she had seen enough of my relationship with Kurata. He was a man who, in a sense, messed up my destiny. I did not forgive him for hiding the fact that he had a wife and children in the country and for machinating, so to speak, to carry on a bigamous affair with me when I was only twenty. Without forgiving him I loved him, and bore him a child. Now I would leave his house and then again be taken back. I spent eight years of my youth in this way. When we parted for the last time, my parents did not consent to my bringing home the child. My mother hated Kurata. She tried to make me hate him, too. Kurata hated my mother, who played a big role in our separation. He gave our child to a couple who were close friends. The couple feared my seeing the child. Although I loved the child even after the separation, I continued to love Kurata even more. To forget him, I took to whiskey and absinthe, which were unfamiliar to me, and while destroying part of my integrity, I tried to change myself through writing. My writing was not enhanced. I tried not to love a man. Literature that would move oneself and others could not exist where there was no love for fellow humans.

A long time passed, and in the midst of the Second World War my child should have been seventeen or eighteen. Unless I saw him then, I knew I might miss him for good, for he was at a dangerous age when he might die as a boy kamikaze pilot. I wrote a letter to the child's foster parents. A reply came. It said that the child had no knowledge of Kurata's and my past, and that even now he thought his foster parents his real parents. If I was to see him, they wanted me to see him unbeknownst to him as a complete stranger. That would be the saddest way of seeing him, and I hated the idea. I gave up the notion of getting together with him. Several years earlier, Kurata's wife, whom he had divorced once but remarried after his separation from me, had died of illness. Kurata's oldest son and the younger sister of Kurata's deceased wife started to visit me often.

Despite the fact that one of them must have been aware of his mother's resentment toward me and the other of her sister's, the two young people occasionally brought me news about Kurata and my child, as though talking about their relatives. Kurata married a young wife. Kurata's first son repeated that this woman resembled me.

Separated by months and years, the intense memory of love from long ago had faded in my maturity. Only nostalgia remained toward the fact that my youth once had such dynamic moments.

When Teiko mentioned Kurata's name and told me what he had said, I only felt as I would toward a close relative, my thought having changed to unruffled reminiscence.

"He asked her to send heartfelt greetings to mother. He said he wished to be forgiven about the old days, Mitsue said."

If so, he would no longer chase me. My heart sank somewhat, and I felt compelled to grab at a void, realizing this was the outcome of that love.

"I want to hear about the child."

I thought the child I gave birth to might be dead. Perhaps they refused to let me see him because they did not want me to learn about his death—I sensed the shadow of this possibility. If he had died, I should not try to see him. I felt that part of my heart had been supported solely by the awareness that a child who was mine was alive on this globe.

"Mr. Kurata seems to live near the Misasa Shrine. Mitsue said she might run into him again. Shall I tell Mitsue to try asking him about your child?" Teiko said simple-mindedly.

"I wonder if he'd tell the truth if Mitsue asked. Tsuruko's younger sister Naoko came again before I left Tokyo. I asked Naoko, too, but. . . ."

Tsuruko was Kurata's wife, who had been tormented by Kurata and me until she died. Her sister Naoko said that Kurata didn't know my child's whereabouts after the war. She seemed to know that the aged foster father who lived in Kobe worked in the proofreading section of an Osaka press, but beyond that she kept her mouth closed. I told Teiko the name of my present companion, who did not necessarily always live with me:

"He says he wants to be there too when I see my child. But if the boy's dead, then I'll be more shaken up about learning it than by not seeing him, won't I?"

Suppose he had died at the front, or suppose he had happened to come to H City from Kobe on some errand and met his inevitable final moment due to the atomic bomb. Since this was not impossible, I was afraid of pursuing only to deepen the wound. With the war disaster further complicating life's problems, my soul was utterly confused.

Having drunk most of the sake, I became lighthearted, and since I was prone to laughing when drunk, I suddenly laughed, shifting my mood.

"Let's wake Miyano. I wonder what would be best for her to do from now on. No matter where we turn, none of our relatives is doing well. Wake her, wake her," I said to Teiko. We heard Miyano's voice from inside the mosquito net:

"I was just thinking of rising. You two were mumbling and mumbling. I have been awake for a long time."

Miyano, cold at first glance, always spoke politely like a stranger, although she and I were cousins of about the same age. She crawled out from the net with a somehow despairing pale face, nearly identical to Teiko's and mine.

"Won't you have some sake? We've left a few cups."

"Sake? I am afraid sake is . . ."

She sat upright by the table. Single-minded, absolutely serious, which was her temperament, she looked as much as to say that it bothered her even to look at something like sake. Whenever I saw Miyano I recalled something. On August 3, six years ago, she and her mother, my mother's older sister, stayed overnight at my mother's and Teiko's house. I had also returned there from Tokyo, where air raids were fierce. After sleeping on the spacious second floor, both left H City early on the morning of the 4th. They had managed to send their furniture to the country in two horse-drawn carts. Having vacated their house, they were escaping from the city. Wearing work trousers and carrying rucksacks, the two trodded off. My seventy-year-old aunt had tied her *setta*, strong leather-lined sandals, to her feet. As we thought this was the last time we would see them, a faint pain nagged at everyone's heart. After the war, this aunt lost the family's entire fortune, which she had placed in an account with the South Manchurian Railway, and died of illness soon after discovering the loss.

"The sick man is waiting at home. After visiting Tsuyako at the hospital with you and shopping a little, I have to go home as soon as possible. So I want to ask your opinion tonight."

I found Miyano's tragic situation after the war ironic. From childhood, she lived in Fengtian, Manchuria, her father and older brother occupying important posts at the South Manchurian Railway. At nineteen, Miyano married a local wholesale drug dealer. However, when it was discovered that he was dealing in illegal opium, Miyano's father, who was an extremely religious Buddhist, hated the deception and took her back to his house. After that Miyano remained unmarried for a long time. Her father and brother both died, her father from old age in Fengtian and her brother from tuberculosis at the Japan Red Cross Hospital of H City. The Manchurian Incident showed signs of enlarging the war, and, chased by the flames of war, Miyano and her mother returned to H City. They lived in H City for a long time. Since they had many relatives, they recommended that Miyano remarry, one by one bringing concrete proposals for candidates. Miyano refused to marry, and at times she declined so angrily that the bearer of the offer withdrew, shocked. She sharply rejected marriage as *kichanamashii*, which meant impure in our dialect, inviting laughter from all relatives, who commented that marriage was not simply a matter of impurity. When a man wanted to marry her, she said he must be staking out her father's inheritance left with the South Manchurian Railway. Miyano opened a sewing class and took students. Having contracted vertebral caries, she wore a cast and a corset. Around the time the war ended, the infection stopped, improving her complexion and making her plump. She was nearly forty then.

A man lived alone near their house in the country. He was a bachelor and middle landlord who had never married because of the tuberculosis he had suffered in Tokyo in his youth, and he was engaged in humble many-sided farming. He was not yet fifty. Drawn to Miyano during the war, he brought her grains, vegetables, and eggs. Before dying at an old age, her mother suggested that Miyano marry this kind and lonesome man. Bereft of her mother, when Miyano realized that after all she could not draw even a cent of the savings she and her mother had left in a single South Manchurian

Railway account, for the first time she seemed to realize her isolation. She consulted as many relatives as possible by writing or talking. I received a letter in Tokyo. I replied affirmatively. What a nice mate she had found at this late stage, I thought, vulgarly envying the luck of a man and a woman of mature age marrying almost as if for the first time. After marrying, Miyano never wrote of her feelings about the marriage. At the end of the second New Year's card after moving into that house, she added that her husband had had a stroke, though light, and was bed-ridden, half his body paralyzed. I had been concerned about the possible relapse of tuberculosis which both of them had suffered. I had not expected to hear, however, that in a little over a year after their marriage half her husband's body would become paralyzed. The news of unpredictable human affairs left my heart overcast. Asking someone to care for the sick man, Miyano had rushed to see me, running with small steps, so to speak.

"Just because he got sick, you can't very well abandon him, can you?" I had no choice but to say.

"I have no intention of abandoning him, nor do I have a home to return to, but there is no telling whether he will lie in bed for five or ten years, is there? Suppose he stays like this as long as ten years, and I care for him? When he dies, they may tell me, you have no children, so please leave. Then what?"

"Would anyone say such a thing?"

"In that kind of situation, there is always some relative who might. He has many relatives. You write novels, don't you? Please tell me if you have a good idea."

"Even if I write novels, I can't see everything," I laughed a little. I thought that Miyano perhaps found it worse than meaningless, perhaps found it a grave loss, that her husband had collapsed after one-and-a-half year's marriage.

"Even while caring for the invalid, I have to farm; otherwise we can't eat. I feel miserable because it is as if I had lost myself again, all the way at the end."

Miyano did not love her husband, I thought. Thinness of affection was reflected here and there in her words. I said a little cruelly, "But you can't tell who'll die first, can you?"

"That is so. At our age."

Teiko silently listened to our brief conversation. She was by nature reticent. Never commenting on Miyano's broken life, she crawled stealthily under the mosquito net, looking sleepy. As though following Teiko's back with her eyes, Miyano turned her face to the net.

"Oh," she raised her voice, surprised. This was because she saw slugs not just around us in the dining room but climbing up all over the mosquito net and gathering near the ceiling.

"How awful. I never saw so many slugs in my life. I am getting a shiver," she said, narrowing her shoulders.

"It's good that you were not in H City on August 6, Miyano. When looking at this swarm of slugs, I tremble thinking that soldiers who died on this parade ground are back in the shape of slugs."

It was still drizzling the following day. Miyano and I went out into the city in the rain to visit our younger cousin Tsuyako who had been hospitalized for three full years in the Red Cross Hospital. Having decided to buy some food for Tsuyako at a store on a busy street, we walked along the streetcar road. A dingy little streetcar tottered like a lazy man in the middle of the Fifty Meter Road now under construction. A strange landscape was in view. In the center of the city where the traces of devastation were still raw, a wide road called by that name was being constructed with no apparent purpose. The miserable roadside stands that stood helter-skelter in the postwar confusion had already been moved to the river bank, which flooded every year during the rainy season. Only a strange-looking Chinese-style noodle shop remained there all by itself.

Around the middle of the not yet finished Fifty Meter Road, close to the streetcar rails, the dirt was raised just there, and the little Chinese-style noodle shop stood tilted on top of the mound. I had learned from a reporter, with whom I walked on this road four or five days ago, why this shop alone remained there. It was not that the shop was left unheeded. The others disappeared on receiving a small amount of money for being forced to move, but the noodle shop sat there, refusing to accept compensation. The man who ran the shop was from a third country. Referring to the present freedom of the third-country person, the reporter laughed gleefully as though he was the victor. The house atop the dirt forming a tiny hill had dirt steps in front and back, down to the Fifty Meter Road. On the streetcar side of the tilted and almost collapsing shed, a signboard for Chinese noodles hung. A german shepherd, leashed on top of the steps carved on the back side, was lying flat. Since the dog was out of proportion in comparison with the shed, it looked larger than the shop. Rhododendrons and garden jalaps were in bloom from around the shed to the steps. When I briefly explained about the shop, Miyano, who was walking at my side, laughed.

"Isn't it interesting that only the third-country person is holding out like that."

"But do you know why just that house is standing on the raised dirt mound?"

"Why?"

"It's said that the whole city rose three feet. In other words, the Fifty Meter Road is at the original level. That house still stands on the raised place, but underneath—" I closed my mouth.

"Bodies? Shambles?"

"Both."

We passed by, suddenly averting our eyes from the Chinese-style noodle shop atop the mound of dirt. The rain did not stop falling. Men who looked like construction workers were planting saplings in the rain along the Fifty Meter Road for a future tree-lined street. At first I did not understand that they were to line the street. I asked an old worker as we passed them.

"What are you planting?"

"Saplings to line the street."

A shadow of pathos stole into my heart. Although the constant sorrow never left me, at this moment it shook my heart more strongly than ever. The fact that new trees had to be planted along the new road, now after seven years, overlapped in my mind with the character of this Fifty Meter Road. Like others, I could not overcome the premonition that the road might be for future military purposes.

"What trees are they?" I again asked the man planting them in the rain.

"Plane and lindenbaum. We won't live until these become big

trees and grow thick foliage, though.''

The old man looked up at my face. I, too, looked back at his half crying, half laughing tan face.

At the entrance to the Japan Red Cross Hospital we asked at information where Tsuyako's room was. I found it surprising that Miyano had never visited this woman during the three years of Tsuyako's hospitalization. I was angry myself that none of us relatives sufficiently visited Tsuyako, who had tuberculosis of the kidneys and whose throat was also now affected.

Yet I had not stopped by at her room when I recently visited this hospital. With a girl from this city whose face had lost its shape due to the atomic bomb, I came to visit another girl whose appearance had also become half human and who was having an operation at this hospital at this late date. On that day I had not felt like visiting Tsuyako. Since Tsuyako, the daughter of my mother's youngest brother, was born in Seoul, I had never met her. From photographs I had occasionally seen, I knew that she was a beautiful woman who resembled her mother. However, my feeling toward her was not necessarily unadulterated. Twenty years ago when, having left Kurata with much agony, I started to write a little in Tokyo, my father, who was a landlord, lost everything and died. Money sent to me in Tokyo became scanty. I fell ill. There was no prospect of my novels selling. I was trying to live by writing. I wrote my greedy uncle, who had bought land and several houses in colonial Seoul, asking for money. In spite of the fact that I knew he was greedy from my own childhood experience, I had dreams about a cousin who lived far away. No reply came. I wrote repeating the same words. My uncle's wife answered. She wrote that they could not respond if a niece who had never even sent them midsummer and year-end cards asked to borrow money.

When Tsuyako reached marriageable age, my uncle and aunt, who were then in Sariwon, Hwanghae-do, and did not wish their daughter to marry in a colony, wrote asking me to find someone for her in Tokyo. I owned a house and lived with my mother then. I asked my mother to write to my uncle that, if he cared for his daughter, he should have cared for another's daughter, too. My mother wrote nothing of the kind. If I thought of my uncle in this way, my mother said comforting me, I should take care of my young cousin. Carrying a much too formal photograph of Tsuyako in long *furisode*-sleeved kimono, my mother and I made the rounds of the houses of relatives and acquaintances looking for someone for Tsuyako to marry. A relative's family became interested. Letters and photographs were speedily exchanged between Tokyo and Korea, and a young man was chosen. He became definite. He and his mother were about to go to Korea to see Tsuyako. Then suddenly my uncle wrote that Tsuyako was preparing to marry a promising youth who worked for the South Manchurian Railway.

After the war, my uncle and aunt were among the first to return by black-market boat. They had lost everything. They were both past sixty. Now they were both teachers in an elementary school branch on a plateau in the mountains of H Prefecture, where there wasn't even electricity. Of Tsuyako's two children, they kept the six-year-old. I no longer resented those people who would not even send five yen as a token of sympathy to me who had asked for one hundred yen. However, a trace of the scar of life that had been carved in my heart twenty years ago still remained, pulled taut. With my pity for Tsuyako nuanced, I felt somewhat concerned about our meeting.

On opening the door to what was called a model ward, we saw, in a certain kind of fresh cleanliness maintained in the large, bright room, five gloomy, pale, and lean women lying quietly. Both Miyano and I spotted Tsuyako immediately. It was not possible to hide mutual recognition of the resemblance between something in her features and ours.

When Miyano and I entered the room, Tsuyako was crouching, having gotten down on the far side of the bed. She seemed to recognize us immediately when our eyes met, but, smiling faintly with a fleeting expression, she remained crouched. Tsuyako was not as drawn as I had imagined. After finishing passing water, she politely greeted me on her bed on our first meeting and exchanged words as an old acquaintance with Miyano. Since I was no good at greeting anyone properly, I was flustered by this and quickly asked about her illness. Tsuyako answered, now in bed.

"I have to pass water thirty-five or thirty-six times every twenty-four hours, so I don't have time to sleep."

"How old were you when you first took ill?" I asked my younger cousin, who had just passed thirty.

"About a year after my parents left Korea, I also left with my two children and went home high in the mountains where they live. After another year or so, my legs were incredibly cold, and I began to pass water frequently," Tsuyako said in a frank and honest manner.

"My parents live on a plateau deep in the mountains where things are inconvenient, you see. There was no doctor, and it was a job to visit a doctor in town. By the time I saw a doctor, it was fairly bad. After staying in the doctor's clinic as a patient about half a year, I was hospitalized here."

"I wonder why you contracted the kind of illness that affected both your kidneys," I said full of compassion.

"—Before crossing the 38th parallel, my husband died of tuberculosis."

"I heard about it from my mother."

"After that I crossed the 38th parallel with two small children, with or without food, and I had a really hard time getting to Pusan. That kind of thing, I feel, was also a cause of the illness," Tsuyako said calmly, as if talking of someone else.

"I have sent my boy to my husband's parents' place, but I feel sorry for my father because I'm in this shape. If I recover, I would love to live with my children in the mountains where my parents are, perhaps as an elementary school teacher. If I don't get better, I will be a burden on my father until I die," Tsuyako said, as though telling the thoughts that were on her mind all this while.

Tsuyako also slowly spoke, intermittently, about her father, who worked at a branch school deep in the mountains. He got up at three in the morning whenever he came to visit her at the hospital. He walked twenty miles down the mountain trail in rubber-soled workers' *tabi*, changing his clothes and shoes before boarding a bus. Miyano and I said to Tsuyako that she shouldn't talk too much now. Despite the fact that I pitied her, I did not feel my chest so gnawed by this individual's misfortune. At heart, I involuntarily compared Tsuyako with the young woman who was still groaning in a ward almost straight above this one, whose entire body had been burnt by atomic bomb radiation. When I first saw maidens who appeared half human due to radiation, I felt as though I had been pierced through and cried despite the presence of onlookers, thinking of their present and future. I rarely cried about my younger brother Tetsuji as an individual. When compelled to out of resentment for the sake of all, I cried alone at midnight.

While looking at Tsuyako and listening to her story, I could not help noticing that here, too, the war disaster pierced the abdominal walls of life in general. For me, Tsuyako was in one corner of my resentment of the whole. She was certainly included in the circle of that resentment. There lurked in me a certain psychology that was difficult to tell others. It was difficult to tell others, since it related to death. A poet who witnessed the same thing in this city had reawakened this city's devilish memories from the beginning of the Korean War, and he had killed himself as though unable to withstand the traumatic sense of crisis he harbored about the future. Around the same time, a similar psychology developed inside me. I disliked suicide. However, the thought that I might commit suicide or that I might suddenly die due to the resurgence of the atomic bomb disease never left my mind. There was a black dot in my heart concerning this return to H City. It meant a valediction to my home, ruined city though it was—my ultimate silent valediction to my close relatives and dear acquaintances. I wished to see them once again without making it look final.

"Is there anything we can do?" I asked about Tsuyako's immediate needs, but she answered with a slight shake of the head, "Thank you. But I am fine because the nurses take care of everything in this model ward."

When we said good-bye and went out to the corridor outside the ward, I thought it was good to have seen her, although I was also aware that my visit took a conscious effort.

"The moment I glanced at her, I realized that she looked exactly like you," I whispered to Miyano as we walked along the corridor toward the entrance.

"You look more like her," Miyano instantly replied, "you have the same face."

We went out to the spacious entrance which was now restored to its prebomb appearance. As we were going down the low stone steps, a white-robed nurse whose face I remembered well passed in front of the flower bed. She was one of the head nurses who had served me food and told me of many things when I came last. Since I remembered her name, I thought of calling to her. I didn't. It was because her words heard on my last visit darkly flapped their wings in my heart, and I could not bear to hear them repeated. The young nurse, named Fukuhara, had shown me the traces of the deep wounds on her limbs incurred under the debris. Lying beneath the wreckage of the nurses' dormitory and encircled by fire, it was not on August 6 but on the evening of the 7th that she had crawled out to the hospital entrance.

"Even doctors, nurses, and patients who survived were half dead and bloody. We didn't know what to do. Wounded outpatients kept coming in droves. Since I couldn't stand up and walk, I tended them by crawling around. Every single one said please give me water, let me drink water. Water, water, they said, as they died one by one. Like watering plants, I crawled around pouring water into their mouths saying, Here, water, here, open your mouth. Here, water. Here, water. But finally there was no longer a drop of water anywhere. I hate it! I shouted in a loud voice and picked up a baby from the side of the body of a mother. What were you born for? Weren't you in the warm stomach for nine months and finally born? You shouldn't have been born, I said to the baby."

Fukuhara's feelings directly touched my heart.

"The dead filled the corridor, each with a piece of paper that said 'Dead.'" A crazy man started to hop over them. Referring to that flash he said, 'A wide yellow sash wound around him,' and went hopping over the bodies as if they were stepping stones, hugging his head. The following day he said, 'lemme have so-u-up,' and died while having it."

There was no limit to Fukuhara's stories about the misery at the hospital.

If I called to her and if she resumed her story from that time, I felt that it would burden Miyano, who was to return to the country before the day was over, with cruel images. Before accompanying her shopping, I called Shunkichi from a department store pay phone. Shunkichi was Kurata's son who visited me often, sometimes staying overnight, after Tsuruko's death. My mother, who by then had forgiven Kurata, was kind to Shunkichi. He worked at a small company, founded after the war in H City, as *senmu*, executive director, a title which had a postwar ring. He answered the phone as if he had been waiting for the call.

"I saw your name in a newspaper panel the other day, so I knew you were back. I didn't know where you were, though. I wrote you a card care of the newspaper," he said lightly like the wind. Arrogant as ever, I thought. I said I wanted to see him once.

"It doesn't have to be once. Won't you come to my place today? In the evening fireflies come out and it's lovely," he said. I knew Shunkichi's temperament because I had lived with him and the other children during my marriage to Kurata: his words were mixed with diplomatic flattery. Shunkichi said he would come and get me where I was. The more he insisted, the more I half doubted his true intentions. Part of me pondered learning of my child's whereabouts by seeing him and easing the nostalgia toward my old love, which still lingered in me. I said to Shunkichi on the other end of the line:

"I'm going to be with a relative for two hours or so. She's returning to the country, so, after seeing her off, time permitting, I'll come to your place."

In a lively way Shunkichi gave me directions to his house in the suburbs. Miyano was shopping inside the department store. Soon she and I went out to the entrance and opened the umbrellas we used both for rain and sun, Miyano her rusty red one and I my green one. We went to the rainy streetcar road and got on a streetcar. I don't know when I'll see this cousin again, I thought. Then I began wishing to see Kurata. It was not the choking passion of old. It was a flow of sweet feeling with a tinge of intimacy like that I harbored toward a close relative. I thought that Kurata might understand my dark state of mind as a result of the war disasters.

Kurata, a dozen years older than I and a follower of socialist ideology in the line of Osugi Sakae, an early twentieth-century anarchist, first mentioned the socialist's name when I was leaving him to go to Tokyo for the first time, and he suggested that I try to see him. Although Kurata dropped out of every movement due to his naturally nihilistic character, I wanted to believe that the throbbing of antiwar sentiment was still burning in his soul.

Shunkichi had a family, a wife and children, and lived apart from Kurata, but I thought I might somehow chance to encounter Kurata at Shunkichi's.

We arrived at the depot of the bus that would take Miyano back to the country. Even after sitting down on the waiting room bench I remained silent, but realizing that we didn't have much time, I said in a small voice:

"In your case, you never know what happens when. Living alone with an invalid must be strange, but, well, I guess you should stay with him till he dies."

"Yes, well, I guess that's so."

"There's no escaping. If you escape, you'll only regret it."

In a sense I also applied these words to myself. At four in the afternoon, the bus Miyano got on left. I recalled Shunkichi's words that he would be home by four. If I were to go to Shunkichi's house at the foot of a mountain range on the other side of the big river which flowed from a mountain village, I would have to take a streetcar and then transfer to a bus. To get back to Teiko's house, it wasn't much of a walk to the site of the old campground in the grass after getting off the streetcar. Returning to Teiko's house where slugs were creeping and visiting Shunkichi's house were both depressing. Hesitantly I bought a gift for Shunkichi's children.

Rain was also drizzling at the foot of the mountain near twilight. Three bicycles stood side by side at the entrance to Shunkichi's house. One was a beautiful bicycle with red enamel paint on the body. One was a child's bicycle. With a Go board placed in the center of the guest room without proper furniture, and with a Go handbook by his side, Shunkichi was alone placing black and white stones. Under the eaves on the verandah side hung a cage with a canary. Stones and moss were placed deliberately in a small yard. I perceived an odd atmosphere.

"Somehow this is oddly old-man like," I said to Shunkichi, who was putting away the Go board.

"Yeah, I've aged suddenly."

"How old are you?"

"I'm thirty-two. Girl students call me ojisan."

He was the age of Kurata when I came to know Kurata.

"At thirty-two you're into this kind of old people's life style? It's as if you're almost sixty."

"That's how old my old man is."

"At thirty-two your old man wasn't arranging Go stones alone as if he'd been abandoned. He despised caring for bonsai plants."

"I've aged early because I don't know when I'll die."

As he said this with a fleeting smile, I saw wrinkles all over his face. I had been bothered before by the appearance of the weak-minded Shunkichi, who resembled the beautiful but not striking Tsuruko and took after Kurata's tall, angular body and big, bony hands and feet. Although it annoyed me that his face resembled his mother Tsuruko's and his bodily features his father Kurata's, I was also surprised to see how enervated he was, sitting cross-legged in front of my eyes.

"My hair fell out completely once, but while I was anticipating death, hair after hair started to grow, you see, and I've managed to live seven years."

In this city, no matter who meets whom, this kind of dialogue cannot be avoided.

"I stayed in this house the whole time. But my old man was in the mountains of Ujina. Do you remember that August 6 is his birthday? My wife made *ohagi* rice dumplings for him early in the morning and left, saying that she was going to bring them to Ujina—that was before eight o'clock. The train seems to have gone through the area that became the target unexpectedly fast, and by 8:15 when the bomb fell it was fairly close to Ujina. But I didn't know it, so I thought she must have died near the target area. From the following day I walked around searching for her from Hatchobori to Kamiya-cho, which were still on fire. The dead, the dead, there wasn't even space to walk. I couldn't tell men from women, so I looked into each face."

Shunkichi was exposed to the residual radiation in the target area, he said.

"On looking back, because the whole city burned for three days, and even after the flames subsided the situation was such that women could not walk, I understand that she couldn't walk home from

Ujina. Since she didn't come home for three days, I thought she was dead and looked for her body for three days in a row."

"Your wife was in Ujina?"

"Yeah, she came back looking innocent with the old man on the fourth day. But I began to spit blood after a month."

"When I think of that radiation disease, I can never forgive America," I said, my voice trembling.

"Radiation disease is something like a devil who sticks around with unshakable determination all your life."

Shunkichi's wife placed supper plates on the table and brought a pourer filled with heated sake. In contrast with thin Shunkichi, whose only strong features were his thick bones and his height, his short wife was plump, her face pink like a young girl's. I had heard from Naoko that she had a fine disposition. The two boys were moving excitedly around Shunkichi and me. At the frugal supper table, Shunkichi and I became inebriated enough to become somewhat glib.

"Do you believe the excuse that they used the atomic bombs to end the war?" I asked Shunkichi.

"Don't take me for a fool. Who would believe their statements and excuses about atomic power? Ask J. R. Oppenheimer if he did or did not advise the president to use atomic bombs to seize the initiative in the war. Or was it slaughter in H and N cities for the sake of experiments in the atomic era? How long will they continue to believe that their discovery and deep knowledge of atomic power have embellished a brilliant page in human history?"

After a pause, I said, "When you speak like that, even your face starts to look beautiful. Then, why are you living this way like a hermit?"

"My health's no good."

"Does your old man say the same thing?"

"He's no good, either."

"Is he ill?"

"Ulcer, you know. He's trying to live by fleeing from this floating world. Neither my old man nor I can join the peace movement and have the same influence you do."

"That's not true. You have influence. Don't talk nonsense. If the whole society joins, of course there's influence.''

Shunkichi drank sake in silence. Suddenly I said:

"Do you know about the child? Mine? If you know anything, would you tell me?''

"I don't know anything about his recent past,'' Shunkichi answered, gloom over his eyebrows. Being a gentle person who did not like to see another in agony, he said with deliberate humor: "When he was small, his old man over there brought him on New Year's Day every year, so we saw him, too. It was funny that he called the old man over here Dad. Once he saw our toys and wanted them. I heard there were many over there because they loved him, but he wanted ours. He especially seemed to crave my long sword. After he left, we were missing many things. The old man over here, I heard, gave them all to him!''

I was afraid of asking whether my child was alive or dead. If he had died, it was better not to learn it. If it was in vain to try to find out about the child, it seemed meaningless to stay long.

"Would Papa know?'' I asked about Kurata, using the name Shunkichi and the others had used in childhood.

"I think he probably doesn't know what happened to him after the war. If he did, he would say something to us. He doesn't say anything. He is reserved about the boy's present mother, too. She's extemely afraid of the child's seeing you.''

This rang a bell in the depths of my heart.

"You and even Naoko have visited me, but not my child.''

I swallowed the word death, which came up to my throat.

"Kurata knows nothing, does he?''

After a while I started to rise.

"I've stayed long. I'll be off now.''

"Going home? You can't.''

"Why?''

"Because it's raining hard. There are no more buses, so if you're going home I'll have to take you on my bike. I'd rather not.''

In deciding to stay there was a fantasy about Kurata. It was a fantasy containing lingering thoughts. Before I realized it, I had counted him among those whom I should see while in H City. Shunkichi's youthful wife, who had hung a mosquito net in the other room and was putting the children to bed, came out and started to prepare my bed in the guest room.

"This house was destroyed, too, wasn't it? I thought there was no damage up to here," I said to her.

"Yes, the walls are leaning quite a lot and crumbling everywhere. Half the ceiling blew off, and on rainy days it leaked all the time as if there were no ceiling at all. Last year at last we had just the ceiling fixed."

Shunkichi and I went out to the entrance and waited there while she hung the net. Of the bikes on the dirt floor, the red woman's bike shone. Leaning against a high desk, I said:

"You're lucky. To buy a pretty bike like that for your wife and to bike together—it's a nice life."

"I want to take good care of my wife."

Hearing this, I no longer felt that the words carried an insinuation about my past. Turning around, with no special thought I eyed the wall against which the desk stood. On it hung a *shikishi* poetry card with the words "Human passions are a void." I see, I thought, understanding Shunkichi's mood which permeated this house. Below and to the left of the calligraphy, signature-like letters said "Hansen-An," Half Saint Hut.

"What's Hansen-An?"

"The house where my old man is. Instead of a normal vertical wooden plaque with the address and name, a horizontal one saying Hansen-An hangs there."

I felt a blow.

"Is this your old man's *shikishi*?"

"Of course."

With this I held my silence. Just as had always happened in the old days, my legs suddenly began losing strength due to a profound sense of despair concerning Kurata. Long ago when I was leaving he said, "I don't want you to become happy through a man, nor will you be able to. Please find happiness in your work." Despite his socialist views, he despised me as vulgar for going to see the summer festivals, Bon dances, and other popular entertainment. He even called me vulgar for wearing *komageta*, flat clogs made of a single piece of wood, on a fair day. Now, once again I realized his illusion. That was because I thought the philosophy of Hansen-An was the illusion of his life.

I slipped inside the mosquito net. Shunkichi brought two electric lamp stands.

"What am I supposed to do with two?"

"One's a big lamp, the other's small. You're going to read the evening paper, aren't you?"

Shunkichi put the single-sheet evening newspaper inside the net.

"Thank you. But one lamp will do. D'you have any sleeping pills? I always take some."

"I'm afraid we don't have any sleeping pills. Why don't you drink some sake with egg?"

There was no way I was going to be able to sleep with something like egg wine. Shunkichi went out to the kitchen with his wife and made a clattering noise. After a while, his plump wife handed me a cup of wine with egg, laughing. In a big white cup, the hot sake and the raw egg were separate, and there was a stinging smell of sake. At midnight I still couldn't sleep. I had kept the lamp light on. The big net, dark blue from age and with stains in many places, hung limp. Here and there I saw slender white hairs stuck to the net. It was uncanny. I knew that Kurata's mother, who had lived with me long ago as my mother-in-law, died in this house a year ago. So the white hairs seemed to have belonged to Kurata's aged mother. Yet I had an illusion that they were Kurata's.

I shut off the light. It seemed to be dawn. I gathered and pulled the blanket over my eyes. When I tried to sleep, memory sprang back. Seven years ago when I escaped from H City, which had gone up in flames, and found shelter in a house in a mountain village, a man walked along the only village road saying the same thing every day. From the railing of the second floor, I stared at that man, who was past middle age. He walked around, tenaciously spreading the rumor: "I hear that every single person who was in H City that day is going to die." He was a rich man who had moved to that village years earlier. Therefore he did not see H City on the day of the bombing. There was no basis for totally negating what he said. Even today, there was nothing that could completely bury the man's words.

As I tried to sleep, a big, vague, white hand appeared before my eyes. It was a hand that disturbed me all the time. It was the hand of the man who released the atomic bomb. That hand pressed the button, pulled the switch, causing the first atomic bomb to drop. What did he look like, the man with that hand? Above this pilot, there was an officer who commanded it. Above the officer were capitalists, statesmen, and scientists. However, I wished to see just once the face of the owner of the hand that actually dropped the atomic bomb. I wished to find an answer in his eyes to the question as to whether or not the wine he drank today in his own country was as bitter as death. Or rather, I wished to ask the soul of the man who pulled the switch with that white hand whether or not he was able to live now free of agony.

While seeing a vision of the white hand, I slept a little as it was getting light.

My stay in H City continued several more days. It was now July. I had distanced myself somewhat from thoughts of suicide and homicide. It seemed that I had started to think I should not die.

The rainy season was not over. Sometimes there was a torrent. Before and after that, it now rained and now stopped raining. In the early afternoon one day, the older of Teiko's two daughters came home in the rain, carrying a young bamboo branch. The green bamboo leaves, wet from the rain, seemed alive and breathing.

"What's the Seventh Night, *tanabata*, about?" the girl asked me.

"A cowherd star and a weaveress star meet each other on the evening of July 7 across the river in the sky called the Milky Way, after a long time. After a whole year."

"That's tomorrow night."

"I see, the bamboo branch is for that, then."

"I've got to go buy *tanabata* decorations with Mom. Everybody's going."

Teiko went out to buy decorations with the two children. My mother, who never used to nap before, was taking a nap in a corner of the six-mat tatami room. Since at night slugs only multiplied, my mother stayed up almost all night getting rid of them for Teiko, me, and her grandchildren. During the day when slugs didn't come out much, she sometimes winked. I too lay near my mother's feet. As I was starting to fall asleep, Teiko and the children came home with hurried sounds of clogs, talking cheerfully.

"I bought the eighty yen set because they said they'd price it down to sixty yen."

Waking our mother and me, Teiko spread papers of different colors for the July 7 decorations all over the place. Bright yellow, red, or purple paper squares, gold and silver square *shikishi*, and narrow *tanzaku*; pink treasure boats, papercut eggplants, and gourds; circular and angular paperfold balloons and lanterns. . . . The children and Teiko, and also my mother, blew into the balloons and lanterns making them swell. I vaguely watched more and more swollen balloons and lanterns, then lay down again.

"Oh my, this is the Milky Way," Teiko showed the children, lightly pulling a long blue and pink paper with cuts that filled both her hands.

"We're supposed to cut these square colored papers and gold and silver papers in *tanzaku*-shaped strips, write something on them, and hang them, right? I wonder what to write."

"You're supposed to write wishes and poems," my mother responded. The older child said:

"At my friend's house, they already hung all the papers. She wrote 'Father' and 'Mother' and hung them."

"Big sister, what are we supposed to write? Do you know?"

"When I was small, grandmother used to cut pieces of cloth of different colors into *tanzaku* because there was no square colored paper in the country, write words on them, and hang them up. I wonder what words she wrote. I don't know too much about the July 7 festival."

I felt interminably sleepy then.

"All you need is to write whatever you wish and hang the papers."

Hearing my mother say this to Teiko, I said on the spur of the moment: "Write 'Against war' or something."

With that I fell asleep. When I woke, all the papers, lanterns and treasure boats, numerous stars and balloons, were hanging from the twigs of the green bamboo which were sticking through and tied to the looped metal handle of the little chest of drawers in the three-mat room. From the top of the bamboo, a pink and light blue Milky Way streamed down left and right.

"How beautiful. Fully bedecked," I said, as if my eyes were refreshed. Unless it were the evening of July 7 according to the old agricultural calendar, one saw neither the traditional Milky Way nor the stars, so I had no particular interest in the July 7 festival celebrated in the wrong season. However, I could not deny that there was a comforting scene of a certain down-to-earth beauty before my eyes. A fragment of sad poetry was there. I noticed the writing on narrow strips of paper hanging from the green bamboo.

"Yeah?" I said, looking at Teiko. On the blue, red, gold, and silver *tanzaku*, only the words "Anti war" and "Milky Way" were written.

"Don't you have anything else to write? It doesn't have to be just 'Anti war.'"

"The children make lots of noise, and besides, I can't think of what else to write. Big sister, why don't you write, too."

I suddenly found it appealing. Taking a brush from the inkstone box by the side of Teiko, I wrote on yellow and pale pink *tanzaku* strips. I wrote "Peace" on one, "Liberty" on another, and "Stars of love, please protect our peace" on still another, and attached them to bamboo leaves with thread. By the evening, Teiko and I had hung countless *tanzaku* from the bamboo twigs on which we wrote, half with amusement, "Sincerity," "Courage," "Stars, protect our peace," etc. At night, slugs gathered around the bamboo for the July 7 decoration and started to creep. My mother began to pick them up with throwaway wooden chopsticks and put them in a can of salt water. I mumbled to no one in particular:

"Somehow, I can't stop thinking that these slugs might be the ghosts of the soldiers who died on this parade ground."

My mother put down the can and the chopsticks in the shade of something in a corner of the room. With no context she said:

"When there's war next time, let's escape together to Miyano's, shall we? I hear there's going to be another big war."

I felt a sharp, gnawing pain in part of my chest. Again it gnawed and gnawed. It was sad that my seventy-four-year-old mother, worried that there would be another world war, was thinking about escape.

"Mother, don't think about moving to Miyano's. There's never going to be a world war."

"There really won't be?"

"No. It won't be possible even if some want to have a war."

My sister, who remained at the foot of the July 7 decoration, said, looking worried: "Even if it stops raining tomorrow and the weather's good, I don't know if we will be able to take this pretty bamboo outside. I've started to feel nervous. All our *tanzaku* have writings different from other people's."

Toward evening the following day it started to clear up. There was clear blue in the southeast sky. With her children, Teiko walked from street to street where hundreds of burned out people's houses comprised a town. After going around looking, Teiko returned breathing fast and said:

"Big sister, it's okay, it's okay."

"What's okay?"

"I saw it written. Here, there, everywhere. We must put ours out quickly. Big sister, please come out."

Wearing *komageta*, I went out with Teiko and walked, looking between the houses. Rows of shabby houses identical to Teiko's stood side by side. This was a gathering of people in bizarre situations. Only atomic bomb survivors and returnees from the front lived here. On paths between shacks that stretched as far as we could see, vegetables grew and summer flowers bloomed. Here and there under the eaves of houses in the back alleys, a green bamboo stood with July 7 decorations. Perhaps bought at the same store, pink treasure boats, gold and silver stars, circular and square balloons, and lanterns swayed in the breeze just like those of Teiko's family, together with *tanzaku* of many colors. One *tanzaku* said "Anti war." A few uncut square colored papers read "Peace, liberty, independence." "Father" was written in a child's hand on one, and "Mother" on another. Some *tanzaku* said "Milky Way" or "Tanabata Festival." At another house, writing in pen on yellow paper read:

Inscribing a stone from a distant day
shadow falling on the sand
crumbling—midway between heaven and earth
a vision of a flower.

The paper with this poem, from the epitaph of the poet from this city who had committed suicide in Tokyo, hung from the stem of green bamboo leaves. I felt my heart stir. I stood in front of the house for a while. Although personal experiences differed, I felt deeply that I saw a certain stance of the heart flowing through the rows of these shabby sheds. Four or five houses down, *tanzaku* saying "Oh, stars of love" peeped from among many balloons, and a lovely chain of small gold, silver, blue, and red stars hung from one that said "Peace."

This was dusk of July 7, 1951.

STONE'S SLEEP

Nakayama Shiro

I

It was in order to pick up my father who was badly drunk that I visited the Nashimotos.

At the time, I was eking out a living on unemployment insurance, having just resigned from the company I had served for many years.

Before my resignation, periods of despondency had set in about twice a year, lasting from a week to ten days when short, and nearly a fortnight when long. In the past year or two, however, the frequency of these cycles had accelerated dramatically, and despondency had become a chronic condition.

A sense of exhaustion would assault my entire body, making me feel too sluggish to do anything.

When a cycle started, the desire for work which I had maintained until that moment was suddenly lost, and, feeling like abandoning everything, I would crawl into bed and stay there for days on end. During that time, all I did was eat; I did not even think about anything.

People thought I was lazy.

There is a yellow-covered book called "The Atomic Bomb Hibakusha Special Handbook," and those who possess a copy can receive a free physical checkup twice a year. But I have never been to a designated hospital. The notebook was issued to those who had experienced the bombing within a two-kilometer radius from the epicenter, or who had entered within a three-kilometer radius within a week of the bombing. Both my father and my mother had received one of those books. My Tokyo-born wife didn't have one.

At our home only my mother made appointments by phone and went to the hospital for checkups. This was because seven years ago she had been diagnosed as suffering from leukemia as a result of the bomb and had been hospitalized and even been given a blood transfusion. Since then, she has simply come home from her checkups with the information that she has high blood pressure and an abnormally high white blood cell count.

I had often given the excuse of a cold when I skipped work, without bothering to ascertain the cause of my enervation. My superior seemed to ascribe it to the exhaustion endemic to the nerve-racking job of stockbroker.

I started to find it painful, however, to offer false excuses for missing work: although my superior urged me not to do so, I submitted a letter of resignation to the personnel office, voluntarily resigning from my job.

The phone call came within days after I had quit the company. I was in bed, assailed by a gloomy mixture of anxiety and futility as a result of having deliberately denied myself access to income without thinking about the consequences.

I took the receiver from my flustered wife. My father, she indicated, had collapsed on the tatami floor, having felt poor while drinking whiskey at the Nashimotos. I could see the color fade from my mother's face as she stood beside me at the telephone table.

"With father's high blood pressure, I knew it would come to this," I reflected painfully as I took the receiver, which was cold to touch, from my wife's hand and put it to my ear.

The tipsy voice of the other party, an elderly man, sounded a little arrogant; he seemed to lack the ability to explain the situation in a concise, coherent way.

"Who's this?"

"This is his son. . . ."

"His son? Aren't you supposed to be at work? What are you doing home this time of day?"

"I'm home because I quit the company."

"That's funny. Your father was saying today that you work at T Company."

I resented the impolite tone of this man whom I had never even met. Out of vanity, my father must have mentioned the name of the first-class company where I had worked. It was probably difficult for him to admit that his son was unemployed.

"More important, how's my father? Can you tell me quickly?"

In response to my question, the other party slowly explained what had happened. He added that my father would probably be all right, although no doctor had been called. Then, with ponderous verbosity, he gave me directions to his house, including streetcar numbers, so I could come for my father.

"I'll catch a cab to your place in Fukagawa, so just give me some landmark, any landmark, so I can get my bearings."

My tone had become feisty.

My mother and I hastily prepared to go out. Both of us assumed that my father had collapsed with a cerebral hemorrhage. The fact of my unemployment came home to me in that instant, and I realized that I should never have given up my job.

The Nashimotos' house was a fair distance west of the Tomioka-cho streetcar stop. Noting the town name, Ishikiriba, on a wooden plaque, I had the taxi stop at a liquor store with a Coca Cola sign and asked where our landmark, the kindergarten, was. The place was easy to find.

"I was shocked when your father suddenly said he felt sick and lay down without a word on the tatami. But he started to snore right away. So I thought, don't worry, he'll be all right. We didn't go for a doctor. Even so, I'm sorry you had to come all this way."

There was none of the arrogance that I had felt on the phone; in front of my eyes was the smiling face of Nashimoto, who was about the same age as my father.

"I told my husband he would upset all of you if he phoned himself. I told him I would call you, but he wouldn't hear of it. I'm so sorry about this.'' Kayo Nashimoto stood at her husband's side apologizing. Spoken in familiar Hiroshima dialect, her words sounded strangely leisurely by contrast to the situation. Kayo continued:

"Whiskey has so much alcohol in it. I poked my husband in the back and said he could make someone sick by pouring and drinking whiskey as if it were sake. But *he* wanted to drink, so he kept ignoring me, saying it's all right, it's all right. Really, he doesn't know when to stop. . . .''

Eying Nashimoto with a mixture of irritation and contempt, as one would a drunk, Kayo sat behind him criticizing the way he had offered drinks to his guest.

"There's no way to apologize once something terrible has happened. He should know that. . . . Really, he has done an awful thing,'' Kayo repeated again and again, looking as if she could not overcome her anger at her husband.

Nashimoto, as if embarrassed, reached up and stroked his bald head. Watching this gesture, I was reminded of the expression *toshiyori-kodomo*, senile child. Both my father, lying there drunk at someone else's house, and Nashimoto, fiercely scolded by his wife, seemed to me like school children. Their behavior was no different from that of children who merely satisfy their desire without thinking of the trouble they cause others.

"Why are you making the guests wait for tea?'' Nashimoto said, sounding important.

Kayo continued to complain about him while making tea.

"Please don't worry. In this case, of course, the one who drank too much is to blame. Even if it were offered to him, my father should have restrained himself. They say drinkers are insatiable. Anyway I'm sorry he gave you so much trouble.''

Before arriving at the Nashimotos, I had resented the two old men: why did one make the other drink until he collapsed, and why did my father drink himself into such a state? In the end, I thought, it was my father who had become drunk who was to blame.

Suddenly the topic of conversation, my father, woke from the loud voices and sat up, straightening his jacket.

"Is there something urgent?'' he asked, seemingly wondering

why my mother and I had come to the Nashimotos. "How did you find your way here?"

My mother and I were aghast.

Unable to contain herself any longer, my mother explained what had happened in a tone quite similar to Kayo's tone when she scolded Nashimoto, adding, as Kayo had done, "You should think of your age when you drink."

Looking pale and somewhat bloated, my father nodded, exhaling breaths that reeked of alcohol, and said, "Oh. That's what it was."

"How can father behave like this?" I thought, resentfully.

But because we had been spared the worst eventuality of my father collapsing with cerebral hemorrhage, we all managed to avoid taking offense, or making a barbed retort, to each testy comment someone else made. Since Mrs. Nashimoto's scolding had started the moment we rushed in, the awkwardness and stiffness that usually accompanied a first meeting were instantly stripped away.

But what if my father had died from a cerebral hemorrhage or something similar? Naturally Kayo was furious at Nashimoto.

Nashimoto was a childhood friend of my father's deceased older brother. Today they had met for the first time since the 1923 Kanto earthquake. So they drank, while renewing their old acquaintance, until they passed the limit and my mother and I had to rush over in a state of panic.

In the car on the way over, I had been dumbfounded at the thought of the unexpectedly sudden death of my father. The thought of hospitalization procedures and funeral expenses made me resent his foolishness. I felt like using a harsh word or two: "Think of your age, father," or "you should drink in moderation."

On the other hand, grief wrapped my body like a cocoon, making me think about parting by death between father and son. Although my father and I did not talk to each other much because he disapproved of my older wife, I started to picture in my mind the grief of reminiscing about him. When my father suddenly disappeared from the house, only his clothes, small daily use items, and the traces of his pen in his notebooks would be left, and I would remember him through that familiar handwriting. Then his unpleasant features were obliterated, and only good ones appeared close-up. "Blood is dirty,'' I recalled my mother having once said to me.

He had not fallen with a cerebral hemorrhage, and the moment I saw that expression around his loose and lax mouth which, when drunk, he habitually displayed in the effort to cover his inebriation, the cocoon of grief that had wrapped my body fell away.

I got rid of the state of mind into which I had fallen in the taxi, as if I had nothing to do with it, and exchanged a wink with my mother, which only we two understood: "He only lay down, exhausted from too much drinking, nothing more."

At a pause in the conversation, my father abruptly said, "This is the keloid from the flash," referring to the scar on my face.

Taken aback, I felt my body stiffen.

When he pointed to show Nashimoto, the tip of my father's lukewarm forefinger touched the keloid scar on my cheek.

I was shocked. Although it was partly the hatred of an immediate relative's fingertip, the surprise came more from the realization that this was probably the first time that my father's fingertip had directly touched my keloid scar.

Through the muscles like crab legs on the left side of my face, I momentarily felt my father's body heat. It was strangely tepid. Although still drunk, my father too seemed surprised and immediately withdrew his hand. Quickly pulled it back—that was the gesture. It was a matter of just a brief second, but both my father and I were confused as in a chance meeting in an unaccustomed place.

"This is how the burn from that time is now," my father said stammering, bringing together the fingertips of both hands.

As I wished to rub out the tactile feel of the part of me that my father's fingertip touched, perhaps my father, too, may have wanted to wipe away the feel of his son's bumpy, slippery keloid scar sticking to his fingertip.

The body heat carried by the same kind of blood as mine generated hate that made me almost shudder. Was this feeling because the body heat was perceived with the keloid as a medium? I clearly felt spasms in my back muscles along the spine like a little child who has convulsions.

Taking off his glasses, Nashimoto brought his face close to my keloid scar. His eyes were like an old man's, narrowing before a lucky porcelain find. I was relieved. I twisted the keloid side of my face so that Nashimoto could see it more easily.

"Well, it's fine if it's only this. No one can tell when looking at you from the front. How lucky that you aren't a girl. If you were a girl your parents would have a hard time."

Putting on his glasses, Nashimoto said this with a laugh as if in jest; he no longer tried to look at me after that.

"Their child got hit by the flash, too," my father said suddenly, looking at me.

So that's why Nashimoto stopped looking at my keloid, I thought.

Nashimoto faced me, however, and asked, "How old were you at the time of the flash?"

"I was fourteen," I answered.

Nashimoto looked thoughtful for a while, his head inclined.

"Then, our Kazumasa is a year younger than you are. So you were a third-year student in middle school," he said, looking at me and nodding to himself.

"Yes," I responded vaguely.

I thought that Kazumasa, whom Nashimoto mentioned, a man who was apparently about my age and moreover with a keloid scar on his face like me, might later open the sliding door and come into this room to greet us. I started to feel depressed as I imagined the situation.

Whenever I encountered someone on a train or bus with burns on his face, I immediately moved far away. I had done so in Hiroshima and did likewise in Tokyo.

In other words, when looking at the man's burnt face, I felt as though I were objectively gazing at my own; so I could not bear to look him straight in the face. I knew well that, while conscious of each other, we pretended unconsciousness. I could not bear to observe his pose of trying quietly to repulse the passengers' staring eyes, or his restlessness due to paying constant attention to the eyes of people around him, even as he turned his body diagonally away from them with an air of being engrossed in something else.

Partly to avoid falling into that situation, I would change cars when I spotted a man with a keloid face. When the man got off at the same station as I, each of us would send a searching eye toward the throng. Momentarily my eyes and his would meet. Then they would part right away.

Through several past experiences, I found it painful to encounter a human being with keloid marks on his face.

I didn't want to meet this man called Kazumasa. Inside my body, depression spread with the dullness of a sinking piece of lead. I gradually became conscious of vertical wrinkles gathering between my eyebrows. And I felt I had to leave the Nashimotos' place as soon as possible.

When I made up my mind to that, Nashimoto almost shouted, twisting his body toward the kitchen: "Hey, Kayo, if Kazumasa were alive, he would be as fine a man."

I looked at my father. Silently he shook his head a few times.

On entering the tatami room, Kayo gazed at me with a complex expression, but finally she nodded as if accepting something.

"Is everything all right now?" she asked, a question that anyone would ask.

"But after all, how good that you survived. As long as the child's alive, no matter what his face is like, parents are happy, aren't they?" she said, looking both at me and my mother.

"Our child had gone to Zakoba for labor service, and there he encountered the flash. . . . And where, I wonder, did you experience the flash?" she asked me, correcting her sitting posture.

"It was on the west side at the foot of Tsurumi Bridge."

"Then you must have gone through a lot of distress."

Before I answered, Nashimoto, silent until then, opened his mouth and explained to Kayo about me: "I hear that's the burn from then, but it's not so bad, is it? I wish Kazumasa were alive, too." Deeply nodding, Kayo looked at me.

"How hard it must have been," she said.

"Yes."

"At one point we thought we had lost him," my mother said briefly. After that, she asked, "Did your child also have burns?"

Suddenly looking distracted, Kayo muttered, "That, somehow, isn't very clear."

After a while she added, "His whereabouts were unknown. So, it's not known what happened to him. . . ."

"....."

Hearing her unexpected answer, my mother and I had to reflect upon ourselves for asking a careless question.

"It's not at all certain where he fled and where he died. The only thing we picked up was the lid of his lunch box at the ruins of Zakoba where he and his friends were at work. That's the only memento of that child."

Kayo explained that Kazumasa probably had suffered from fairly bad burns.

As she explained it, this was not the story of someone who directly saw Kazumasa but the vague testimony of someone who, while looking for other people, thought he had heard so-and-so say so. If we were to trust that story, it follows that Kazumasa was picked up by a military truck at Takano Bridge and was sent to a clinic.

"Do you think he went to Kanawa Island? I was nearly sent there, too."

"I also thought of that, and immediately went to Kanawa Island, Ninoshima, and to first aid stations and morgues east and west . . . , but no matter where I went, I couldn't find him. Even now, I keep hoping he died instantly."

Nashimoto continued: "Because Kazumasa couldn't be found, Kayo was sick at heart, and she was often bedridden. Isn't it just in the last two or three years that you became healthy?"

"Yes. When I think Kazumasa might have waited, calling for me, forgetting his wounds, my chest hurts so much I can't do anything. As I often tell my husband, I really don't want to live long," Kayo said, and tightly pressed her chest under the sash.

"At that time there was nothing we could do," my father said by way of introducing a long story. "When I went to Hijiyama that evening to find this one, three first middle school students were just sitting there on the ground. They held one another's hands as if forming a circle, so I went near them and asked if they were all right. 'Ojisan (sir), we three can't see well. We're holding hands tight so we won't lose one another. Where are we?' they asked. Their consciousness was already hazy. 'This is Hijiyama. Good for you to have come here when you can't even see,' I said, impressed. 'One of us could see until a while ago, so we could flee here together, but when we got here, none of us could see. Ojisan, we're sorry to bother you, but would you let us drink some water?' Their faces had lost their shapes, and they were, so to speak, monsters. Their clothes were burnt and torn, and when I looked at the hands that were held, the skin was coming loose like the skin of a rotten peach that didn't peel neatly—I thought, oh no, they won't live at this rate. I had heard that burns that cover more than a third of the body were fatal. Since the boys had burns nearly all over their bodies, it's natural that I thought so. At that time we were instructed never to give water to those with burns, but I felt it was far more humane to fulfill their last wish, so, taking down the canteen that hung from my shoulder, I let the three boys drink it all. I thought I'd look for water somewhere if I found my son.''

"Indeed that's pitiful," Nashimoto sighed deeply.

My father continued: "When they finished drinking, the one who could talk said, 'Ojisan, now it's all right if we die. Ojisan, we can't remember your face because we can't see, but thank you very much. Let's hope you soon find your son and our senior at school.' 'Keep your spirits up, okay?' I said, jotting down the three boys' names and addresses. Then I went to search for my son, but I couldn't find him after all, and I gave up and went home. On my way home, I felt concerned about the three middle school students and went back to where they were. They were holding hands in exactly the same posture as I had left them, but they had already breathed their last. Thinking that at least I would tell their parents where they died, I went again and again to the addresses I had taken down, but those places forever remained burnt fields, nothing but sagebrush growing amidst the rubble. They were near the target area, so I assume their entire families were destroyed.''

"That must be so. It can't be otherwise," Nashimoto nodded many times.

I looked at Kayo's face. I was worried that my father's story might deal her a blow, and the very sign that I had anticipated started to surface in Kayo's expression. First it trembled under the skin, then faint convulsions ran across the surface of the skin. As she listened, Kayo must have linked Kazumasa's death to the deaths of the three students in my father's story. For that reason, her complexion began to turn pale.

"This one was after all lost for six days or so. No good, give him up, I repeated to my wife, and I also forced myself to accept it, but then on the seventh day we finally learned of his whereabouts," my father said after a while.

I detested this expression, "lost for six days." Each time I heard it, I felt as though my private part was touched. In fact, that I was lost as many as six days was unmistakably my private part. The reason is that some, who had been much nearer the epicenter, ran through the flames and reached their homes despite much graver wounds than mine.

Whenever this was mentioned, I felt that it pointed to the weakness of my will. If I had come home mustering my last drop of strength, my mother would not have had to look for me near the epicenter; she would not have had to be exposed to secondary radiation and contract leukemia by the atomic bomb.

I was tasting humiliation yet again.

The Nashimotos had been listening as if stifling their breath, but the moment they heard this, Kayo's face froze like a noh mask. I did not overlook Nashimoto's eyes, which quickly caught that change.

In the old man's peaceful face the eyes shone, although just for an instant.

It didn't suggest that he was blaming his wife, but something that had been hanging somewhere in his heart for the past twenty years seemed to have stirred a reflex inside of him.

To me those eyes seemed to say, Perhaps ours might have been found.

Kayo seemed to have felt her husband's momentary glance falling on her.

"That was really lucky," she responded briefly.

Somehow it was as though she was defending herself before Nashimoto.

I found it hard to breathe.

Inside her eyes, which did not quite focus, clearly there was agitation. They said: Is it possible that I did not use all my might to look for him then? Or, is it possible that I was so upset that I overlooked his name on the list of patients and lost him forever?

I realized how inappropriate and insensitive my father's story was.

"If a neighbor had not contacted us, we would not have found where he was. We had given him up for dead." As my father explained this last point, Kayo's expression gradually relaxed.

Simultaneously, something like the mistrust that had emerged a minute ago on Nashimoto's face also disappeared. There was serenity in his expression as if he would never be able to feel that way again.

Nashimoto's voice was bouncier. "What irony. 'Tokyo's dangerous, move away,' they say, so I send my wife and child to Hiroshima, and look at the result. I just can't forget it no matter how hard I try. As you see, this area didn't burn or anything," he grieved in an exaggerated manner, then asked me: "So, how old are you now?"

"I'm thirty-four."

"I see. If Kazumasa were alive, he would be thirty-three," Nashimoto said, deep in thought, his eyes meeting Kayo's.

However, it seemed hard for them to imagine the thirty-three-year-old Kazumasa. Kayo said of me, "Such a fine man, your parents must have nothing to worry about."

I felt ashamed.

As though he had completely forgotten about having made me resentful on the phone, Nashimoto nodded at Kayo's words: "True, true."

II

There were two faces that I often recalled over the past twenty years.

One was that of Furukawa, the plasterer.

The other was the face of a man with a private first class insignia on the collar of his khaki colored open neck shirt. I didn't know his name, and I don't even clearly remember his face.

These two faces sometimes suddenly appeared before me, but at other times, when I tried to remember them, they grew mixed with the faces of people who actually lived around me and did not easily emerge. There were also times in my dreams when I saw them with strange vividness—for example a wrinkle carved in the facial skin, a slightly dry voice, or a movement of the eyes or fingertips.

Furukawa, the plasterer, died of stomach cancer in 1949, and as for the private, I never met him after parting at the camp because I learned neither his home town nor his name.

Calling these two "remote faces," I made it my habit to reminisce when alone.

When I heard the story of the lost Kazumasa at the Nashimotos', the remote faces loomed up before me.

—It was the sixth day after the bomb.

I had been placed in a private house halfway up the eastern slope of Hijiyama. The sign at the entrance read "Military Signal Corps Temporary Camp," and there were many soldiers. Before reaching the camp there was a deep bamboo grove, and next to it a spacious garden in front of the entrance, where evergreen trees were planted so that they almost covered the garden. I glimpsed the summer flowers planted under the trees innocently abloom. The building, which stood as if embraced by the deep green wings of the mountain, escaped damage from the explosion-generated wind because it was on the slope opposite downtown, and the slate roof appeared cool in the green shade.

When I came to this place on the private's back, it was late afternoon and the sun's rays had already weakened. I opened my eyes wide in wonder at this quarter. After the brilliant sun and sky of the summer morning melted in an instant in dense, yellow rays, the ensuing phenomena around me belonged to the grey, sticky world of scorching heat, disintegration and decomposition. This tranquil space, unrelated to that world, felt to me like a dream world.

There was dignity, however simple, inside the building so that at a glance I associated it with an old samurai house. A stone was placed in a corner of the entrance inside the door, and it seemed that normally water was led through a bamboo pipe. The long corridor of wide, thick zelkova panels and samurai-style fixtures left a strong impression on me in my deranged state of mind.

After receiving first aid in the infirmary from a military surgeon in glasses who looked like a medical school student suddenly made to wear a military uniform, I was again carried on the private's back, this time to the big hall in the farthest corner of this building, and was laid down on the tatami.

In putting me down, the private took off my backpack containing my padded hat, lunch box, canteen, and military training handbook and put it under my head for a pillow.

"Right now the city is a sea of flames, so you can't go home. When the fire subsides enough for you to go, I'll tell you. Wait here till then, all right?" the private said many times, as if making sure.

The reddish yellow clay surface of the scraped part of the mountain appeared close to the open window, and water drops shone on the dirt, a cool breeze blowing through the room.

Although I was only concerned about going home, I fell asleep despite myself, fatigued from long hours of wandering. In the consciousness that started to be fuzzy, I was drawn into pleasant sleep.

It was midnight when I was awakened by a dull pain that seemed to thrust up from inside the body, and by beastly cries, which seemed to crawl on the damp dark ground. I dimly remembered being shaken by someone once before that.

When I tried to open my eyelids, I noticed that they would not move, as though covered by a lead film. As my murky consciousness slowly awakened, my mind recalled what had happened during the day, and I realized that this abnormal sensation was a reality.

I felt unusually heavy from the neck up, the movement of the air which I myself stirred stimulating the skin of my face, causing sharp pains, and before I was aware of it, I was groaning.

Bestial cries filled this dark room. Miniature red lamps went on and off, and the wireless was beeping. In that slowly spreading faint pale light, only the black back of the soldier who faced the wireless suggested humanity.

Thinking of the world in which I was placed at that moment, I experienced a chilling sense of isolation.

What saved me then was the sound of human conversation. I strained my ears to sort out human words from the groans.

The words were spoken by an old woman who had damaged her throat with cigarettes and alcohol. The listener was a man whose age matched that of her voice.

"When I said Grandma will die with you, 'Run, Grandma,' that's what she said. A second grader, she said something a god would say, that sweet little child. . . .''

The old woman cried hard.

''I asked a man in the same town who came just then to see if there was anyone who failed to escape, and the two of us tried to lift the beam in order to save the girl, the tip of whose hand was showing under it, but the beam didn't move. My mind was so agitated that I shouted, 'Someone please come,' but there was no one, and at that moment I thought, how can I believe in the gods or Buddha? In the meantime the fire came nearer, and she started to shout, 'Grandma, I'm hot.' 'Grandma will be with you,' I said as I tried with all my might to lift the beam, but it wouldn't budge. I gave up and prepared to jump into the fire, when the man struck the pit of my stomach as hard as he could and left holding me. She shouted from behind us, 'Grandma, I'm hot'—her voice is still in my ear. . . .''

''But that's not your responsibility, you see?''

''How must she have felt? When I think of that I don't feel like staying alive. I'm so sorry, so sorry that I couldn't die in her place. . . .''

''Many people had experiences like yours. You shouldn't be overwhelmed.''

'' Grandma, I'm hot'—that voice sticks in my ear.''

The old woman continued to cry for a while.

Dawn was approaching.

Listening to the old woman's story, I thought I must go home no matter what.

''I'm going to where she is as soon as possible,'' she said, then seemed to stand up.

''You mustn't go to extremes,'' the male voice followed the woman leaving.

The sun had not yet risen.

When the old woman left I fell asleep again and did not wake until someone shook me for the doctor's round. Dull pain covered my entire body, and I had a severe headache.

When the base of my neck jerked, sharp pain ran straight through the brain. At that instant, a tepid liquid dripped from cheek to chin, then from chin to neck.

I had burns on the left side of my face and the back of both hands, and they became infected. When the bandage was unwrapped, the smell of pus stung my nostrils.

"Infection," the military surgeon diagnosed, lightly pushing the flesh around the burns.

When the treatment was over, the private who had carried me on his back came over.

"Do you think you can eat this?" he said, offering a triangular shaped rice ball placed on the lid of a mess tin.

I realized that I had not eaten a morsel since breakfast the previous morning, but the odor of the burning protein clung to the mucous membrane of my nose from the time when my body and clothes burned, and nausea overrode my appetite.

The private divided the rice ball into small pieces and tried to push some through my infected lips. Finding that it was impossible, he brought watery rice gruel in a mess tin and poured it into my mouth spoonful by spoonful. The taste of soft rice grains and salt spread warmly across my tongue.

Tears started to come up although I didn't mean to cry.

"No need to worry."

The private went to fill my canteen with water and moved the position of my pillow when I was having a hard time in direct sunlight, perspiration and pus oozing down from my forehead to my eyes. Again, when I told him I wanted to urinate, he carried me to the toilet. As I turned my eyes to the outside trees through the little window in front of me while passing water into the urinal, which was made to look like a green bamboo cylinder, somehow I felt that it was impossible to go home. And I thought that the sun's golden rays scattering over the tree leaves would soon fail to reach my eyes. I would no longer be able to feel the familiar smell of the water that rose when I urinated. I thought I wanted to see my family just once before dying.

"Can't I go home yet?" I asked each time the private came. He always repeated the same answer: "Don't worry. I'll tell you without fail."

I no longer had the strength to walk.

Wanting to go home so badly, I started to long for the private to come.

The ward was extremely noisy, with groans of the wounded calling family members.

There were many people: a middle-aged woman who called her family members' names and, when there was no response, broke down in tears in the presence of others; a mother who had been crying and screaming from the start; a man who walked around looking at each wounded person without even calling names.

I tried to concentrate my nerves in my ears and to stay awake so as not to miss any little voice.

While doing that, all the news that reached my ears was tragic. Imagining only dark things, I started to think about getting home as soon as possible. I never thought about the factory where we had been mobilized, our work, or our teachers.

The burnt portions of my body started to suffuse a rotten odor, pus dripping incessantly on the tatami floor. Although I was at first bothered by the odor, soon I became insensitive and only counted the passing days. Already five days had passed since I was brought to this camp. I should have gone home the day I came here, I regretted, even if it meant a night trip. On the third day, or on the second day, I would have had more strength to walk home than now, I thought. On the fourth or fifth days, only my mind was lucid, and I felt my vitality fall away with certainty, drop by drop like the dripping pus.

As my consciousness became hazy, I gradually started to think that I was a dying person who could no longer go home. The private continued to encourage me. With no vanity or decency, I was totally dependent on him. And I resented my own lack of strength.

However, I was in luck.

The good fortune arose when the private, who was then off duty, carried me on his back out to the cool shade of the garden. Without that coincidence, I am not sure if I would have gone home at all. Unable to establish contact with home, I might have died without sufficient treatment amidst the many wounded, or been sent to a place where my parents' eyes never reached.

Running a high fever, I was in an isolated world.

My body, filthy with pus, suffused a sweet and sour odor. If I moved even a little, a groan burst from my mouth.

"How about freshening up a bit," said the private, who couldn't bear watching me like that. Carrying me easily on his back without minding my dirty body, he went out to the garden covered with summer grass.

Liberated from the unusual odor of mucus that filled the room, I deeply inhaled the fresh air outside.

The half-sleeve cotton shirt that I wore was stained with blood and pus, and some of it stuck to the open wounds so that it could not easily come off, but the private moistened those parts with water and took it off, trying not to hurt my wounds. The coolness of the well water he pumped up stimulated my totally enervated heart.

To get rid of the unpleasant feel of the pus that stuck inside my mouth, I rinsed my mouth with the water the private pumped into a mess tin. I drank just one sip at the end.

Then I was aware that I was alive, but at the same time I felt insecure and lonely about being in a place where I knew no one and where there were only wounded people and soldiers. The private pumped the well water again and again into a bucket and wiped my body with the cotton towel I had, marked kamikaze.

It might have been sheer coincidence that I was able to find Furukawa the plasterer, but it is also possible that the urgency with which I desperately sought an acquaintance in the world of unknown people made me discover him.

Furukawa was running around visiting every possible aid station in town in search of his daughter.

On discovering Furukawa, who came out of the bamboo grove wiping his sweat, I shouted excitedly, but I had no voice. My throat uselessly convulsed, only emitting intermittent hoarse sounds through my lips. From trying to open my mouth as much as I could, my infected lips burst, and tepid pus ran to the tip of my chin and down my neck.

I asked the private to bring Furukawa.

Furukawa at first gazed at me with a strange expression, but when I told him my name he looked awfully flustered and stared at me dubiously.

I did not understand Furukawa's reaction. Unaware of how strangely disfigured I was, I faced him exactly the same way as if meeting him on the street.

Just barely understanding that it was me, Furukawa was now startled and asked how I had come through the disaster. Held by the private, I told Furukawa about my situation at the time of the bombing and afterward.

Furukawa explained that he had been searching on foot every day since his oldest daughter had not returned. A Prefectural Girls School student, she was, like me, mobilized to work.

"What a cruel thing the American devils have done," Furukawa said resentfully.

I asked about the damage in town, where my home was, and about my family. I was afraid to hear his answer.

He remained with his eyes closed for a while, seeming to organize his thoughts, but then said, "Oh, everyone was safe at the leader's."

Before thinking, I pushed my body forward: "My father and mother and big sister are alive, are they?"

My father was the leader of a wartime town association. Furukawa told me that he had set up a temporary office in the field and was very busy distributing food and issuing identification cards for those bombed out.

Furukawa promised that he would contact my family as soon as he returned home. He asked the private to take good care of me and then left. On his way out he carefully checked the list of patients posted at the entrance, but when it was clear that his daughter was not there, he left looking downcast.

Feeling that someone from home would come instantly when contacted by Furukawa, I waited expectantly; but it was late at night when my father came to see me.

His voice sounded a little higher pitched than usual.

On hearing it, I raised myself, forgetting the pain, and turned my body in that direction.

The moment I recognized my father in the faint candlelight, I went forward, tripping over wounded people nearby.

My father momentarily displayed an expression of shock, but

quickly assuming a manly attitude, he said, "Good for you that you are alive," as he firmly held me in both arms.

My father had intended to carry me home on his bicycle, but when he found that I was badly enervated, he went back again to arrange for a horsedrawn cart.

The following afternoon my mother returned with the cart.

Clinging to her, I shouted, "Now I don't care if I die."

My mother, who had kept searching for me, looked haggard and pale.

Carried by the private as when I had come to the camp, I went out to the street where the cart was parked. When I was placed on the cushion in the cart, I was aware that my mind, which had been taut until then, suddenly went slack.

III

"Take a look at this before you leave," Nashimoto said, pointing toward the garden when we were paying respects to Kayo at the entrance. Having exited before us through the back door and gone around, he was standing outside. Guided by him, we approached the bushes near the wall.

It was an ojizo-san, a stone bodhisattva.

The small jizo was about eighty centimeters tall. Under the lotus-shaped pedestal was another stone pedestal. It was square and made of well-polished granite.

On the left side of the granite pedestal was inscribed "Kazumasa, age thirteen," and on the right side, "Praise the Buddha."

The main body was made of blackish sandstone. It was a strikingly innocent-looking ojizo-san, but even so it was properly equipped with a tin staff in the right hand and a rosary of agate beads hanging on the left hand. Each bead, though small, was carefully polished.

After asking Nashimoto's permission, I quietly lifted the rosary and placed it on my palm.

Besides the rosary and staff, a small wattle hat and straw sandals befitting his height were hanging from his neck.

"Just like departing on a journey," I said to Nashimoto. It was exactly what I thought.

A smile surfacing on his face, Nashimoto stroked the head of the ojizo-san with his gnarled hand.

Each item seemed to have been ordered separately, for both wattled hat and straw sandals were well made. Such care went into the tin staff, too, that its head was shaped like the top of a *sotoba*, a wooden grave marker, several brass links hanging from it.

On the ground around the pedestal, small pebbles were heaped in piles. Nashimoto explained they had brought them from the ruins of Hiroshima, and I conjectured that they must have picked them up at Zakoba where their son had been working.

The surface of the pebbles, discolored and light brown, was the best proof of that. As though still emitting heat, they appeared gruesome to me.

"We had a stone mason in Toyoshima, Shikoku, chisel this jizo. It was a much bigger job than one would expect. A round hole is carved out of the pedestal so that the core of the image fit into it," Nashimoto praised the workmanship.

It was a completely unaffected, simple-feeling jizo-san, which, I thought, reflected the personality of the stone mason who carved it.

"Is the sculptor who carved this in Tokyo?" I asked.

"Now he has withdrawn to Toyoshima. He teamed with me in the old days, but he's retired too, and this was his retirement piece. All the more, he did a fine job," Nashimoto said in a tone as if praising his own work.

Listening to his explanation, my heart was drawn to the epitaph, if these two lines can be called an epitaph:

> Kazumasa, age thirteen
> Praise the Buddha

I felt as though I were looking at the inscription on my own tombstone.

"Each season I let Kazumasa eat the first food of the season. If eggplants are around, for example, I offer him some first, and in between times I offer his favorite food."

In the way Kayo spoke, there was not even a trifle of the agitation that she revealed a while ago; it suggested calmness after emotions had been washed away by the flow of twenty years.

"There's nothing else we can do for Kazumasa but decorate flowers throughout the year and offer incense," Nashimoto said as he swept with his hand the dead leaves on the ojizo-san's shoulder.

In his gesture I perceived his love for his child—it was as if he were giving instructions: wear your straw hat when it's hot, wear your straw sandals when your feet are sore, drive them away with your staff if you encounter poisonous insects.

"I think of how much he must have wanted water then, so every day I offer him fresh water poured in a lunch box lid," Kayo said, looking at me, or rather, at my keloid marks.

"I wanted water then. If I can drink water I don't care if I die, I thought," I responded, recalling the heat that made me feel burnt to the core of my body. I thought of my thirst then.

"Well, as long as we watch him like this, I believe that Kazumasa's soul won't wander, and that he can attain nirvana with a peaceful heart," Nashimoto said as he faced the ojizo-san, keeping his hand on its head, as though speaking to be heard by a living son.

From the incense holder by Nashimoto's feet, ashes had fallen on the ground.

I looked at the deep red azaleas blooming in a corner of the garden. They were quietly burning alone.

I recalled what Kayo had said during our conversation a while ago:

"When someone I went to look with received a few pieces of bones in an envelope at the temporary crematorium, I felt both pity and envy for that parent. On looking back, I have no idea which was better. She was handed bones like fragments of chinaware which they said were her child's, but she said she couldn't believe that. In the end she broke down crying. Kazumasa didn't even leave bones in my hands. Even now I wake many times during the night, feeling as if he is coming home saying, 'I'm home!' Even in my dreams when I think that I have to unlock the front door because he's coming home, or that somewhere he must be waiting for me to come and get him, I feel as if I can't sit or stand. I want to die quickly and see my boy."

She added, "My chest hurts so much that I think I'll contract cancer if I continue to live like this.''

At this, Nashimoto angrily said, ''Don't say what's useless to say. We have no choice but to think that everything is a matter of fate. Kazumasa is a child who was born into this world with that predestined span of life.''

Remembering that conversation, the thought took on a sense of reality—the thought that a man one year younger than myself who bore that fate existed with me twenty years ago under the mushroom cloud.

I recalled the sight on the evening of that day.

. . . The doors of the covered freight train were opened at the foot of the mountain to carry the wounded.

I was watching it from the bluff.

A soldier's thick voice was gathering the wounded. From the forest and anti-air raid side caves, wounded people in tatters crawled out and moved down the slope of the mountain. Helped by soldiers, they disappeared into cars one by one.

Partly because it was nearly sundown, I felt strangely lonely in a mixture of frustration and insecurity and tried to slide down the slope on my bottom, like many other wounded people.

Then it occurred to me that this freight train might be going to Ujina Port. Because this side track for the exclusive use of the army was connected to the Ujina Line, it was perfectly plausible that the train was bound for Ujina.

It seemed to be going to the first aid station on Kanawa Island. I recalled having gone to the armory on the island for labor service. I went back and forth between the island and Ujina Port on the army's landing craft. Although only four kilometers by sea from Ujina, to me the distance felt infinite.

I drew back the foot that I stepped on once, and returned to my former posture.

While I was doing this and that, the freight train closed its heavy steel doors and departed. When the angular cars with white and black camouflage markings disappeared from view, I was assaulted by a feeling that resembled regret.

I started down the mountain, thinking of going to the factory where I worked as a mobilized student; I would go home after getting treatment at the medical office.

Due to the violent impact from the bomb, every joint in my body had lost its exact combination of bones, and as I walked, pressure was added here and there with irregular, dry noises. As I myself was sometimes aware, I held my burnt arms raised to the chest with hands hanging, and I uttered a voice that was between a scream and a sob as I wandered in the mountain with insecure steps.

Then, I encountered the private first class and was taken in at the first aid post. . . .

Recalling the scene then, I felt that it was something like fate that today, after twenty years, in a corner on the outskirts of Tokyo, I would meet a jizo built as an offering to console the spirit of a lost person.

He may have died vicariously for me, I thought.

The freight train and the jizo overlapped in the corner of the retina of my eyes, then the train gradually vanished. Then the ojizo-san began to shine in gold, and a beautiful halo towered behind him. It spread resplendent, rose, and shot through my eyes.

Suddenly, a smile flickered on the jizo's face.

It was the smile of a buddha who, having gone through a hell of agonizing cries, has finally reached the world of nirvana. It was an image of the buddha who was liberated from all passions and attained a high realm of immortality beyond birth and death. His lotus blossom pedestal was not the mortal world which I trod.

I was sad because it was as if it reflected, by contrast, my unenlightened attachment to this world.

When the halo vanished and I faced the innocent jizo, I thought of many things.

The lost boy was still thirteen to the Nashimotos; undoubtedly he was not thirty-three. I was sure that the childlike face he showed on leaving the house on the day of the atomic bomb must have been retained unchanged for twenty years; the face the Nashimotos always remembered was no ugly keloid face burnt by the atomic bomb. It was the face of a boy with smooth skin. Should he by chance unexpectedly come home, he would be just as he was in the old days.

What Nashimoto lovingly stroked was the memory of one who became a buddha. A question arises: what if his son were alive with ugly keloid marks like mine? He would not stroke his face, I thought.

What if the son married an older woman who didn't please his parents, and what if he couldn't work like a normal person? He might be better off being an offered jizo.

Stroking the smooth cheeks of the stone buddha, I felt almost jealous.

Between my father and myself lay a deep gulf that could never be filled.

Although as strong a memory as mine may not have remained in my father, the words he threw at me then struck me as something decisive, casting a deep shadow over my later life.

With what thought did my father regard the offered jizo for the lost son of the Nashimotos? I felt curious, but soon a violent rebellious impulse gripped my heart.

. . . My father and I shared an unforgettable memory.

It was soon after I was bombed. In those days, I feared human eyes. In fact, human eyes lacerated me more sharply than words could.

For this reason, I walked with my body stiff, paying close attention to the external world so that I would miss no eyes that regarded me with the smallest evil intention. Whenever I met such eyes, my brain snapped as if by reflex so that I only thought about how I could avoid having people see my keloid marks.

I spent many hours confined at home, looking at my face reflected in a mirror. In it, a lump of ugly flesh covered the left half like lava rising out of a crater. My eyebrows were burnt away, and the corners of my lips and eyes were pulled taut. My neck, which inclined to one side, refused to go back no matter how much I tried to push it to the opposite side.

Disregarding the pain, I picked at the thick lump of flesh with a pale purple gloss and tried to tear it from my cheek. As I continued this vain act, I suddenly felt lonely and started to cry.

Tears flowed as though a dam was broken, and, without trying to wipe them, I let them drop on the keloid marks on the back of my hands. I remained crouched with the mirror in my hand, until no more tears came. Finally, when the keloid skin felt pulled because of the tears that dried, I stood up.

Knowing that people called my keloid marks "burns" or "boiled octopus," I tried never to walk outside by day except when commuting to school. When there was no choice, I took a back alley that was covered with rubble. I avoided trains.

One day, my father came to my room to tell me he had a job for me. I had just returned from school and had not been able to forget an unpleasant event I had encountered there.

I was looking at my ugly face with a mirror in my hand.

Seeing my father, I put the mirror in a drawer of my desk.

I did not respond to the job my father told me to do. It was an errand that could not be done without going out, and that day I just could not do it. I told him that I didn't want to go out.

Then, my father angrily asked to make sure: "You won't go no matter what?"

"No, no matter what," I insisted.

"There you go, that's why you get burns on your face."

Hearing these words, anger rose throughout my entire body. Not knowing what to say, he ascribed my burns to my nature. Driven by violent resentment, I was aware that my body convulsed.

"I got burnt because of the war. And moreover. . . ."

Unable to finish my sentence, I tried to grab at him in blind hatred.

"It's not because of the war. You got burnt because you have that kind of nature."

". . . ."

I stared at my father in rage.

"I will no longer think of you as a parent. All my life I will never forget what you just said."

Grabbing something nearby, I hurled it to the ground. Although tears flowed endlessly out of remorse, I continued to stare at my father, clenching my teeth.

My mother came, alarmed by the noise.

Fixing her eyes on my father, she shouted angrily, "There are things you can say and cannot say. No father anywhere in the world would say such a thing."

"It's true, of course. People with a good attitude don't get burns even if they're bombed," my father said, and walked away, his back to my mother and me.

"Really, what kind of father he is to say such an awful thing. . . ." We cried aloud.

"Give me back my old face," I shouted, banging my head against a pillar.

My mother also shouted, "I hate America. I'll hate it even when I'm dead."

Was this how my own father viewed the keloid marks on my face? I was overwhelmed by a dark feeling.

My father had not walked around looking for me from love of his child. He had walked on the burned field simply out of parental duty. So it was natural, I realized, that others teased and laughed at the keloid marks on my face.

It was a dark night.

My father was asleep, snoring loudly.

Soon, a clear image of the jeep that had come to school during the day loomed in my mind. I sighed deeply.

The jeep carried two American soldiers and a Nisei interpreter.

Students with cicatrized keloids were collected in the school master's room, and one by one their scars were photographed. The lens of the large camera that the visitors brought in shot a cold light to my eyes. My neck, pulled taut by the keloid scar, was bent roughly by an American soldier's hands with soft golden hair, and in the same way, the keloid scarred back of my hands were put together one over the other in an unnatural way.

The ugly photograph of my naked upper body was probably going to be numbered and eternally preserved as part of the material meant for those who dropped the bomb.

I came home feeling humiliation all over my body, but I did not reveal to my parents that I had been photographed by the American soldiers for my keloid marks.

Listening to my father's relaxed snoring, I thought I no longer wanted to live. . . .

However, in front of the offered jizo, I am actually alive like this.

I let go of the ojizo-san. Since coming to the Nashimotos', I felt that I had recalled too many things. This must also be so for the Nashimotos.

I thought for the first time that, judging from my age, in forty years there would be no atomic bomb survivors, and that someone would beautifully talk about them as if in a tone of narrating a fairy tale. I realized how ugly and small my obsession was.

Right then it was the moment of an evening glow.

The lotus blossom seat burnt, and the moment the contour of the ojizo-san was lit in gold, the entire body shone as if burning. It was an elevated moment. When the flames subsided I felt that I had been given peace as if my heart had been washed.

After joining my hands in prayer for the peacefully sleeping ojizo-san, I took a step backward. While stepping backward, I thought that the most becoming name for this ojizo-san might be "Warawa Jizo," Boy Buddha.

"Well, then, shall we go?" my father said.

"Yes, let's," I nodded, feeling fatigued.

"I had too much to drink today, but I had a really good time after many years."

Nashimoto came out to the street to see us off.

My father, by now sober, had a secure gait.

Nashimoto stood there until we turned the corner.

As I looked back while turning, Nashimoto waved his hand once again with a gesture as though stretching. In response, I also waved with all my might.

My father walked several meters ahead.

 # PHOTOGRAPHS

At 11 a.m. on August 9 a plutonium bomb with a force equivalent to 22,000 tons of TNT exploded over Nagasaki. Within one-millionth of a second, the temperature rose to several million degrees centigrade, giving rise to a fireball and a mushroom cloud shown in this U.S. Army Air Force photograph.

Hiroshima's Industrial Promotion Hall, subsequently known as the Atomic Bomb Dome, was one of the few central city buildings to survive the blast. In the right foreground are the ruins of the Sei Hospital, which stood at the hypocenter. The board tied to the post at the lower right of this October 1945 photograph by Hayashi Shigeo bears the message that its author is still alive.

Urakami Cathedral, the hub of Catholicism in Nagasaki and Japan, was 500 meters from ground zero. Its ruins are shown in this October 1945 photograph by Hayashi Shigeo.

Hayashi Shigeo recorded the ruins of the steel-frame Hiroshima City Water Works, 550 meters from the hypocenter, in October 1945.

Hayashi Shigeo's October 1945 photograph shows the virtual leveling of central Hiroshima and the scope of destruction in the vicinity of ground zero.

Relief workers and family members search the rubble of Nagasaki for survivors and remains of the dead on August 10, 1945. The photograph by Yamahata Yosuke was taken 700 meters from the hypocenter.

A wounded Hiroshima policeman issues casualty certificates to victims of the bomb. Matsushige Yoshito's photograph was taken on the afternoon of August 6, 2.7 kilometers from ground zero.

Two girls return home with bags of rice rations in Yamazato township, Nagasaki, in early September 1945. Matsumoto Eiichi is the photographer.

A boy, carrying his injured younger brother on his back, searches for their father near the Nagasaki railroad station on August 10, 1945. The photograph is by Yamahata Yosuke.

A Nagasaki family cremates one of its members. Matsumoto Eiichi's photograph was taken in September 1.3 kilometers from the hypocenter.

In May 1973, 23,000 items that had been taken to the United States for research twenty-eight years earlier, including clinical records, slide specimens, and human remains, were returned to Hiroshima.

POETRY

POEMS BY ATOMIC BOMB SURVIVORS

From *Nihon genbaku shishu*

Umeboshi*
Ikeda Some

Oh yes, at that moment, what shall I say,
together with the glass case in the dining room
I tumbled
Rumble rumble each time it shook
I squeezed out to the top of the roof.
Squeezed out?—there was no way I could get myself out
I was helped out I suppose
by the gods or by the Buddha.

Oh what distress what pain
I wish I'd breathed my last quickly
then I'd be able to go to the other world, I thought.

It was on the morning of the third day
that someone put an *umeboshi* in my mouth.
"This old woman's dead, alas
poor woman

---

*Pickled plum.

namu Amidha namu Amidha,''
he stroked my face.
''I'm alive I'm alive,'' I said
then he kindly dropped
a big *umeboshi* in my mouth.

This thing *umeboshi* is a good thing.
It was thanks to that *umeboshi*
that I grew stronger.

City in Flames
Nakamura On

Under a pale blue glow, the black sun,
dead sunflowers, and a collapsed roof,
people lifted their faces voicelessly:
bloody eyes that exchanged looks then
loosely peeling skin
lips swollen like eggplants
heads impaled with shards of glass—
"how can this be a human face"
everybody thought at the sight of another
yet each who so thought had the same face.

Flames soon wrapped the city
at one house there were only a mother and a seven-year-old girl
crushed under the roof the mother could not move
the girl alone survived
while the girl was trying to move a pillar
the flames came there too
"run by yourself"
the mother, with her free arm,
pushed the child away.

Without even uttering a cry of horror
toward a place without flames

from the west and from the east
naked figures their skin loosely peeling
you couldn't tell men from women
a procession of ghosts continued;
in the middle of all this
suddenly
an old woman in the procession stopped
pulling in something like a sash that was coming off
when the flames had already come so close!

Someone, unable to take it any longer, said
"come, throw that away, let's hurry"
then she answered
"these are my intestines."

A Skinless Throng
Yamamoto Yasuo

In the big shelter at the foot of Mount Hiji
a skinless throng
looking up
or lying face down
or sitting with legs crossed
were crying "give me water"
they were all still alive
their spasmodic cries and groans
filled the air-raid shelter from the farthest dark corner to the
    exit
like a huge musical instrument
they resounded making a ghastly howl.

My wife and I
carried on a shutter
our dear child, burnt alive, naked
into the naked group.

Inside the shelter an army doctor was applying oil
on dying people
"For this child, please do something for this child."

This was the first-aid post we had found at last
"Let this child live—"
"Here's another terrible case . . . , "
the doctor went over the swollen red-black back and legs of the
    child
with a cloth soused in oil in the pot
when I pointed at the big open wound
left split like a ripe pomegranate
which had shed the last drop of blood
leave it alone, it'll heal itself, look
I have neither medicine nor bandage, the doctor said
as I realized
the doctor himself was naked with burns all over him
my wife and I bowed palms together to the doctor
dirty like an old statue of the Buddha, only his eyes glowing.

Was he going to make it?
again placing him on the shutter
saying "so lucky, so lucky,"
we went back holding it at both ends.

Ah what fools parents are
such cruel burns and
such deep wounds could never be cured.

That night my son
in the debris
of the house blown to pieces in the explosion
lived out the remaining few hours meted out by the atomic
    bomb
like the flame of a candle burning itself out
"are there *yokan* cakes in the Pure Land? and
there's no war in the Pure Land, is there . . . "
he muttered

and twitched his body and breathed the last
of his sweet life of thirteen years and three months.

That army doctor, too, probably died before long
the naked group without skin
crying in the dark shelter
probably all died
cursing mankind's brutality called war. . . .

To the Voiceless
Yamada Kazuko

No matter what you say
it is cruel
already forgotten by everyone
and buried away
are the buddhas
left alone
are the buddhas
no matter what you say
it is cruel
on a night when the moon inclines
come over as ghosts
talk with your mom
let's talk, with our backs turned.

Ten Years
Yamada Kazuko

An incredibly long night and
an incredibly short day and

an incredibly long night and
an incredibly long night and
an incredibly long night and
an incredibly long night and . . .

Wail
Yamada Kazuko

Oh Shoji
Oh Yasushi

Oh Shoji
Oh Yasushi

Ohh Shoji
Ohh Yasushi

Ohh Shoji my boy
Ohh Yasushi my boy

Shoji my boy
Shoji my boy.

To the Lost
Yamada Kazuko

When loquats bloom
when peach blossoms in the peach mountain bloom
when almonds are as big as the tip of the little finger
my boys
please come.

The Wind
Yamada Kazuko

Knocking on the door of the back entrance
who is it?
koto koto koto koto
shaking the gate in passing

who is it?
mom's working on a side job at home
mom's waiting
mom still has your briefs and undershirts.

Floating Lanterns
Kosono Aiko

Flickering flickering
bobbing bobbing
blue lanterns
red lanterns
swaying swaying
they float
to a far place
to the Ten Trillion Lands
they float away
countless numbers of them
a hundred a thousand ten thousand,
many more
continue
floating
it was
long long ago
the dreadful atomic bomb
was dropped on Hiroshima
and many many people
died
in this river
those people today
have come for a visit
from the Ten Trillion Lands to Hiroshima
lighting a red fire
lighting a blue fire
"let's not
ever drop

another such dreadful bomb
be peaceful forever
let's protect Hiroshima
let's protect Japan
let's protect the world
let's protect the cosmos''
rocked by the waves
recalling their distant past
they whisper
flickering flickering
bobbing bobbing
red lanterns
blue lanterns
swaying swaying
they float away
to a far place
to the Ten Trillion Lands
they float away
countless
numbers
a hundred a thousand ten thousand
many more
continue
floating.

Burnt Eye
Shimada Isamu

Again August 9's here
listen, the day your right eye
was smashed is back
the day
your eye, lovely
as a candy
was gouged out
is here
again—

after your eye was taken
always wearing a white eye patch
you went to school
how angry you must've felt
how mad
how inconvenienced
from time to time
you took off your eye patch
and under the desk
you were stroking your keloid scar
I knew it
I
thought if I said it
you'd cry
so I kept quiet
this year again
your day's here
the day of the pikadon's* here
you were
called a cripple
called a one-eye
you were
reading books with your left eye
your right had been taken by the pika
would you
perhaps wish for a rosary
would you
perhaps wish for the Madonna's necklace
August 9's here
you were six, weren't you
you've become twenty-five
you'd like to marry, wouldn't you.

---

*Flash-boom, or the atomic bomb.

Peace Park/Laughter
Matsuo Shizuaki

Incredible laughter heard
the invisible seen
the forest of horror sitting in the farthest corner of the eye
we quickly covered our white chests, but—

Yoshio who had often played with our Hiroko died that year
The words of Yoshio's mother who came food-hunting for
    vegetables gushed out, coated with tears
"On the second day, when poor Hiroko was brought here to
    the country
from the burnt windows of City Hall and the Red Cross Hospital
many bones of the dead to which pieces of flesh were still
    attached
    were thrown out and piled up
that's when Yoshio was dug out from the dirt
without a single scar he was dug out from the dirt
a dozen days later
he cried it hurts it hurts
no matter how and where I touched him he cried
after that neither his ankles nor neck
nor hips could move—he couldn't even lift or lower his arms
they didn't bend
besides have you ever thought of a doll's eyes?
his eyes only saw straight ahead
'how come only I'm this way'
he said, crying with his tearless eyes
with his eyes under eyelids which had lost eyelashes
in the third month Yoshio became a doll
a doll's eyes are open but can't see
why I wonder did the gods keep those unseeing eyes open?
what were those unseeing eyes seeing
yet before he died
he had finally become well enough at least to crawl around
the day he died he
wanted to see his oldest sister who had loved him

crawled from his bed to the yard to see if she might
   be coming
he waited single-mindedly for three hours in the cold air
but his sister had died four days earlier of 'medullary leukemia'
if we died, who would care for someone like Yoshio?
my husband and I often prayed
'would that he would die before us'
what parent ever wished that a child would die first?!''

Now from the restaurant across the river a burst of laughter rises
   to the night sky
now the fountain powerfully spouting up in the square suddenly
   stops.

How much can words sustain space—
when we sit facing fresh laughter again
it becomes an incredible peal, more sharply whetted
and splits us in two
the funnier the laughter, the harder for us to laugh.

The Atomic Bomb*
Sakamoto Hatsumi

When the atomic bomb drops
day turns into night
people turn into ghosts.

Untitled
Tanoo Kinue

After the bomb dropped
mom says
boiling rice she has carefully saved
''what's so fun about
making war''

---

*This and the following two poems were composed in 1952 by primary school students.

she says
"Takashi my son, Takashi my son
please come back healthy"
she cries
making rice balls.

Untitled
Sato Tomoko

Yoshiko
with burns
in bed
said
I want to eat a tomato
so mom
went out food hunting
in the meantime
Yoshiko
died
"by feeding you nothing but sweet potatoes
I've killed you"
mom cried
I too
cried
everybody
cried.

That Guy
Sakamoto Tadashi

Flinging himself back, still clinging to the bed, his protruding
Adam's apple convulsing up and down, he groaned, I'll die, I'll
die. The two of us grabbed him and held him down, and gave
him a morphine shot.

His liver was so poor that his urine specimen turned deep red
before our eyes, and, refusing three days to touch his trays prepared without protein and grease, he sulked and sulked saying,
I'll starve to death. Shouting vile words at him, at last I gave him
a glucose shot.

Having lost his senses from a high fever, he had a grayish dark
face. His skin which enclosed 38,000 white cells idly sagging
around his eyelids, that guy, ugly as a monkey, from time to time
mumbled, you quack. There, there, I said holding him in my
arms, and injected Ringer's solution through a staggeringly fat
needle into a vein which had risen to the surface.

But one day the guy spewed blood like a fountain of heavy oil,
dyeing the sheet even while we watched. As I turned to him in a
hurry with a needle for a blood transfusion, he received it meekly
and said in a faint whisper, doctor, I want to live, and with that
he stopped moving, his eyes open.

Song of the Prime Minister
Okamoto Jun

However much deadly ashes scatter
however much polluted rain falls
whatever scholars say
whatever hubbub the populace makes
the minister's face turns "over there" and greets
—please, please, anything you like.

Beta rays
gamma rays
nebulous radioactive clouds cover the archipelago
fish cattle vegetables trees and grass
all turn into a leaden soggy mass
young and old, men and women turn into sea monsters, even then
the minister leaves it up to those "over there"
—please, please, anything you like.

Now no woman no man
has a human shape
the islands are shattered fragments of oyster shells
an eroded desert
where bones and ashes dance directionless
the wandering ghost of the minister
is singing somewhere like a marsh cricket
—please, please, anything you like.

Tanka from Hiroshima

City flattened distant mountains are in view
mountains they are thus they escaped burning

街崩えて居ながら遠き山の見ゆ山なればかく焼けのこりたり

Unobstructed view of the low Ujina hills
how wide the ruins of the city that burnt

見とほしに見ゆる宇品の山低く焼けくづれたる街あとの広さ

Imai Tokusaburo

Body and limbs burnt out of shape the voice
is still youthful she's a maiden

五体みな焼け崩れたる人の声いまだ若きは乙女なるらし

Kanda Mikio

I must first get my children I thought and rushed out
on the street the schoolers were coming home crying

先ず子らを迎へに行かむと馳せ出れば通りを児童^{こら}が泣きてもどり来

My children my children thank God you're safe
firmly I clasped the two children's hands

子らよ子らよよく無事なりししつかりと二人の子らの手をにぎりしむ

Kurihara Sadako

Those killed without ceremony we gather
without ceremony and place in the bonfire

無造作に殺されし人を無造作にかき集めきて榾火^{ほたび}にふすかも

Sasaki Yutaka

Clawing at the air "I'm hot I'm hot" a girl says
curselike in a shadeless city

虚空つかみ熱いよ熱いよと少女のこゑ呪ひのごとく日蔭なき街

Fukagawa Munetoshi

Rice ball in her hands   lost
a half naked old woman walks the street

握飯手にささげつつおろおろと半裸の老婆路上をありく

Yamazumi Mamoru

Infected his lips cannot close a middle school student
faintly with his tongue stutters ''(M)other''

化膿して口もつむげぬ中学生かすかに舌で「アカータン」とつぶやく

A five-year-old we burnt in the sweet-potato farm
in the same small hollow today we burn her little sister

五才の子焼いた小さな薯畑のくぼみで今日はその妹を焼く

Sugita Hatsuyo

All night through groaning was heard
near dawn the voice became quiet perhaps he died

夜もすがら呻きし声が暁ちかく静かになりて死にゆけるらし

Hasegawa Seisaku

Each time I see a boy's body I bring my face close
to see if he's my boy as I travel in search

少年の屍と見れば顔よせて吾子ならじかと覗きては行く

Charred beyond recognition yet
the shoes he wears are my boy's shoes

焼け爛れ見分けもつかずなり果てど穿てる靴はまさに吾子の靴

That I could have been here one hour earlier   my hand
feels a faint trace of the warmth of the flesh

今一時間早かりせばと手に触ればかすかに残る肌のぬくもり

Masuda Misako

Koreans we discriminated against in this town
from its sky the atomic bomb indiscriminately fell

朝鮮人よと差別受けたるこの町の空より原爆は差別なく降る

Ueno Haruko

Alas, my wife still hopes
though setting his plate already for a month in vain

ああ妻はなほもたのむか陰膳も一月すぎてむなしけれども

Imai Tokusaburo

Voice serene she sang the Song of Ariran
the Korean maiden was soon dead

声涼しくアリランの唄歌ひたる朝鮮乙女間なく死にたり

Kanda Masu

Again and again I count his white blood cells
since it is below several thousand I don't tell the patient

幾回も繰返し数へし白血球数千に足らざれば患者には云はず

If I know my white blood cell count is decreasing
my energy will wither I don't check my own

白血球減るとし知らば我が気力衰えぬべし己のは調べず

Koyama Ayao

Her ears burnt by the atomic bomb my younger sister
does not ask to have earrings

原爆に耳を焼かれし我が妹はイヤリングなど欲しがらぬなり

When I approached she rose from before the mirror
what was my younger sister thinking of

近づけば鏡の前をつと立ちし妹よ何を思ひて居しか

Nitta Takayoshi

In the hypocenter the evening is light in the falling rain
a boy, wet, is planting wheat

爆心地夕べあかるく降る雨に少年濡れて麦を蒔きおり

Fukagawa Munetoshi

Staring with bomb-blind eyes
the youth listens to a mazurka

原爆に盲し眼ふかく据え青年はマズルカの曲にききいる

Inside the coach chartered for orphans
there is singing there is laughter and balloons fly

孤児らのため貸切られたる電車のなか歌あり笑いあり風船がとぶ

Ishibashi Teruko

Under the beam you dead wife told me to leave you and run
because of your eyes I remain alone

梁の下逃げよと云ひし亡妻よその瞳故未だめとらず

Imamoto Shunkoh

Knotgrass and wild parsley sprout by the water
for my sick husband I catch mud snails by the river

犬蓼も野芹も水に萌えており病む夫に蜷をあさる川岸

Rain nears inside the evening window
    signs of the onslaught of pain
I wrap my husband's arm in silk floss

雨もよう夕窓のうち疼き兆す夫の腕を真綿にくるむ

Utsumi Seiko

The fire pressing under the beam I abandoned my wife
I cannot forget her wailing voice

火の迫る梁の下敷きの妻を捨て泣き叫びゐし声を忘れず

Kuroda Hotsumi

Palms joined my friend asked for water
that I gave none has become my lifelong regret

手を合わせ水欲る友にやらざりし我が終生の悔恨となる

Kono Chizuko

Girl students dance and wail before the monument
come out dead sister, like light

女生徒がいま碑のまえで舞って哭く、亡妹もででこい光のように

I want money summer's gone fall's departed
my mother has become an *oden* seller I want money for her

銭が欲し夏去り秋逝きおでん屋のおかみとなりし母に銭が欲し

Forever she's a girl of thirteen years
the image of my dead sister in my heart

いつまでも十三歳の少女なりわが胸ぬちの亡妹の映像

Little sister made into a ''ghost'' you appeared in my dream
silent tears filling yours eyes which will never become clear

「お化け」にされた妹よ、夢に現われて無言、冴えることのない眼
に涙がいっぱい

Masuoka Toshikazu

Snail-like I crawled on the ground and sought water
about that living hell I cannot tell my children

でで虫のごとく地を這い水求む生きし地獄は児らに告げ得ず

Kanamoto Misaki

Tanka from Nagasaki

In an instant they lost homes and parents
from today they are orphans, these children

一瞬に家をも親もうしないしこの子らたちよ今日よりは孤児

To the children living in a branch school on the mountain
a Catholic Father has brought snow white bread

山の分校へ避難して住む子等たちに神父が持ち来し真白きパン

Ota Jisaemon

In the Cathedral in the ruins of boundless expanse
I stayed one night criticizing God

茫漠の瓦礫の中の天主堂に一夜明かしぬ神をあげつらひ

Suga Takashi

My friend breathed faintly
I placed a small cross on her breast

絶えだえに息する友の胸にわれ小さきクルスをかけてやりたり

Yamashita Haruko

Collecting scraps of wood beneath a bridge I burnt a girl's body
I cannot forget the sound of the water that night

木切れあつめ橋下に少女の骸焼きし夜のせせらぎを今も忘れず

Ochiai Kei

A lonesome child my daughter once was
on this owl-hooting moonlit night where does she cry

淋しがりの娘なりしが梟鳴くこの月の夜を何処に泣くらむ

Suda Iwaho

Over the burnt image of the Virgin Mary the wind is cold
dusk approaches the Urakami Cathedral

火に灼けしマリアの像に　風寒く　昏れせまり来る　浦上天主堂

Oshima Takeyasu

White blood cell count is low
dazzling my eyes young leaves rustle tossed in the wind

白血球すくなきわれを眩しませ若葉木さわぐ風に揉まれて

Mihara Hanako

No trace of the atomic bomb   dyeing Mount Hiko
morning after morning the sun rises

原爆の跡かたもなき彦山を染めて朝々陽は昇るなり

Matsumoto Sueko

Slow Buddhist chanting is heard amidst other voices
floating lanterns, bobbing, leave the shore

ゆるやかに読経の声もまじらひて流灯はゆられつつ今離れゆく

Tatara Yukiko

Near the hypocenter blooms in dust
in front of Jizo a red heavenflower

爆心地にちかく埃をあびて咲く地蔵の前の赤き曼珠沙華

Moriuchi Masa

Haiku from Hiroshima

Out of the infernal fire   corpses in the summer river

業火脱がれ来て夏川の屍となる

Ichiki Ryujoshi

Blue fire on bare bones   burns   a star   falls

青き火の肉骨　燃えて　星　流る

Okamoto Ogaku

Because people go I must go too skin dangling

人ゆくゆゑ行かねばならぬ皮ひきずり

Charred black   they hold perhaps a cicada-catching pole
  perhaps they are brother and sister

黒焦げて手握るは蝉竿らし兄妹らし

Kozaki Teijin

A smile at a bite of tomato   the boy is already a corpse

一口のトマトに笑み少年早や死骸

Strength to turn a body in a girl who looks for her mother

屍体裏返す力あり母探す少女に

Shibata Moriyo

Their whispers like ghosts of the dead   flies swarm

さゝやきの亡霊に似て蝿むるゝ

Seo Tetsuo

Like stakes
tombs
stand side by side
hammered in

杭のごとく
墓
たちならび
打ちこまれ

Takayanagi Shigenobu

Swollen with burns   unable to make a weeping face he weeps

火ぶくれて泣く表情にならず泣く

Hatanaka Kyokotsu

Crows came   the corpse is headless

烏来て骸に頭なかりけり

Kaneyuki Fumiko

An empty shell I walk   flowers hit my eyes

抜け殻となって歩く花が眼につく

Sasaki Isami

Setting sun shoots the wasteland ghost-like

西日さながら亡者の如き荒れ野を射る

Hanabatake Tomio

Hiroshima is without light a white white city

ひろしまは光げのないしろい白い街

Shoji Tokie

To the jeep that quickly came I refused autopsy

疾くと来しジープに解剖拒みけり

Okada Nobuyuki

In the spring mud a child runs this way   my dead child?
  I thought

春泥に馳せくる子あり亡き子かと

Gyotoku Sumiko

[Haiku left by the girl]

Cicadas don't cry   you make me remember Masanobu-chan

蝉鳴くな正信ちゃんを思い出す

Gyotoku Satoko

Over a floating lantern   faces together an orphan and his
 big brother

流灯に顔重ねあふ孤児その兄

Obori Chie

A-bomb anniversary   regretting that I was a soldier ill in bed

原爆忌兵たりしこと悔いつ病む

Kumagai Masao

Nothing to clutch   ten fingers remain open

すがるべきものなし十指開きしま゛

Sawaki Kin'ichi

Sprouts have cracked the A-bomb scorched land

ものの芽の原爆焦土割りにけり

Shigemoto Yasuhiko

I pull away summer grass   here's a grave marker

夏草を抜き捨て此処に墓標あり

Date Shiyoshi

Upstairs A-bomb disease patients   downstairs A-bomb corpses

階上は原爆症階下は原爆屍

Tanaka Kikuha

Firefly in an orphan's hands powerfully glimmers on and off

孤児の掌の蛍は強く明滅す

Taruma Yoshikazu

Burnt land holding moisture   white radish flowers bloom

焦土しめりもてば大根花開く

Tsutsumi Mannen

Autumn at night ABCC's lights dominate

夜の秋ABCCの灯君臨す

Narusawa Kaken

Fire flowers glow   bones must be burning under the river

花火映え川底の骨燃ゆるらし

Utsumi Kanshi

Hiroshima anniversary   night train with many empty seats
  passes

ヒロシマ忌空席多き夜汽車過ぐ

Emoto Seitoh

Tree-budding rain falls bringing something cheerful to Hiroshima

木の芽雨明るきものをひろしまに

Ochi Saijo

A long prayer   in drought ants race on the ground

ながき祈り旱の蟻は地に迅し

Kaji Daisuke

Concealing a keloid she is already a mother

ケロイドを秘しつつすでに母となる

Suzuki Ippa

A jet now severs Hiroshima's Milky Way

ジェット機いまヒロシマの銀河截る

Takeuchi Takashi

Demonstrators' groups taint Hiroshima A-bomb anniversary

デモ隊の広島をよごす原爆忌

Tanaka Naoko

Peace Festival   none of my business   I shoeshine

平和祭かゝはりなしと靴磨く

Numata Toshiyuki

I feel bad for the bodies not all burnt this being all the wood
  we have

焼け足らぬ死体にすまぬ薪の量

Suzuki Motoyuki

God suddenly averted His eyes at 8:15

神はっと眼をそむけたり八時十五分

Fujikawa Genshi

Haiku from Nagasaki

Not even a trickle granted   I resented the stars I resented
  the heavens

一したたりもくれぬ星をうらみ天をもうらみし

Kubota Kaoru

I look across wide and far   where is the Lord   autumn wind

見はるかす天主はいづこ秋の風

Kimura Ryokusui

Rainbow vanishing   a cross stood on the hill

虹消えて十字架の立つ丘なりき

Mori Tsuneo

Behold, God, this is the inferno   the summer sky is dark

神よ見よこれが地獄ぞ夏天暗し

The summer cloud becomes a colossal log   beats the Cathedral

夏の雲大丸太となり天主堂打つ

Minenaga Kazumitsu

Whether or not I listen   ghosts sob on the atomic field

聞かずとも聞いても原子野の鬼哭

Taniguchi Seinosuke

I lay her dead body on the roadside   night dawns early

亡き骸を路傍に据へて明けやすき

Shimomura Hiroshi

Evening cicadas cry   dry, the image of Jesus

夕蝉や乾きゐ給ふ耶蘇の像

Muto Tsuguyo

Sand flowers   on this land were many secret Christians

浜木綿やこの地に多きかくれ耶蘇

Takenaka Jakutoh

The day when tens of thousands of souls crave water A-bomb
   anniversary

万の霊水欲る日なり原爆忌

Umehara Takuroh

Water generously sprinkled   Urakami streets let people pass

おしみなく打ち水浦上人ら通す

Tsuji Masao

Picking up the ant on my palm I put it back on the bombed land

掌の蟻をつまみ被爆の地にもどす

Uesugi Ryusuke

From the dark river   clapping hands   the A-bomb
　　anniversary comes

暗い河から掌を叩き原爆忌来る

Iwata Yuka

Floating lanterns   darkly etch keloid faces

流るる万灯ケロイドの貌くまどりて

Suzuki Hakuro

Footsteps of the A-bomb anniversary   here's water to the brim

原爆忌の足音に水満たし置く

Matsumoto Kazao

Bomb anniversary comes   in predawn colors grapes ripen

爆忌来る未明の色に葡萄熱れ

Saheki Shintaro

Nagasaki anniversary   a single bird hurtles splitting the
　　blue sky

長崎忌一鳥づしんと蒼空割る

Koga Tofu

From palms joined in prayer   my parents   charred black
  keep slipping

掌に合わす黒焦げの父母こぼれやまず

Gods asunder   luminous birds descend to mass

神々砕け光りの鳥らミサに降る

Sumi Haruto

Turned into cicadas they sob they sob   children with burns

蝉となりしえしえと鳴く火傷の子等

Matsumoto Kazao

Scattered ghosts fly dragonflies in all directions over our land

飛散の霊たちがとんぼ縦横に祖国

Tahara Senki

One side of the face shuns light   August anniversary

片頬は灯をきらいつつ八月忌

Kushibe Masayuki

War don't be   green apples to children

いくさよあるな青きリンゴを子供らに

Ando Harue

From *Genbaku kusho* by Matsuo Atsuyuki

1945

(Bombed on August 9, two children died, ages four and one; found the following morning.)

Dead children by my side without trees or house   day begins
　to dawn

こときれし子をそばに、木も家もなく明けている

Nothing can be done   I place the children on the ground,
　flies swarm on them

すべなし地に置けば子にむらがる蝿

(Eldest son, too, dies; first year in middle school.)

Flaming heaven, I go to find water for my dying child

炎天、子のいまわの水をさがしにゆく

The last night of this world by mother's side   a moonlit face

この世の一夜を母のそばに、月がさしている顔

Two outside, inside the shelter too the moon starts to shine on
　a dead body

外には二つ、壕の内にも月さしてくるなきがら

(I build a pyre of wood myself and burn the three children.)

Dragonfly   I pick up wood to burn the children

とんぼう、子を焼く木をひろうてくる

Wind　　putting fire on the children, one cigarette

かぜ、子らに火をつけてたばこ一本

Flames　　big brother in the center they huddle together turning
　　into fire

ほのお、兄をなかによりそうて火になる

(The following morning, I pick up the children's bones.)

Morning mist　　bones of siblings close together as before

朝霧きようだいよりそうたなりの骨で

Ah the life of seven months　　bones like flower petals

あわれ七ケ月のいのちの、はなびらのような骨かな

Children's bones by her bedside　　sadly her breasts fill

まくらもと子を骨にしてあわれちちがはる

(The children's mother, too, dies, thirty-six years old.)

Over and over about rice rations　　this then was her will

くりかえし米の配給のことをこれが遺言か

Everything lost in my hand　　four certificates of death

なにもかもなくした手に四まいの爆死証明

(I burn my wife, August 15.)

Burning sun　　I put fire on my wife and drink water

炎天、妻に火をつけて水のむ

The imperial edict of surrender   the fire that burns my wife
  now flares

降伏のみことのり、妻をやく火いまぞ熾りつ

(Caring for the oldest daughter, from summer to winter.)

Ration book   truly just the two of us we are

配給通帳、しんじつふたりとなりました

Sun shines on pampas grass for a long time I have not laughed

萱に日の照るながいこと笑わない

The sky with leaves fallen   in bed since summer

葉をおとした空が、夏からねている

Bush clovers bloom   wearing her mother's clothes she begins
  to resemble my wife

萩さくははのもの着てつまに似てくる

Unsure faint hair of girlhood   too, motherless child

たよりなげな陰のうす毛も、母のない子

Fall insects sing   stroking the child's legs truly we are two

虫なく子の足をさすりしんじつふたり

Finally no longer needed, I hang an ice pillow to dry
  under the eaves   autumn clouds

やっといらなくなった氷嚢を軒に、秋雲

Gradually getting her used to walk, today up to the bridge   water
  spider

歩きならせてきようは橋まで、あめんぼう

Flowering buckwheat a single stalk for a grave   we have survived

蕎麦の花ポツリと建てて生きのこっている

(We move to Sasa, rationed rice bowls and other things wrapped in a scarf.)

Going away to be sheltered we are two so we take two plates

身を寄せにゆくふたりなら皿も二まい

PHOTO ESSAY

THE BOY WHO WAS A FETUS: THE DEATH OF KAJIYAMA KENJI

Domon Ken

An unusual case at the Hiroshima Atomic Bomb Hospital is drawing attention. A boy who was a five-month-old fetus at the time of the bombing died of acute medullary leukemia from secondary radioactivity, although his mother, who had only walked around near the target area, is completely normal.

Kenji (11), first son of Kajiyama Takeshi (44), a farmer in Toyoshima-Uchiura, Toyohama Village, Toyota-gun, Hiroshima Prefecture, was a sixth grader at the village school, the Toyoshima Elementary School. For six days, starting on August 7, 1945, the day after the atomic bomb was dropped, his mother Mitoyo (41) walked around such places near the target area as Aioi-bashi, Ote-machi, and Yoshijima-machi. She was searching for her aunt, who had been in labor service in 4-Chome, Kanda-dori, Ujina. Mitoyo was then five months pregnant, and Kenji was born on January 4, 1946. Kenji started to lose weight from around last November [1956], complained of pains and dullness in the limbs, and on May 23 this year was admitted to the hospital attached to the Hiroshima University Medical School. Diagnosed there as having acute medullary leukemia from the atomic bomb, he was hospitalized for treatment in the Harada Hospital in Aga, Kure City, but since he did not improve he was moved to the Hiroshima Atomic Bomb Hospital on the fifth of last month. At that time, his white blood cell count was 301 (normally 6,000 to 8,000), red blood cell count was 1,720,000 (normally 4,000,000 to 4,500,000), and hemoglobin was 36 percent (normally 95–100 percent), indicative of severe blood changes. He died at 4 a.m. on the morning of the 21st, becoming the twenty-fifth victim this year.

Mitoyo, on the other hand, has been normal except that her hair fell out at one point. Although she was examined at the same hospital, no changes in her blood were discovered. She is said to have no symptoms indicative of atomic bomb disease.

According to Dr. Kaneko, head doctor of the pediatric department of the Hiroshima Atomic Bomb Hospital, Kenji was hospitalized with a high fever of 102 to 104 degrees and complained of pain in the joints of his limbs. His liver and pancreas were swollen. He had terrible anemia in the last stage of medullary leukemia, and nothing could be done. There had been examples of leukemia in children born of mothers who were bombed, but this was the first case in which the child of a mother who did not directly experience the bombing contracted leukemia. Since no symptoms of atomic bomb disease have been found in the mother, this will create a stir in medical circles. (*Mainichi*, June 22, 1957)

Leukemia patients and patients with hard-to-heal anemia on the third-floor internal medicine ward appeared the same as ordinary internal medicine patients who had nothing to do with the atomic bomb, and they somehow did not make photo subjects. I stayed exclusively in the second-floor surgical wards and kept taking pictures of patients with keloid scars. However, I wished to photograph at least one internal medicine patient who would provide proof of the insidious, persistent character of the "nail marks of the devil."

When I expressed my wish to a second-floor patient, he told me that a twelve-year-old boy who had recently been admitted to the third floor was dying of leukemia. Thinking that a boy would make a good photograph simply because of untainted sorrow, I went up to the third floor. It was the afternoon of September 19.

In the middle of the corridor, a small boy was playing by himself. Thinking that he must be the child of a patient, I waived my hand gesturing at him to come to me. I thought I would give him a caramel. However, the child withdrew and ran into a nearby ward. Before the door closed, I caught a glimpse of the face of a boy lying in bed. The name card on the door said "Kajiyama Kenji."

As I entered sheepishly, a fortyish man, tanned and unshaven, met me with eyes that threatened to tear. Sensing that he must be the father, I offered my calling card and a gift of cakes, but I could not begin to tell him the purpose of my visit, which was more important. Perceiving his sorrow directly from his grave eyes, I could hardly say that I had come to take pictures of his dying child. He did turn out to be Kenji's father, Kajiyama Takeshi. Besides him were Kenji's mother Mitoyo, petite and healthy looking like a farmer's wife, and his uncle Mr. Kitayama, a wounded ex-soldier, in a cast from chest to abdomen. The child who had run in was Ureo, Kenji's five-year-old brother. I learned that Kenji had a big sister in the ninth grade and a little sister who was a second grader, but that they were taking care of the house.

Whatever the case, I was surprised by the arms and legs flung out of the comforter. They were literally skin and bones. Could one become as thin as this? I felt a shiver running down my spine. And the patient's eyes, opened abnormally wide, gazed at me without a twinkle. Black eyes wide open in the depths of the cheekbones on the paper-white face from which every sign of life had receded! Those eyes seemed to see completely through my "intentions." I could do nothing but utter conventional words of comfort as one who had happened to hear about Kenji's illness on visiting the Atomic Bomb Hospital from Tokyo, and listen to Mr. Kajiyama and Mr. Kitayama.

On August 6, 1945, Mr. Kajiyama had been summoned to the Hamada Unit of Izumo, Shimane Prefecture. His wife escaped the bombing because she was at home on Toyoshima Island in the Seto Inland Sea. When the unit disbanded and he returned to the island after the war, he heard what had happened to his wife: she went to look for her aunt in the bombed city of Hiroshima; she returned, however, without finding so much as a bone. After a while her hair suddenly started to fall out, and nausea and diarrhea continued. A lot of fuss was made at one point when it was suspected that those symptoms might have come from being exposed to the poison from the atomic bomb in Hiroshima, but soon she returned to normal.

Since Mr. Kajiyama did not observe any unusual signs in his wife, who was in front of his eyes, he listened to the story as no more than a story. On January 4 the following year, their first son Kenji was born, a plump baby; then a girl and a boy were born. For the past ten years, the family had lived totally oblivious of the atomic bomb.

"In the red-against-white mounted warriors' battle in the school athletic meet last September, the red team was totaled, while just one horse of the white team remained uncrushed. The warrior mounted on that horse of three boys was our Kenji. I feel as if I see the lusty face he had then," Mr. Kajiyama said, casting his face downward.

Soon after that, Kenji started to say that his knees *hashiru* (ran). In Hiroshima dialect *hashiru* means "hurt" or "feel lazy." He was examined by a doctor on the island, who said it was rheumatism. "If the doctor had then recognized it as leukemia caused by the atomic bomb, Kenji would not have been as beyond remedy as this," Mr. Kajiyama regretted. Even if the doctor had noticed it, after all it might have made little difference to his fate given that there is no special cure for leukemia. A boy of fighting spirit, Kenji continued to attend school while coaxing the pain in his knees, and became a sixth grader. In May this year he joined the overnight two-day school excursion to Iwakuni, Miyajima, and Hiroshima. The day after his return, a growth the size of a thumb developed under the left knee, and the pain did not stop. He had a penicillin shot, then surgery. However, when that growth was cured, another developed somewhere else, tormenting Kenji. While diagnosis remained uncertain, a fever of over 102 degrees persisted, and Kenji became visibly emaciated. A growth developed under the left side of his chin, too. Takeshi, his father, went from hospital to hospital, carrying him on his back. Finally it was diagnosed as the atomic bomb disease at the hospital attached to Hiroshima University, and on September 5 he was sent to the Atomic Bomb Hospital.

"Big brother's legs are thinner than mine. More *komai, komai* than my legs." Ureo stroked Kenji's legs sticking out of the comforter. *Komai*, I guessed, was Hiroshima dialect for "thin." The mother gently put the quilt over them. "He says 'my legs hurt, my legs hurt,' so I stroke them all night. When I am stroking his legs, he starts saying his back hurts. When I stroke his back, he says his

Cranes with get-well messages hung from the ceiling of Kenji's hospital room.

Kenji, cheer up Takahashi Tsugio
Kenji, get better soon Takano Eikichi
Get better soon

Kitayama Sadako
Undefeated by illness

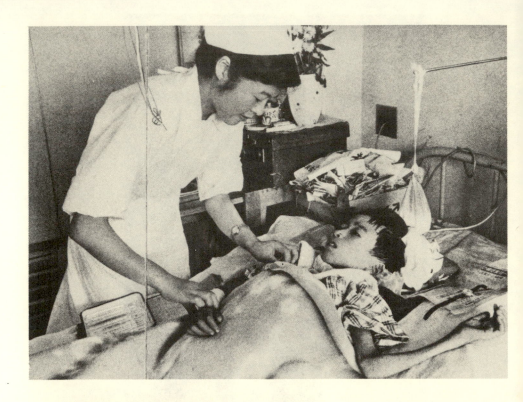

A nurse takes Kenji's pulse. It was a rare moment when the boy's eyes turned away from the photographer.

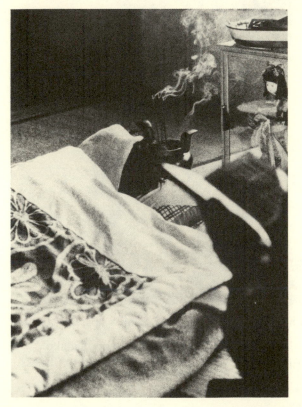

Kenji's body in the hospital room for the dead.

Kenji's father before his grave. The marker reads "Shaku Jikai" (posthumous Buddhist name) in front and, on the side, "Died September 21, 1957, Kenji, Kajiyama Takeshi's oldest son, age 12."

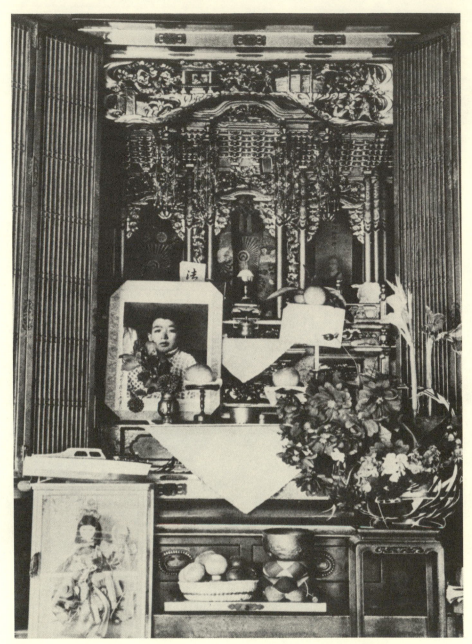

The miniature shrine at the Kajiyama home with a picture of Kenji.

stomach hurts. In the end bones all over his body and also his intestines start to hurt, and he's in such pain. I wish I could take his place," the mother said. "When the fever runs over 104, his limbs are so hot I can hardly touch them."

Since moving to the Atomic Bomb Hospital, Kenji had no appetite at all. Although his mother prepared this and that favorite food he used to like, it was of no avail. Even his brother Ureo delayed his meal, saying, "If you eat, I'll eat, too," but this also failed. At night when Kenji started to suffer, Ureo encouraged him by singing the theme song from "Akado Suzunosuke," a popular radio drama for children about a samurai boy: "Keep it up, you're strong, Akado Suzunosuke, our comrade." "Keep it up, keep it up, don't bow to the illness" seemed to be the password in this ward. Even while we talked, many times I heard the father and the uncle utter these words into the ear of the patient to cheer him up. The boy was also desperately trying. He had a single-minded desire to get better. When the medicine happened to run out and only antifebrile was left, his mother gave him a dose of just that. "Mom, one medicine's missing," he said, I heard.

A thousand cranes and *tanzaku* poetry cards from his classmates and teachers at Toyoshima Elementary School hung from all over the ceiling of the sickroom. Since there was not enough space to hang them all, there was a stack by the boy's pillow. They directly narrated the depth of the islanders' feelings. Following with my eyes each poetry card, some written in a childlike clumsy hand, some written in a teacherlike fluent hand, when I came upon one that said "We are all waiting for you to come back in good health," I shed tears despite myself. How many people were watching him, praying for his recovery—and yet I knew there would be no day when he would leave this room looking healthy.

Mr. Kajiyama showed me a 5 x 7 cabinet-size photo. In this memorial photograph his mother, father, and Ureo sat around his pillow. The press had come and taken this picture two days earlier, I was told. The press had come and taken a photograph! Encouraged by this, I said that I too wished to take a commemorative photograph with family members surrounding Kenji. Obviously I lied. I had not come because I wanted to take a commemorative photograph. However, in the hour since I had entered the room, the sick boy's eyes never left me. Those eyes, harboring the absolute destiny of death, poured over my eyes with lucid, clean sternness. My Leica M3 was on my lap, and sometimes in my hand, but I could not turn its lens toward the sick boy. Face to face with those eyes, my camera work, whose principle was "absolute snapshots with absolutely no dramatization," was felt as no more than fraud, deception, and profanation. The formalized framework of a "memorial photograph" seemed the only way to beg forgiveness from those eyes. "Sensei, take a picture of me . . . ," the boy said suddenly then. I will never in my life be able to forget that slender, clean voice. It was the voice of one who was soon to die. The voice made me all the more nervous. Nor did I understand why he called me *sensei*. Since it was summer, I wore a whitish jacket, and so he might have thought I was one of the medical staff in the Atomic Bomb Hospital.

"Please take a picture of him," Mr. Kajiyama also said. I asked the family to get together near the boy's pillow and pressed the shutter two or three times. I also took pictures of the thousand cranes and poetry cards hanging from the ceiling.

Perhaps because my photography helped divert his mood, the boy said, "I want bread, I want bread." His mother ran to the store on the first floor. By the time she returned with bread, however, Kenji no longer tried to eat. Even so, because he had an appetite for the first time since he was hospitalized, the parents were happy, talking about it as if it had been because of my visit.

Around four o'clock, when a nurse came to take his temperature and pulse, she spoke to the boy. At that very instant, I pressed the shutter once. It was the moment when those eyes turned toward the nurse.

The following morning I heard a rumor that a telegram had been sent to collect relatives. I held back from going up to the third floor. I had almost completely given up taking pictures.

That night I was putting my photography notes in order. I think it was past one o'clock when I went to bed. It was a chilly night, rare for early fall. I fell asleep. Suddenly I clearly heard the sharp cry of a crow. I woke alarmed. Another cry—I heard it clearly again outside the window.

"Kenji has died," I thought. I looked at my watch. It was 4:10. I thought of getting up right away, but somehow I fell asleep again. When I sprung up surprised, it was already six o'clock. Morning mist floated amidst the trees of the Peace Park, and another fresh morning had come. I thought Kenji, however, was no longer in this world. Washing my face with great haste, I ran out of the hotel.

When I arrived at the hospital it was exactly seven. I rushed toward the room for the remains. I knew that at the hospital a patient who breathed his last was immediately moved to that room at the north edge of the Japan Red Cross Hospital. It was adjacent to the autopsy room. I also knew that the corpse of a *hibakusha*, one exposed to the atomic bomb, was autopsied within several hours after death. Before, the corpse of every *hibakusha* was carried to the Atomic Bomb Casualty Commission at Hijiyama for autopsy by the American side at American initiative. Around the time the Atomic Bomb Hospital was established, it was decided that corpses that were with the Japanese side would be examined by the Japanese side at Japanese initiative. However, even then the autopsy results and a set of dissected organs seemed to be sent to the ABCC after all. Of course this is my conjecture. If I asked a person involved, he would no doubt deny this. However, in Hiroshima I met no *hibakusha* who contradicted my conjecture. . . .

Kenji was lying on a futon on the floor in the resting room, his face covered with white gauze. By his pillow was an elaborate toy motor boat with batteries. Kenji loved boats more than anything else. Incense smoke was floating. There were his mother with eyes swollen from crying, his big sister whom I saw for the first time, and his father with an even more painfully subdued expression than before.

After nine o'clock, the medical staff shuffled in and started to get ready for the autopsy. Miss Kubo, the head nurse, also came and handed the mother an envelop of *koden*, an obituary gift, from the hospital. Seeing me, Miss Kubo looked surprised. She seemed to find it puzzling that I was sitting there, knowing of Kenji's death so soon. "A crow cried," I said. Miss Kubo did not seem to understand.

The autopsy ended in a little over an hour. The metallic sound of the electric saw that was carried from the autopsy room to the waiting room was cruel. It made me vividly imagine the saw's teeth relentlessly severing the spinal cord. Fortunately, however, neither Kenji's father nor his mother seemed to have any idea of what that sound meant. Kenji's body came back again in the original shape. By then the resting room was full of people. They were people who had rushed from Toyoshima by boat. The head priest of Hongakuji, the Kajiyama family's temple in Toyoshima, was there, too. Kenji had studied with him. Soon the Buddhist scripture was read by the priest, then his sermon started. Rather than a sermon, it was a reminiscence on Kenji's cleverness and bravery. "At this point, it would be impossible for you to give up, even if I tell you to give up. I encourage you to cry as much as you like. Crying as much as you like may be the best offering for Kenji," he said, while crying himself. Turning his back to the people, Kenji's father cried aloud, man as he was. Those present all cried. Thinking of photographing that situation, I held my camera over their heads, but tears instantly filled my eyes, and I could no longer see the finder or anything else. . . .

Past mid October, an unexpected letter arrived at my house in Tokyo from Kajiyama Takeshi.

> It is now very cool in the morning and evening. I don't know how to thank you for taking pictures in my child's lifetime. He loved photos. Since September 21, that memorable day, when the horrible atomic bomb from twelve years ago ruthlessly took away the life of dear Ken, there has been no joy, and I just sit blank in front of the miniature shrine. I call his name, but the photograph has no voice. As you know, his mind was lucid until a moment before death, and he was talking about when the *sensei* who had photographed him would send the pictures. When Ken said "Sensei, take my picture," I never dreamed that he would be blown by the merciless wind so soon. From parental greed, we were longing for the day that he would look

as healthy as before, but the horrible radiation ate into the marrow of our dear Ken's bones, ate into his stomach, instantly driving him to hell's torment. He passed into the other world complaining of pain. How cruel the torment was for one year. Please understand how badly we wished to help him.

We could not talk in leisure with you whom we met for the first time, since we were occupied in tending the patient. We moved from hospital to hospital, spent a large amount of money, and in the end I am so sad that we were parted by death from our dear child. I am so sad. How cruel the atomic bomb is to an innocent child, Sensei. Receiving letters of compassion from strangers everywhere, we only bow our heads in thanks. I don't know how to thank you for the big offering as well as the illustrated children's books and candy for Ureo. I should have asked your address, but I didn't think of it because I was carried away taking care of Ken. When things gradually calmed down after Ken's death, I regretted that we didn't know your address, so I asked a newspaper reporter and got it. Ken would have liked to see the photos you took. I cry each time I remember the words he said, emaciated and in pain: Sensei, take a picture of me.

Together with Ken's big sister Kayoko, little sister Marie, and little brother Ureo, we sit in front of the miniature shrine whenever we have the leisure and pray to the gods and the Buddha for peace and for the elimination of atomic and hydrogen bombs.

When he fought as a mounted warrior in the school athletic meet, I am sure none thought Ken would become a buddha after one year. I myself never dreamed of it. Kayoko, having lost her little brother, and Marie and Ureo their big brother, look lonely in front of the miniature shrine. Ureo sings the song of Akado Suzunosuke which his big brother liked, and the sisters sing "Come, come, turtle, turtle dear," a nursery rhyme Ken used to sing when in pain. This is a cause of tears.

Sensei, why did we have to make an innocent child a victim of the atomic bomb? I would like you who live in Tokyo to ask the government people to prohibit tragic bombs. Ken-bo had hope for life until a second before death. At three o'clock in the morning of the 21st, when we had him take just one wrapper of powdered medicine instead of two as usual, he asked for another wrapper and took it.

Then five minutes before four, his petals scattered at age twelve, September 21 being the last day.

I feel I still see him return from school and say "I'm home!" I see the school things he used to use and recall how he played in good health. Image after image appears in my eyes as I spend sad days. He had pictures taken by the gentle *sensei* three days before his death. Now I think he is looking at the beautiful photographs in the flower bed in the other world, and playing with his favorite boat in the pond. He doesn't have pain as in this life. I look at his photo and say: Ken, when you're sad, come home to your parents.

If you come to Hiroshima, make sure to visit Kajiyama Kenji's home in Uchiura, Toyohamamura, Toyota-gun. May we have a picture of Ken-bo taken right before death, so we can keep it near the miniature shrine? And, Sensei, let me ask you to work in the movement in Tokyo toward prohibition of atomic bombs.

Ken, who so patiently fought his illness, was also wishing for the prohibition of atomic bombs and praying for peace as he departed, saying, bye Dad, Mom, sisters, and brother.

So that there will be no cruel atomic and hydrogen bombs again, please work in Tokyo and get rid of this tragedy. Let me beg you.

Perhaps I should call it lingering attachment. On reading Mr. Kajiyama's letter, I felt like going back to Hiroshima. I wanted to take a straightforward picture at least of Kenji's tomb.

Toyoshima, a three-hour boat trip from Ujina Port, is a small southern island covered by tangerine orchards, with a circumference of seven miles and a population of seven thousand in a few thousand households. The Kajiyamas' house was halfway up the hill where a narrow winding stone pavement led me. It was a fine two-story house with a slate roof, which stood out in the area. Cultivating a tangerine orchard of two acres and owning a modern engine-operated boat, the old family was among the most prosperous on the island. For Kenji, who was the heir of the Kajiyama family, a small but happy life as a diligent fruit grower on a peaceful island should have been promised. . . .

Kenji's tomb was on the hill, which had a wide view of the Seto Inland Sea. On the front of the brand new gravemarker of Japanese cypress, his posthumous name was written: "Shaku Jikai" (Buddhist Merciful Sea). On the left side, it read "Died September 21, 1957, Kajiyama Kenji, Takeshi's first son, twelve years old," and on the right, "Tragic child of the atomic bomb." In front of the grave marker, a small, not yet ripe tangerine had been placed. I heard that some of Kenji's classmates visited this grave together from time to time. In the strong sun, the white "death flowers" made the eyes smart. While Mr. Kajiyama was lighting incense sticks, I quickly pressed the shutter three times. I had nothing left to say now. Whether good or bad, this finished my photography concerning Kajiyama Kenji. I asked the head priest of the Hongakuji Temple to recite a sutra. Hands joined, I prayed from my heart for the repose of Kenji's soul. The sutra chanting permeated into the grave marker, spread across the blue sky, and flowed to the surface of the distant sea.

CITIZENS' MEMOIRS

MY HUSBAND DOES NOT RETURN

Tada Makiko

Since my husband worked at the Electric Railroad Company (Dentetsu) during the war, thanks to the effort of the section head we lived in a Dentetsu house beneath the gasoline tank in 4 Chome, Minami-machi. The Ministry of Communications storehouse was there, and around August 1945 they offered work winding wire on drums. They paid thirty yen a day to men and fifteen to women. Because the pay was good, my husband went there to wind wire on days off at the company; I, too, went to wind whenever I had time.

On August 6, he went to wind drums, while I stayed home because I had been told that I was on duty for ration distribution. But they later told me that after all I was not on duty, so I rushed to the warehouse after eight o'clock. Though the air raid alarm had been cancelled, I heard an airplane, and I was looking up in that direction as I walked. The moment there was the flash, it felt as if thickly mixed paint was thrown at me, and I thought that heaven had fallen. At that instant, I was burnt from face to shoulder to navel. Our oldest son Mutsuzumi, behind me on a tricycle, did not seem to be burnt as badly. Because it grew pitch dark around us, I crawled under the eaves of a house and, on all fours, put my son under my stomach, stopping his ears with my elbows and my ears with my hands. I'm hot, I'm hot, my son cried. When I came to, it was whitish around us, with a violent wind flying. My backbone and pelvis hurt so much that it felt as if I had been smashed by a rock. My husband ran from the drums saying, "Take your clothes off quickly, they're burning."

Not only my clothes but my body was burning pale, and all that was left of my jacket was a hanging piece of the left sleeve, and it fell from my shoulder like a rag. Although I wore khaki army pants, my legs were burnt, like my arms, except under my underwear. Mutsuzumi, too, turned yellow from chest to shoulders, and tattered skin was hanging. My husband had been in the shade of a drum so he had neither burns nor injury.

Returning to the air raid shelter in front of our house, I held my child, my upper body still naked. I called and called, but my husband didn't come, so I went into the house though I felt scared. The tap water was dripping slowly, so I washed my face there, but I just couldn't get rid of something sticky, and when I touched and pulled it with my hand, the thin skin-like thing stuck and wouldn't come off. I had to get money and clothes, but it didn't seem possible because the house had been flattened. My husband said we would be in trouble if we didn't get our money out, even a little. I said, forget the money, let's go to the doctor's, what good will it do if our child and I lose our lives? My husband pulled out a piece of clothing, but since I couldn't wear it, I put it over my shoulders and went to look for a doctor. Minami School was no good, the Monopoly Bureau's hospital was also no good, and as I was walking, naked people with peeled skin came toward me asking for help. We walked toward the prefectural hospital, my husband almost carrying me. Since I was burning hot, many times I picked up rags or cotton at a fallen house, wet them in a rainwater tank and put them against my chest. My husband scolded me, saying that I shouldn't do that kind of thing because germs would get in, but I couldn't walk otherwise. When we reached the hospital, it was packed, and they wouldn't treat us. After three long hours they put mercurochrome on our child but told me that adults should have patience. My chest was burning, my stomach ached like when I was in labor, and my eyes became hazy. But my husband said he had to go home and see if it was still there, so he left me and my child. I spread the coarse straw mat I borrowed from a guard and lay down with my child, but I was crazy with stomach pains. Then, after bleeding badly, two bloody lumps passed and I fell, my eyes reeling. When I came to after a while, I pulled a root of the brushwood and poked the lumps with it, and it was as if I were poking a liver. I began to feel a little better while lying down, but, according to my child, I became weird around then, and whenever I saw people I tried to strip their clothes. I remember asking a soldier to help me up. He didn't, because, he said, I wasn't the only injured person. I felt sorry for my injured child and put him on my back as I crawled on the road. When we got back to the streetcar road our neighborhood was a sea of fire, and though I called my husband, I remember that I had no voice because of stomach pains and lack of strength. I also remember that I wandered about trying to find where Team 23 of 2 Chome, Minami-cho, was sheltered. At last I met my husband late at night and went to sleep in the air raid shelter in the embankment. Probably I felt relieved; my eyes couldn't see, and I have no memory of what followed after that for a while.

According to what people say, I went quite crazy, and because I sang songs every day and made rub-a-dub rub-a-dub noises, people hated me so much I couldn't stay with neighbors. I lay alone on the one-tatami-mat-size patch of grass that remained under the torn roof of the Gas Company and just made noises, my body burnt all over, unable to tend the heavy bleeding by myself. When a shed was built where our old house had been, neighbors carried me home on a shutter, I am told, but I have no memory whatsoever. When I suddenly came to, though everybody was saying it was hot, I was cold and short of breath, and I started to walk, looking for a place where I could sleep restfully; but, because I had no sense of direction, I could not go back to my bed and wandered around dripping blood until midnight. After my mind became much calmer in the late fall, when I was unsewing some clothes that had been left unburnt so I could use them, I felt poor again, and just as I started to move my needle I lost consciousness, eyes failing. After that it became a habit, and even now, when I do any chore that makes my shoulder tense, like laundry or sewing, I always grow faint and lose my senses.

That fall, Mutsuzumi and I would eat all the rice my husband cooked to fill the eighteen-cup pot for breakfast and lunch. He would cook rice again in the evening, and we would wake in the middle of the night and finish it up before morning. In the morning, I remember, I would feel so hungry that I could not wait till he cooked rice. Sometimes I toasted the rationed soy beans and ate two to three cups all at once. I ate and ate like this, but still I was hungry and ate again, and maybe that's why I was able to survive.

At that time doctors were hard to find, so I went to the doctor in front of Kanda Shrine and asked to be examined, but he flatly refused.

"At least take a look at this child. Please put mercurochrome on him, leftovers from what you've used for others is fine. It'll comfort him," I begged from the bottom of my heart, but the doctor declined even that.

I still didn't feel like leaving, so I stayed there hoping he might do something after all the patients were gone. As I watched, I found that other people were handing him rice and clothes besides money. When I saw that, I resented the war so much I didn't know what to do. On our way home, some children playing at the roadside ran home crying at the sight of me and looked at me through the window, terrified. I myself felt how dreadful I looked then, and I resented the war all the more. I thought that we should make this the very last war, construct a peaceful era, and save children from going through such sorrow.

The bleeding stopped at the end of November or so, but I felt poor, and when I went to a doctor around February of the following year, I was told that there were traces of a miscarriage, and I was treated. I became pregnant soon after that. During my pregnancy a painful lump the size of a pickled plum grew by the side of my breast. So I did things like swallowing a killfish or getting a massage to scatter it. Masumi was born on November 11, 1946. I tried heating my breast, thinking of somehow nursing her, but the more I massaged, the more painful it got, and no milk came.

My husband and the midwife only scolded me, saying, "How you fuss," and they didn't take me seriously. It hurt so much that I ran around desperately. The breasts swelled until they almost buried my chin. At last, on the twentieth day after the baby was born, they burst, and a white lump of milk the size of a summer orange [comparable to a grapefruit] gushed out, and after all I had an operation. According to the doctor, when my chest was burnt by the atomic bomb, most of my mammary glands became plugged so that even though milk was produced when the child was born, it had no exit, and that gave me a hard time.

With all this, my husband was too busy caring for me to go to work at the Electric Railroad, so he quit his job and started a green grocery around the spring of 1947.

In those days things were still scarce, there was no wine to drink, few women were beautiful, and maybe because of that my husband called me Makiko, Makiko, and cared for me, a woman with spots in both eyes, worse keloid scars than others, skin stuck right on the raw flesh around the shoulders, and only a little bit of the original skin color left on the abdomen. I miscarried in May 1948 and became pregnant again soon after that. Around that time, my husband started to leave someone in charge of the store and walk around drinking, rarely coming home. He sold the store by the end of 1948 and started to work under the city's unemployment relief measures in the spring of 1949. By the time Kosumi was born in May of that year he had more or less stopped coming home. When a sports fair was held in Hiroshima in 1951, my husband was sent there by the unemployment bureau. Then he got a job with a traveling circus, left, and nobody knows where he is now.

After my husband stopped giving me money, I raised my children by buying tatters or picking up trash, but because the moment something worried me my head became foggy and I lost my senses or bled, I couldn't make a living. In the fall of 1952 I asked the welfare committee for help and started to receive "livelihood protection for the poor," but since there was no way I could manage on that, I've been going to work for the city's unemployment bureau.

Even though I go out to work for the unemployment bureau and get livelihood protection for the poor, I have nothing but problems. First it's the house. The Gas Company was already sending people to tell us to leave in the spring of 1947 when my husband was still here. After he left, two letters came. This is the second one:

November 15, 1952

Hayashi Rihei, Director
Hiroshima Gas Company
1 Motoi-cho, Hiroshima City

To: Mrs. Makiko Tada
2–156 Minami-cho
Hiroshima City

A Letter Urging You to Vacate Your Land

Since your house was built without permission on the land indicated below owned by our company, and a portion of the land is being cultivated, on May 31 we notified you to remove every item on the land and clear out by the last day of October 1952. Today, past the deadline, things still stand as they were. Due to inconvenience in the operation of the factory, we urge you to kindly respond in writing by October 25.

Note
Clarification of immovable property
1. Location: 2–56 Minami-cho, Hiroshima City
2. Area: 23.9 square meters.

The company sent men, two each time, to threaten us: "The company has a lawyer, but you have no one to stand by you. If this goes to court, you'll go to jail, so get out at any cost. If you don't get out soon, we'll have you jailed."

I don't know on what terms the Gas Company bought this lot from the Electric Railroad Company, but when we first came here, someone from the Electric Railroad acted as go between, we signed a contract and paid the guarantee, and we never missed paying the rent until the atomic bomb. We can't put up a shed and live here just because the paper's lost? If they say we can't put up a shed here, where can we go? We can't do anything even if we're sent to jail. We can't leave.

I say we can't leave, but this house leaks when it rains, and dew forms on our quilts on winter nights, so we must fix the roof, but we haven't been able to fix it because we have no money.

Around May last year, the wife of the new owner of the public bathhouse in front of the Telegraph Bureau said to me, "We want you to stop coming for a while." Because I thought, too hastily, that she said so because my children are mischievous, I scolded them plenty, and they became quiet, so I took them to the bathhouse again. But the wife at the bathhouse said,

"If you get in the bath, even customers who are thinking of taking time to wash their hair [for an extra fee] quickly leave, saying it's unpleasant, it's ugly, so I want you to refrain from coming to our bath."

That time, if at no other, heartfelt tears really came out, and it touched my nerves for a while so I couldn't sleep nights. Had my body become that ugly? When I realized it, I never even once went back to that bathhouse. But I think the wife of the bathhouse is the only one who used such awful words. Our neighbors, Dr. and Mrs. Yoshimoto Kitao, have kindly let us use their bath and even invited us to their living room and treated us to nice things to eat, so I'm still living here thankfully, not wanting to go away from this kind neighborhood.

We who work under the city's unemployment relief bureau are all distressed people, so we want them to treat us kindly, but the saddest thing is that some of the supervisors resort to violence. I had a job around October last year with the sewage works in Kannon-cho. Since my pay was 200 yen instead of the expected 210 yen, I asked Assistant Supervisor Nakamura, "How come mine alone is low?" He said, "Because we have to pay 220 yen to rock carriers, we are lowering everyone else's pay by turns."

About a week later, when Assistant Supervisor Nakamura saw me at the work site, he said, suddenly twisting me down, "You wrote a letter of complaint, didn't you? Confess," and he beat me. I had no recollection of writing a letter. Everyone had heard the rumor that Nakamura was unfair. Since he was six feet tall and well built, with a judo certificate, my body really felt it when I was twisted down. I had bad bleeding at the work site, lost consciousness when I came home, and faintly came to when my child fetched a doctor. A lump grew in the chest and a pain in the lower back, so I visited Mishimura Obstetrics, Yano Internal Medicine, and Hirano External Medicine, and they all said I should take absolute rest for two or three weeks. But, after resting two or three days, I went to work, almost crawling, because I needed money. Because of this I am still unwell.

Now I am such an ugly woman, abandoned by my husband, chased out of my house, hard up in spite of the welfare for the poor and needy, and stepped upon by people, but I was born in Hatata-gun, Kochi, to a well-to-do samurai family. My older brother, who had received a certificate of merit from the emperor, was respected in the village. My uncle was once the head of the Kochi Police Department. Since I was born in 1906, I am 48. In my youth, when a beauty contest was held at the Matsuya Department Store in Tokyo, I was among the ten finalists chosen and received a ruby ring. After starting to live here, I had never known any difficulty in livelihood until I met the atomic bomb. I feel I would embarrass my ancestors if I went home in this shape, so I can't go home. Some tell me it is better to get a formal divorce from my husband and divide the children, but I have brought them up till today because I never felt like parting with them. Yet lately, given my poor physical condition, I don't think I can safely raise the three children. Something has to be sacrificed, and I have started to think that it can't be helped.

Mutsuzumi is a fifth grader and goes to school so it's all right to leave him, but Masumi and Kosumi are still small. While it was warm, I took them to the factory and had them play while I worked, but since it got cold it's been tough, as they now catch cold and cry, and so in the morning I try to slip out quietly while they are still asleep. When they catch me, they say, "Mom, ple-e-ase take us with you, we beg of you, we pray to you," each joining her hands as if in prayer. Where they picked that up I don't know. So I try to make my heart the devil's heart and shake them off, but I can't, and I end up running to the work site with them, with the smaller one on my back.

Just the other day, I went to work with the child on my back, and when I came back after a day's work, bad bleeding started again, and my body wouldn't move though I tried to make supper. I thought of cutting work the following day, but the unemployment relief job has off days often to begin with, and if I stay home now because a child has a cold and now because I am not well, I can't feed us four. So I went to work while still bleeding. On such an occasion, I've thought it better to kill the children and die myself, and I hated my husband who had abandoned us so much that I thought, "let him appear, I'll cut him up into pieces."

And I resented even more the war that turned me into this shape that my husband hated. Besides, the ABCC on Mount Hiji comes by car to pick us up, strip our clothes so they can examine us as much as they like, and draw our blood, yet they don't even give us a day's pay or nutrition in return for the drawn blood. All they give us are two cookies for the children. I'll never ever go again, I thought, and I chased them away when they came to pick us up the next time. Though I had carefully told my children not to go, they came directly to school by car and took Mutsuzumi back and examined him. I got mad and scolded him, "Don't go." If we become mere objects of examination, it's a waste of our blood. I wish they tried a little to take care of our health. And I wish they did their research for the sake of peace that will never be disturbed by war again.

NO PLACE TO GO

Tsujimoto Tora

I turned sixty-four this year. I married into the Tsujimoto family at twenty and worked on the farm. When my husband died they had me marry his younger brother, so my present husband is two years younger than I am. After we married, we went to the States to make money, and I worked as a chambermaid at a hotel in Seattle. When we had saved some money, we put out a stall in a market, sold vegetables for about ten years, and with the little money we had made we went back to Hiroshima when I was thirty-seven and opened a grocery store near Tsurumi Bridge. Since we had no children, we adopted an older brother's daughter. We ran the store in the same place for seventeen years. We acquired a fair amount of property. We owned a large house that measured over 130 square meters. We put our daughter through the City Girls' School, had her learn traditional dance and shamisen, and when she was nineteen, we took in a husband for her.* Since he was a maker of airplane parts, we had him build a factory on the adjacent lot and subcontract jobs from Mitsubishi and so forth, which brought him a fairly good income. In August of the year when I was fifty-seven, my husband was fifty-five, our daughter twenty-one, and her husband twenty-eight, *pika*, the flash, came.

---

*In order to continue the family line they arranged a marriage with a man who adopted the family name and lived with the family.

On August 5, I was drafted for a half day labor service, for which I was to receive three and a half yen, to build evacuation quarters near Tsurumi Bridge. I was putting things in rucksacks on the 6th, thinking of sending our luggage to Saijo, when the team leader came and said, "Today you must go to work. It's too selfish of you to go when there is pay and not when there is no pay." I had no choice but to go, so I went, and when I had climbed on top of the roof of a dentist's two-story house in the rear part of Showa-machi and just lifted about seven slates, it flashed and I fell off. An old man from somewhere I don't know pulled me out. I didn't realize that my face was burned when it flashed. I wasn't aware of the burn on my throat, either. Since my left hand was in flames together with the kimono, someone there tore off part of the cloth. My right arm was also flaming at the root, but I didn't realize it until he tore off the sleeve. Both my legs also burnt, but they didn't flame up. Because we were told to wear black things in those days, my padded hat and jacket and work slacks were all black. So when I came to, nothing was left.* I wore a white *tenugui* towel under my hat, so it seems there were no burns in the area under the towel, but the towel was gone, and so were my white work gloves and white tabi socks. All that was on me was a linen underskirt. Anyway, I just felt sick; I wasn't in pain or anything. My husband was hit while he was repairing his bike so he could pick up the ration of wooden clogs for the neighborhood team. He still had his clothes on, but there was a diagonal slash across his head. Our son-in-law had cuts in the corner of his eyes and nothing remained on him but his loincloth. Our daughter's forehead was cut diagonally, and both her face and dress were bloody.

We thought of going to Takeya Elementary School, but we couldn't because it was burning. There was fire in the direction of Takanohashi, too. So we headed for Mount Hiji. When we entered the Clothing Depot, they said those who could move on foot would be tended to last, so we went to the Artillery Depot, where they said "no country people," because they had insiders to tend to. So we headed for Japan Steel. Midway there, a truck came, and all of us

---

*Black clothing offered little protection against the flash, absorbing the heat, while white resisted it and protected the skin underneath.

got on it and were taken to the Japan Steel Foundry. After we were treated with grease we went out to Kaita, and when we were resting at a big inn in front of the station we were served rice balls, but I didn't feel like eating. I faintly heard a voice say you shouldn't drink water when I said "water, water." I only vaguely remember being taken into the train. On getting off at Happon-matsu, I hear people looked at me as if I were in a show, but I don't remember it. When I had an injection at the doctor's place in front of the station, I woke with pain as he shot it into my bone.

Our son-in-law seems to have notified his family, for they came with a rear cart to get me. I remember getting in it. Because the pebbly road was hard for me, my face lost color, so they carried me into the doctor's about 4 kilometers from Happon-matsu. The doctor said, I hear, "This old woman won't last two days," but I wasn't conscious then. I was put in the six-mat room of the doctor's flat, and, understanding it was going to be all over, they called someone who could pray to the Buddha and had him pray at midnight. Then I came to around two in the morning. I tried to stand but my legs wouldn't work. They said that the flesh came off when my feet were touched, so I couldn't move. They lifted a tatami in the room and had me pass my water there, but I don't even remember that. After that, for twenty-eight days I was in ceaseless pain.

After I got a little better I had four to five shots a day, and it was quite expensive. The doctor was very kind, and he gave me a couple of eggs every five days, and also some meat. So I started to be able to move little by little, and after about sixty days I was released. Now, however, our daughter had anemia due to the atomic bomb and grew ill with pleurisy so that she was taken to the National Saijo Sanatorium. I attended her during her nine-month sanatorium stay.

At her husband's house, the oldest son died instantly in the Second Unit on the day of the atomic bomb, the third son died in action as a pilot, and there was no heir left; so our daughter had no choice but to go home with her husband and tend their farm. My husband and I borrowed about 23 square meters of a relative's lot where their villa had burnt down, bought a 3,500 yen prefab set, built a house, made a roof with burnt slates we picked up, and started to live there in the winter of 1947. Our daughter gave birth to a baby girl in 1948 and another in 1950, but around December 20 she visited the doctor, feeling somehow unwell. The doctor said that her chest was poor but, worse, the atomic bomb disease was surfacing. I went to look after her, but she died on January 9. Our son-in-law, also showing signs of atomic bomb disease, has no strength and is inactive, but he is only thirty-four and we cannot leave him single forever. We feel we have to return his entry in the family registry to that of his original family* and have him, as heir, take a wife, but he will not hear of it. Now my face is so ugly that nobody employs me, and my husband falls ill every year. Our savings are all gone, and we can no longer live on my paper bag making and piecework sewing. Perhaps our neighbors found it hard to see us live like that; around February of 1952, the neighborhood team leader came and kindly suggested: "Accept the city's welfare since your husband can't work due to the atomic bomb disease and neuralgia, and you can't work either. I'll be the witness."

So I went to the appropriate section at City Hall and asked: "I am very sorry but could we have some help because we are always ill?"

"Bring your seal," they said, so, thinking that they could help us, I returned immediately with our seal.

"What are you talking about when you have a rich relative, Arita. Consult your relatives about everything. We handle only people who are really alone," they shouted in a loud voice. I came home trembling. The Aritas were the family of my younger sister, whose lot we borrowed to build this house. They built a big house on a busy street and are doing a good business. I visited them to tell what had happened at the City Hall. "What will the city do? You're naive; it's a mistake to go there," my sister's husband laughed. He said, "We are a family of many members, so we can't do as expected," and said not a word about helping us. Not only that; even though we brought him a bottle of sake each year for the rental of the 23 square meters, he urged us to leave: "Leave soon, because we have to find a wife for our son."

Nothing could be done, so I consulted our two nephews. "Aunt,

---

*An individual's birth is certified in the family registry under the head of the family. When the son-in-law married into the Tsujimoto family, his registration was placed under the head of this family.

forget about City Hall; we'll help you, if just a little,'' they said, and they have paid up to 5,000 yen of the 10,000 debt for the medical fees from 1951. These nephews are children of my husband's older brother. My brother-in-law died instantly in the Tenma-cho house at the time of the bombing. My sister-in-law, his wife, badly burnt, ran to her home in Furue and died on August 25. So my nephews lost both parents and house. The older one became a farmer in the suburbs, inheriting the business of the old main family, and the younger one commutes to the railroad wireless telegraph office from the shack he built next door to his older brother's place. This younger brother was still a student then, and he just happened to come back for the summer vacation. Standing in the doorway of the house, he had burns all over his back. His right arm was bent with parts of the flesh stuck together, and he could not move it. After having two incisions, he was finally able to move it, but it has not yet recovered to normal. My face and throat are also still badly scarred, though not badly enough to require an operation. The only thing is that I need to do something about the scar under my lip, for when I eat *ochazuke*, rice to which hot tea is added, it spills outside. This is hard for an old woman.

Arita, my younger sister's husband, is prosperous and has more property than before the war. He is a big shot in the city. So he seems to feel uncomfortable about an embarrassing thing like our hut in his villa lot and urges us to leave each time he sees us. He gathers rare garden trees and rocks and arranges them around our hut. In the storage room he piles up tea things. He seems to want to build a villa as soon as possible. We can't possibly move while it's cold, but— how can we stay in a place where we are urged to leave every day?— we are thinking of carrying the hut somewhere when it becomes warm. I say ''carry,'' but Arita can't be expected to help. We can't hire someone either, so we are talking about carrying it piece by piece ourselves with our nephews' help.

Our daughter's husband is a good person, but since his health is not as expected, I think it's cruel to depend upon him. Our grandchildren always say ''We want to go to Grandma's,'' but I regret there is nothing I can do for them.

I have worked and worked since youth, cared for others as much as possible, raised a child, arranged for a husband for her, was respected by both of them, and I am not aware of ever having done anything wrong; yet I was hit by the flash, and when I think I must depend upon others in old age, this is the hardest for me. When, without a place to go, we're urged to leave again and again, I wonder why I was not able to die then. If the old man from somewhere hadn't pulled me out, I would have been able to die without knowing anything—I sometimes feel like complaining.

However, greed is greed: it's not easy to die by my own hand.

THE MEMORY OF NUTRIAS

Ishii Ichiro

Masayuki, my first son, was born on January 3, 1928. When he graduated from a commercial school in Shio-machi, Futami-gun, in March 1934, people warmly encouraged him to become a teacher, but he didn't because he was by nature shy about standing in front of people. Instead he stayed home to work on the farm. However, to evade the draft, in early July 1945 I had him enter the Police Training Center in Kako-machi, Hiroshima City. I understood that he would graduate in two weeks, but he couldn't come home even after graduation, and he had to encounter August 6 in Hiroshima.

Mr. Harada of Kiya, Tazusa-mura, Konu-gun, was Masayuki's friend from commercial school days who also entered the Police Training Center and fled with him at the time of the bombing. He managed to come back to Kiya on the 7th but he couldn't move, so his father came over around seven in the morning of the 8th and said, "Your son's rather badly wounded. We left him at a school in Kusatsu, so please go see him."

As I learned later, he said to our neighbors, "Nose's gone, ears are gone, he's so badly wounded there's hardly hope." They didn't tell me that then, so I promptly got ready and started for Kusatsu.

Since the Geibi Line didn't operate from around Kumura Station, I crossed the Ota River by boat, went out to the Kabe Line, and walked along the line toward Kusatsu. There was an endless line of badly wounded and burnt human beings with horrifying appearances I had never seen before. At this rate, I thought, Masayuki was hopeless. I cannot express my feeling then, either by pen or by mouth. It was sad beyond words.

I went to information at the Kusatsu school and asked, "Is there someone by the name of Ishii Masayuki?" They said, "His name's not on the list so we can't tell."

In the schoolyard the dead lay. In each classroom the wounded lay. I lifted the straw mat going from person to person, but I couldn't tell because everyone's face had changed. My son's front teeth were gutted, so I walked around with that as a guide, but I couldn't find him. I left and walked to all the camps around there. I walked until the sun went down and it grew dark, but I could never find him. I went all the way to Kako-machi, but there was no sign of him around the prefectural government hall. About ten women were dead, their heads floating in the fire-prevention water tank, intestines out. At this rate my son wouldn't be alive, I thought, wandering near the prefectural government hall. Then, under a pine tree that had survived the fire, I saw someone with a bandage like a hachimaki headband on his head doing paper work. I asked and found he was from the Police Training Center.

"Is there someone called Ishii Masayuki?" I asked.

"Was there someone by that name?" he said, and put the name down in the list. A man washing a mess tin seemed to be Masayuki's friend and said, "Ishii is alive. He's wounded, but I am sure he's been taken in somewhere."

"Is he alive?"

"He's somewhere. There's a camp in Hijiyama and some Training Center men went back there, so he may be there," he said, so I went to visit Hijiyama, but they said, "Ishii isn't here." Because I had no place to stay, I was about to leave for the station, when someone said, "I'm going to Yaga, so let's go together."

We walked through Hiroshima, covered by smoke from incineration of the dead, to Yaga Station. "Anyone for Miyoshi or Toka-ichi?" an attendant called in a loud voice, so I jumped on. Inside, the train was full of wounded people and no one had to pay the fare. Though I carried lunch, I ended up not eating it and slept alone on the bridge at Toka-ichi. Around midnight a siren went off above my head, signaling an air raid. Masayuki's dead, and I'll stay right here, too, I thought, and refused to move. The alarm was canceled after a while, and I went home by the first train in the morning, but Masayuki had not come home.

When we had a Shinto official pray, he said, "Your son's wounded but is alive. If you try to find him, you'll only follow after him and won't be able to bring him home, but he didn't lose his life." But I couldn't stay still. I went to Kusatsu once again on the 11th to look for him.

"I'm back again because I just can't give up. Would you please check the list once more? I've come thinking that I'd pick up at least the bones before I leave," I said.

"What sort of person?" asked one who looked dignified, like a hospital head.

"Someone who was at the Training Center, with nose scraped—"

"Yeah, I treated him. He was a big man who looked very much like you. He's not dead."

Hearing these words, I gathered my courage again and walked around visiting every possible camp, whether the hospital or the temple. As I walked all the way across the town of Kusatsu I came across a police station, and my older brother happened to be there. He was at that time the head of the Kozan police department, and he had led civilian guards in the cleanup of Hiroshima. Overwhelmed by both joy and sorrow, I called "Brothe-e-r" and sprung to him and cried.

"Seeing how things are, you must give up. He won't be alive," he said. That night I went to the lodging where my older brother was staying and slept on a mat spread over ashes. When I returned to Yaga Station the following day there was an air raid siren again. We passengers were made to get off the train and enter the basement of the station. After the warning was canceled, I was trying to put water in my canteen when the train arrived.

"Mr. Ishii, Mr. Ishii, Masayuki's home," Mr. Harada's father told me.

"Is he home?" I said and went toward the train, jumping the fence instead of going through the ticket gate.

"He's home, he's home, you can be sure," he said. I can't forget how happy I felt then.

Masayuki had been running away with Mr. Harada, but feeling his face stretched, he went down to the river and washed his face, then his hands got stuck over his nose, so he realized that his face had been hit. When his foot refused to move, he realized that a bone was broken. Mr. Harada went to find a car, put Masayuki in it, took him to the Kusatsu school, and said, "You musn't drink water, I'll come again, so don't move." Then, as I learned, he laid him on a stretcher in the corridor and left. The following day when Masayuki was treated, he noticed the injury on his chest. His chest seemed as if it was scraped out under the ribs. Sinews were showing around the shoulders, too. Although he was in this bad condition, since everyone around was either dead or injured, he thought it would be all over with him, too, if he stayed there, he said, so he went to the camp in Hatsuka-ichi. When he got to Hatsuka-ichi there was a woman from the Training Center, and she treated him carefully. He stayed there on the 9th, received a pair of sandals and a shirt, and, hearing that the trains had started to run again, went home right away.

When he got off at Shio-machi Station, he saw his teacher from the Commercial School.

"I'm back, teacher," Masayuki said.

"Who are you?" the teacher said. There was no way he could have known who it was, because Masayuki had been bandaged round and round, only his eyes showing.

"I am Ishii," Masayuki said.

"Oh, it's you. Your father went to look for you. You didn't see him, did you?" he said and, staying with him, sent a message home telling them to come to meet him. The doctor nearest our house, near Bingo Yasuda Station, had been drafted to Hiroshima and died instantly by the bomb. There was no healthy doctor nearby, so we took Masayuki to an old doctor six kilometers away and had him treated.

"This is bad. I have never seen such terrible injuries as this before," the doctor said, taken aback. About five people who had been hit by the atomic bomb were there besides Masayuki.

"Don't say 'it hurts it hurts' with that kind of injury. Look at Ishii. He has such a grave injury," the doctor said.

Since glass splinters were all over his face, the doctor treated him about one and a half hours. His face was completely covered with bandages except for the eyes, and his chest too was covered with trianglar bandages. His foot was pierced and a bone was broken, but his chest, shoulders, and face were so badly wounded that he did not even notice it.

I took him to the doctor every day until August 29 or so, but from the 30th we cared for him at home because we were told that he was not supposed to be exposed to the sun. In the meantime, freckles appeared, hair fell, and there was so much pus that before half a day passed it oozed through the bandages wound half an inch thick, so he couldn't lie down. Splinters of glass came out with the pus over a dozen times. On the November 1 festival, however, he was well enough, lying down on the verandah, to watch people passing by making merry.

"It's hopeless."

"It's pitiful."

When I was talking with people who came to inquire after his health, Masayuki said, "What are you saying? Aren't you talking about me?"

Even after the pus stopped, it was as if the root of one shoulder was scraped. Water started to collect there, and he could not move his hand. So around December 10 he was hospitalized at the place of a masseur/doctor in Nihyakuda, Miyoshi. He came home on the 30th, having gotten well. Since he got well in spite of the fact that ten out of ten people had said he would die, I felt as if roasted beans had sprouted.

Masayuki started to walk gradually, and he got to the point of saying: "I won't live long, so please let me have a wife."

"I hear that those who were exposed to the atomic bomb can't have children," I said.

"I don't care if I can't have children, please get someone," he said. So I got a bride for him in October 1947. Splinters of glass came out of his body three or four times every year, he couldn't carry things over his shoulder, he couldn't work with others like a grown man, but even so he did his share of the village work.

Masayuki was forward looking from boyhood, the first to try the *setchu* paddies, a method that combines the virtues of water and dry paddies. This is because he wanted to transplant early: you plant the seeds around April 20 and place oiled paper over the soil to keep an even temperature. Masayuki tried this method twice, in 1951 and 1952. He was able to start to transplant twenty days earlier than usual, around May 28. This improves branching off of the stalk near the roots before the last tilling and weeding, so the yield was good. In 1951 at a workshop in Konu village he learned how to use 2–4D, a chemical for weeding in rice fields, and right away bought a sprayer with his own money and tried it, as he was thinking about how to ease the peasants' labor, if only a little.

Again, he had a scientific mind. Around 1949 or 1950, when fuses often blew due to the electricity situation, he climbed the village electric pole with a battery, and high above he held it in one hand while fixing the fuse box with the other. He often fixed radios, clocks, or electricity. When a neighbor came to ask, he readily went to help. When the electricity went out and couldn't be fixed at night, he took a gas lamp, though it was another's matter, and said, "Do with this for tonight, I'll fix it tomorrow." He was this kind of man, and people said he was kind, he was gentle. Then in June 1950 a girl was born, in June 1952 a boy, and happy days continued.

The nutria is an animal the size of a rabbit that looks like a mouse, and since foreigners love its fur, you can make a little money by raising it and exporting the fur, said a book.

"I can't do physical labor, so I'll keep nutrias and earn some money," Masayuki said. The way to keep them, I learned, was just to change the water every day and throw in the food, but I was worried because a pair cost as much as 16,500 yen, and nobody had ever done it around here.

"They're living creatures, so spend money on them, and it's all over if they die. If you're going to spend money, do it after you find out more about them." I tried to stop him. His mother didn't agree either. Neighbors laughed. Even then Masayuki didn't change his mind, went to the Agricultural Cooperative Association to borrow money, and, though its head did his best to oppose the idea, sent for nutrias from Okayama, saying that he "was going to earn at least the money to buy his own cigarettes.''

If the nutrias' coop is made of wood, they bite all night through and get out, so you have to make it solid with concrete. When the 1952 rice transplanting was over, Masayuki worked under the scorching sun to make the nutrias' coop solid, carrying gravel and making a fence by himself. I think that affected his health. On July 29, around the time the nutrias arrived, a tiny, hard growth formed in his throat, and when he drank water, the water stopped there once before going down, making a gurgling noise.

I am a carpenter, and I always go to the Osaka area to work. I had promised to go to Osaka to work with a young man on August 2.

"Father, my throat hurts . . . ,'' Masayuki said when I was leaving.

"If it hurts, you must show it to the doctor," I said. Around that time, my younger son Kazuo was hospitalized in Okayama with a sinus problem, and his mother had gone to tend to him, leaving at home Masayuki, his wife who had just had a baby, our youngest son who was a third grader, and our two grandchildren. The care for the 8,000 square meters of rice field and over 2,000 square meters of vegetable farm must have been too much for Masayuki. Moreover, since he knew how to use 2–4D and owned a sprayer, if someone came to ask him to spray, he couldn't refuse, and he walked around spraying 2–4D not only on our field but on others' in the hot sun of Doyo, the last eighteen days of summer. This must have hit him hard. When his mother and Kazuo came home from the hospital on August 11, I hear that he said, "I'm . . . in trouble, my throat's hurting.''

He went to the doctor's near Yasuda Station and had x-rays taken, but no glass, no nothing was found. It's probably glass, so go to Arase Hospital, which specializes in surgery, he was told. He went to Arase for the first time on the 13th.

"This is not like taking out normal glass splinters. It's difficult because it's the throat. You can't be operated on unless we really feel ready, so stay here for a while,'' he was told.

"I can't definitely say it's glass,'' the doctor said on seeing the x-rays.

"Well, I'll come back after taking care of the Bon festival,''

Masayuki said and came home. He wrote to me in Osaka: "Father, my sore throat is just glass, so no need to worry. It's the usual thing so please do your work at ease." He observed the Bon on the 14th and 15th, and on the night of the 15th he went with a gas lamp to the Joge River for arrow-fishing and caught many fish: catfish, eels, crucian carps, goppa, dace, etc. On the 16th, after planting Chinese cabbage seeds, he prepared for the hospital stay, put a futon on the rack behind the seat of his bicycle, and left. Because his method of planting was good, though this year others' Chinese cabbages had poor yields, fine cabbages grew on our farm, almost 4 kilograms each. But Masayuki was never to come home again.

He was operated on around four o'clock in the afternoon of the 19th, but no glass came out.

"This is beyond me. Because you got hit by the atomic bomb, try going to the ABCC," the doctor said, and he wrote a letter of introduction. Masayuki couldn't sleep now with a violent headache, but the doctor didn't know the cause, so he couldn't give him any medicine. It was decided that Masayuki should go to the ABCC on the morning of the 25th.

"Not there; I'd rather be taken home. Hiroshima's the atomic bomb place so I don't want to go," Masayuki said. I wonder if he said this because he felt sorry about having to spend money on the illness from which he knew he couldn't recover. As a parent it saddens me to think about it. After finally making up his mind to go to Hiroshima, he asked me to bring the children, so on the night of the 24th, I took his wife and two children to see him. When he was given a dose of medicine on the night of the 25th, his headache eased considerably, so the uncle from the main family, his mother, and Kazuo accompanied him to the ABCC on the morning of the 26th.

"We can't admit you with just this kind of doctor's introduction, you need a formal procedure. Get hospitalized at the Japan Red Cross or some place, and follow formal procedures from there," they said. So he went to the Red Cross. They x-rayed him and found a growth in his chest and said that they would check again tomorrow, but that they wouldn't be able to diagnose the illness definitely until then.

Hearing about this while I was at work in Osaka, I went directly to

Hiroshima, to the ABCC, then to the Red Cross, tracing the steps of Masayuki and the others, and finally we got together after seven o'clock at night on the 26th in a room of the Farmers' Hall where they had settled.

"Father, I'm sorry to trouble you, it's nothing serious," Masayuki greeted me calmly. We went to the Red Cross together on the morning of the 27th and had Masayuki examined. Then the doctor called just Kazuo.

"I am very sorry, but this is an illness of one in a thousand people, an illness that occurs in a young person, something like old people's cancer. There's no treatment. There hasn't been any example of a patient who got better by an operation. If you make an incision in one place, it comes out somewhere else—it's that kind of disease. We can't operate on him. There's an x-ray treatment, but one out of a hundred people gets better. It's a difficult illness, so it will be better for you to take him home," the doctor said.

"I don't care how much it costs, I'll have him hospitalized and leave him in your hands, so please treat him," Kazuo pleaded.

"How sorry I am. I'll take care of the procedure for the ABCC, so let him enter when there's a vacancy," the doctor said.

Kazuo was crying at heart, but he hid his tears as he spoke. "The doctor says electro-therapy will cure it, so things are looking good. I was asking him to do the procedure for the ABCC, so the talk was longer than I had expected," Kazuo said so that Masayuki wouldn't notice, then consulted just me and Uncle from the main family. We decided that Masayuki would enter the Red Cross on the 28th. Leaving just Kazuo to stay at the hospital, Uncle, my wife, and I left Hiroshima by the three o'clock train and came home. We didn't tell the truth to our neighbors.

"They say he'll get better if he gets electro-therapy, so things are looking good," I said, and whenever I could be alone I cried. But I had to worry about the cost of hospitalization—I didn't know how long it was supposed to last—so I went back to Osaka to do carpentry on the 29th.

Masayuki was admitted to the hospital on August 29 and started electro-therapy on September 9, attended by Kazuo and his mother. Around the 13th, because he was progressing very well, the two of them came home. On the 21st, his wife went to see him, and on the 24th the electro-therapy was finished for now, and we thought the couple could then come home together.

"Well, I'll stay just a little longer," Masayuki said, however. On the 26th his condition changed, and on the 28th water was taken out on account of pleurisy. The pain became violent, and by the time Kazuo went to the Red Cross on the 30th, the agony was unspeakable.

"Do something quickly, whatever," Masayuki said. The doctor said nothing could be done. Masayuki got a nitromin injection, but it didn't help at all. He had no appetite, either.

The second electro-therapy started around October 26, but this time, far from getting better, he had an unbearably hard time. Since the lymph glands were swollen and lumpy from the cheeks down to around the kidneys, he just lay on his left side, and nothing could be done. Though he had a bedsore where his hip bone protruded, we could do nothing for him. On the morning of October 29, Masayuki and Kazuo said, "Nose's bleeding," "hot flush," etc., and starting on the morning of the 30th, Masayuki spat blood. He spat and spat till noon and it didn't stop. No matter what shot was given, it was no good, and as he coughed badly, black clots of blood kept coming.

"The windpipe's torn because of the coughing, that's why you're bleeding, nothing to worry about," the doctor said to Masayuki. But to Kazuo he said, "The sarcoma is so swollen that the blood vessel burst. It may stop once by an injection, but if there's a second spitting, I think it is hopeless, so if there are people who you want to see him let them see him without letting him notice." So, when the patient fell asleep exhausted at one point, Kazuo contacted home right away. On the morning of the 31st the aunt of the main family came, and on the morning of November 1, Masayuki himself said, "Please call everyone, I want to see Father."

So right away they sent me a telegram, "Come at once." This was the time of harvesting, when at home we were so busy we could have borrowed a cat to help us, and I had my job, but I left home at once with my daughter-in-law and her two children, took a bus from Miyoshi, and reached the hospital around four.

"Father, this is hopeless, I started to bring up blood," Masayuki greeted me.

"Call mother," he said, so we sent a telegram again right away. The second vomit went on and on from the morning of the 1st, and as for the nose bleeding, it never stopped from the time of the first spitting of blood. Masayuki couldn't wait for his mother to come. She came around 2 o'clock on the 2nd.

"Mother, thank you for coming. I'm this way and hopeless, but Kazuo took good care of me. I have nothing to regret," he said, and after a while added, "Is Eizo here?"

Eizo is our youngest child, and I had left him to tend to the house. I called him so there wouldn't be any regrets, but since he came about noon on the 3rd, he didn't make it. Masayuki slept for good at 10:15 on November 3.

Since the ABCC had notified us that he would be examined on November 5, we had asked to change it to the 3rd, and we urged them again on the 3rd. They told us they were sending someone for an examination on the afternoon of the 3rd, but it was too late. When he died we negotiated with the ABCC right away, and an ABCC doctor came and said that he had wanted to see him while he was alive.

"Please allow us to conduct an autopsy at once, because it will be good for a wide range of people," he said, so we had an autopsy done. As a result, Masayuki's illness was found to have been "vertical cornea's special disease caused by the atomic bomb." We had a wake in the waiting room of the Red Cross, then had him incinerated.

"He was hit by the atomic bomb," the cremator said at a glance. When I tried to pick up a bone,* I found that a leg bone was broken.

As a parent it is regrettable no matter what you say. I am reminded of Masayuki by everything I see, and it is a cause for tears. The nutrias that Masayuki ordered without listening to what his parents had to say are expected to have babies in March, and they are swimming in the concrete coop Masayuki made. Why did Masayuki

---

*After the body is incinerated, the bones are laid on a table for close relatives to pick up with chopsticks and put in an urn.

think of keeping these nutrias? If I come to think about it, those hit by the atomic bomb are hopeless once they fall ill, so the only thing they can do is to build physical strength so that they will not fall ill. Masayuki focused his eye on nutrias, thinking of building physical strength without troubling the family—this thought is unbearable. Now that it has come to this, I think that the only way to help people who survived the bomb like Masayuki did is to help them restore their strength with state aid. I heartily hope that this will be possible.

FATHER AND SON
ROBBED OF BODY AND SOUL:
A RECORD OF
RYU CHOON SEUNG AND HIS SON

Kuak Kwi Hoon

"Ryu Choon Seung's condition seems serious."

In June 1972 I received a sudden call from the Korea-Japan Atomic Bomb Survivors Aid Association of Seoul. Mr. Ryu was a member of the association's Honam Branch where I serve as the director, and he lived in Shintaein, Chongup county, nearly one hour by car from Chonju, the capital of North Cholla province.

He looked healthy when I saw him several years ago at the Seoul office, I recalled, as I prepared my camera and tape recorder for my first visit to his house. Many of the Korean survivors are scattered in mountain areas, but particularly in Honam Branch, the sick live isolated in areas hard to reach by public transportation. This makes it difficult for me to visit their homes.

The Ryus were not at the address registered at the association. After inquiring here and there in the village, I finally located their house near Shintaein Commercial High School. Their house, I said, but it was an *ondol* room* about 2 by 3 meters by the side of the kitchen of a dirt farmhouse under a thatched roof. This was the abode of Mr. Ryu's family of five.

On going under the *samlin*** and opening the door to the room, I

---

*A room with underfloor heating.
**A Korean-style woven gate.

heard a groan from the dark. I could not even see Mr. Ryu. A sweaty smell reached my nose. I stepped up onto the room, and after a while I started to see Mr. Ryu lying down. By his pillow was a boy crouched still, holding his knees and gazing at his groaning father. Mr. Ryu, who was more lucid than I had expected, recognized my face and, holding my hand firmly, started to mumble about his atomic bomb experience and his symptoms. Although at heart trembling in fear of the atomic bomb disease, his facial expression was unchanged.

Mr. Ryu was born in Shintaein in January 1917. His Japanese name was Yanagisawa Haruo. In March 1944 he was drafted to work in Japan in the survey corps of the navy's engineering section.

According to Mr. Ryu's recollection, ordered to go to Hiroshima that day, he went with a colleague, Shin Tae Ryong. They arrived at Hiroshima Station at 8:05 a.m. They were expected to meet someone from the workplace, but he did not seem to be there yet. The moment Mr. Ryu looked at his watch, light flashed before his eyes, and he felt hot. "This is serious," he thought, and, taking off and flinging down the shirt he wore, he ran desperately toward Mt. Futaba behind the station. He kept running while stumbling over the rails and iron fence of the station, and, when he was outside the station, he realized Shin Tae Ryong was no longer to be seen.

He reached the foot of Mt. Futaba, spent the night in a half-ruined farmhouse, and on the following day was carried by a rescue truck to the navy hospital in Kure. He lay with gauze dipped in oil on his burnt face, and after a few days maggots hatched on the burns. "The pockmarks on my face are the traces left by maggots crawling out," Mr. Ryu said. The burns healed in a month. With severance pay of 1,500 yen, he returned to his country in September 1945.

Back home, he easily became exhausted and was often ill. However, he whipped himself to work for a livelihood, now as a lumber dealer, now a grain seller. At one point he lived in Seoul and dealt with quite a lot of goods. However, around 1950 he started to vomit blood and have bloody stools. He consulted a doctor, who noted an abnormally high white blood cell count. "Can this be due to the atomic bomb?" Worried, he visited the Korea-Japan Atomic Energy Institute. "It is not clear whether or not yours is the atomic bomb disease,'' they answered coolly.

Around 1968 Mr. Ryu's greengrocer business failed and his livelihood deteriorated. Doubled by the spiritual blow, his illness worsened. A light fever and headache persisted, and he constantly
coughed. Seeking solace in Christianity, he eagerly attended church.
Even while praying on the wooden floor, however, his knees became
so cold and his legs so numb that often he was unable to walk. Still,
he had no courage to visit a hospital. He not only was concerned
about the expense but feared that the doctor might say that he was
''dying of the atomic bomb disease.''

One day in 1970 Mr. Ryu brought home a heap of tatters. According to his family his behavior grew strange and his illness became
serious around that time.

I visited him for the second time in late July 1972. In the course of
the month his condition had rapidly worsened. Mr. Ryu lay in the
pitch dark room, thin as a ghost, and his wax-white face seemed to
indicate that the moment of death was approaching. His hair and
beard were left to grow. He suffered attacks at intervals of about one
minute, and when he did, his limbs and entire body writhed, and he
gnashed his teeth which he closed to endure the pain.

I could not look straight at Mr. Ryu, who was in front of me. After
an attack, he looked around with eyes that had lost focus. It looked
as though he were searching for something in his confusion. He no
longer knew who I was. Although he was trying and trying to say
something, his tongue became twisted, so that it was difficult to
follow what he was saying. His family was at a loss: ''All we can do
is wait for him to die,'' they said.

Until he reached this condition, he had not even once been able to
eat nutritious food or send for a doctor. A box of pain relievers from
a drug store lay near his pillow. I learned that he had been taking
inexpensive commercial medicine he obtained free thanks to a relative who ran a drug store in the same village. When I asked him what
he wanted to eat, Mr. Ryu barely managed to say, ''I want to eat
meat.'' In a corner of the room was his tray. In a container was
leftover rice mixed with barley; there was not even kimchi to go with
it, soy sauce being the only side dish. This was the patient's entire
meal.

I visited Mr. Ryu two or three times after this, and each time found his condition worse. It was three days before the Fall Evening (August 15 by the lunar calendar, the festival of the ancestors, when people visit family graves). On going to visit the Ryus, I saw a white *chogori* on the roof of their house. This was the custom indicating a death in a family.

Mr. Ryu had finally died. My call turned into a funeral visit. I felt lost, thinking that yet another friend had left this world.

According to his family, he had died on September 19, the day before my visit. In our country, we have a custom that no one comes to help with the funeral when there is a death the day before the Fall Evening. I felt that Mr. Ryu must have hastened to die to avoid burdening his family even after his death.

Ryu Choon Seung had two boys and a girl. Dong Soo was born as his second son in 1954, nearly ten years after Mr. Ryu returned to Korea, having been bombed in Japan. Dong Soo was born with weak legs and never walked. The lower half of his body remained undeveloped, and it was difficult for him even to move by sliding.

Three years after his birth, a third boy was born, but this child, with a small lower body and a head more than twice as big as that of a normal baby, died in his third month.

When Dong Soo was school age, he went to school every day on his grandmother's or mother's back. After entering junior high school, his brother took him to school on his bike.

When a first grader, he was examined by a doctor and his case was diagnosed as polio. His family and teachers believed he had polio, but his father Ryu Choon Seung had a premonition that Dong Soo was disabled due to the atomic bomb. Mr. Ryu was not able to ascertain this because there was then no atomic bomb disease specialist in Korea. In an interview, Mr. Ryu repeatedly asked Kei Hiraoka, a *Chugoku shinbun* reporter who visited the country to cover Korean survivors, "Can the atomic bomb disease be inherited?" This indicates his intense anxiety about the effect of the disease.

Although Dong Soo lived a life of just the upper body, he had an outstanding brain. He graduated from elementary school as the top student, and in junior high he was again always tops and received scholarships. A report card from around then says: "Versatile with the exception of gym."

Dong Soo must have agonized, however, feeling that there was no hope for the future with half the body paralyzed, no matter how bright he was. He stopped talking with his family, and, except when studying, he always crouched or lay near his father. His favorite book was an illustrated and annotated Bible. His agony deepened as he advanced in grades, and he attempted suicide three times, although each time his family found him before it was too late. In November of his third year in junior high school, he insisted that he no longer wanted to go to school, and he finally withdrew. Day after day he stayed home, depressed, watching his sick father.

When Ryu Choon Seung died, Dong Soo clung to his father's body, and would not leave the room until the funeral was over.

Worried about his future, I visited him a few times and tried to persuade him to resume his schooling, but each time Dong Soo stared at me as if lost, without any response whatsoever. I decided to watch for a while, having no other resort.

In June 1974 a Japanese religious body contributed two million *won* to Korean survivors. Since it was decided that the fund was to be used for their living expenses and medicine, I thought of buying a wheelchair for Dong Soo and contacted the family.

"Dong Soo? He went completely insane and died. Not eating a thing, he dried out and died," Lee Ye Chong, his mother, told me. I heard that the date of his death was May 20. It was as if misfortune, as in the saying, was really meant to come on another's heel. In Korea, nothing is done about atomic bomb survivors' medication and relief. If so, what can be expected to be done about the second generation? No survey has been conducted on their situations and clinical symptoms; no interest has been shown. All the more reason, when I think of the second generation of our country, for me to ask with anger, "Who created this misfortune?" unable to stop thinking of their future.

KOREANS . . . AND AMERICANS AND CHINESE ARE ALSO VICTIMS

Kim In Jo

I went to Japan in the spring of 1924 (the 13th year of Taisho) when I was ten.

My father went to Japan in 1923, the year of the Kanto Earthquake, as a recruit in a mine in Kyushu, and returned after working about a year. He took me on his second trip to Japan.

Leaving my mother, young brother, and sister, I held my father's hand as we went to the pier for the Shimonoseki-Pusan ferry. Our boat, the Keifukumaru, was the first ferry I saw, and it looked like a small mountain. Although I could not see it clearly since it was night, I said to my father, "It's like a small mountain," and I still remember that he laughed. As we walked on the pier toward the boat it looked beautiful, lit with many electric lights. On boarding, I noticed new straw mats spread on the floor. I went out to the deck with my father and saw my mother and my younger brother, who had come to see us off. When I called to my mother and my brother, my mother waved her hand and shouted something, but I could not hear.

Soon the boat left the pier. Both those on the ferry and those seeing them off waved their hands, and some were in tears. I did not cry then, but before I knew it tears filled my eyes as the ferry advanced toward On Ryuk Do Island outside Pusan Bay, blurring the sight of my mother and others seeing us off.

We went inside and slept, and when I woke, the boat was already about to approach the pier. "Where are we?" I asked my father. "This is Japan," he answered. We transferred from the ferry to a small boat and landed at Moji.

We took a train to Osato just outside of Moji to go to the house of father's acquaintance. There I ate a banana for the first time in my life.

My father worked at the Osato Sugar Company. I wanted to play with young children, but I did not understand what they were saying. Without verbal communication, it could not be helped. Even so, in about three months I began to understand somewhat, and occasionally I even went to get friends to play with on my own accord. Every day I enthusiastically learned Japanese.

Moving from Place to Place and Settling in Hiroshima

In about a year my father called my mother and family members. Since I clearly comprehended Japanese by then, I was able to teach my younger brother and sister little by little. Soon I enrolled in the third grade of elementary school. I was thirteen, but I had quite a hard time because of linguistic barriers.

Due to my father's changing jobs, we moved many times. We moved to Enoura, Hikoshima, Shiohama-mura, Fukuura-mura, etc., in Yamaguchi prefecture. When we were living in Yoshimi-mura outside of Shimonoseki, my uncle, a tofu maker in Hiroshima, came and took us to Hiroshima. It was decided that we would live at 320 Fukushima, Hiroshima City, near my uncle's house. It was the fall of 1927.

The place was five or six houses behind Fukushima Higher Elementary School. The following day I went to school alone and registered.

My homeroom teacher was Ichiro Tanaka, and the schoolmaster Rin'nosuke Hosokawa. I was a fourth grader. What left the deepest impression about this school was Mr. Hosokawa's words at a morning ceremony: "Students should not wear watches. It is important that we do without them until everyone can wear one." Among the many people I met in my stay of over twenty years in Japan, I will never forget Mr. Hosokawa, not even in the next world.

The year after my family moved to Hiroshima, various festivities were held at the West Military Training Field to celebrate the Emperor's coronation. A ceremonial song was composed, and I remember celebrating until late at night, singing that song.

I graduated from school at sixteen. Right away I started to work at a rubber factory at Kannon-cho, Hiroshima. The president was Tetsuzo Arinori. Though still a youth, I was behind none in work.

After two months or so, I was told to stay at Mr. Arinori's house. Rubber machines were there, and orders came from other factories. I enthusiastically learned my trade. My monthly salary as a live-in worker was fifteen yen. However, soon the "Manchurian Incident" occurred, and the president was drafted. Moreover, the factory burnt down during his absence, so I lost my job. Eventually I took a job at a restaurant that belonged to someone by the name of Kiichi Oki, an acquaintance of Mr. Arinori's, and worked daily from eight in the morning to midnight, no, until after two. I stayed there for about five years and became a first class cook, but I quit because the service trade did not suit me.

Next, through the introduction of an elementary school classmate whom I happened to see, I started to work for a greengrocer called Jitsuzo Kimura in the public market at 9 Chome, Otemachi, Hiroshima. Here, too, I worked hard, stocking and selling goods. When, after a while, marriage was discussed in my native place, Pusan, I went home temporarily for the wedding and returned to Hiroshima with my wife Yoon Ge Hwa. This was February 1937, when I was twenty-three and my wife eighteen. The "Sino-Japanese Incident" occurred in July of the same year.

As the war rapidly spread, we were in a state of national mobilization. The national control ordinance was issued, severely restricting mercantile activities. Then the Pacific War started.

I had three children to support, but I worked for the sake of Japan's victory as a member of the transportation corps through the Land Transportation Automobile Company of Hiroshima prefecture. Nearly fifty people worked at the company. Twenty-seven were my compatriots, all drivers; half died by the atomic bomb. I was the leader of the first of the four groups.

My younger brother also received a draft notice in 1942 and was called to the Naval Engineering Division in Kure. My heart ached as I accompanied him to Kure.

A Prefectural Assemblyman's Words

In 1943 we had a fourth child. Everything was rationed, including rice, wood, green vegetables, and even a single scallion, so my wife had a really hard time taking care of our children. I think American airplanes started to attack Japan in the summer of that year. I was also drafted to evacuate buildings in the city as a member of the Patriotic Labor Corps. "One hundred million of one mind" was a phrase used in those days, but this in fact meant the total of seventy million Japanese and my thirty million compatriots. Even so, we were often told that we were too talkative.

One day I was stopped by Mr. K, an acquaintance who was a prefectural assemblyman, and treated to some food at his house that evening. Pointing at the framed calligraphy on the wall that said "One hundred million of one mind," Mr. K asked me: "What do you think of this?" "It's fine," I answered tentatively. He struck the table and said in a trembling voice, "I am asking what this means."

"I am a descendent of a Korean immigrant. After pointing a scornful finger at us all this while, what do they now mean by saying one hundred million of one mind? I can't allow them to do this," Mr. K said, and he tore the frame in front of my eyes. "I think you understand if no one else, Mr. Kaneko (my Japanese name was Seizo Kaneko), whether such a slogan is to our benefit or not—" Silence continued. "Mr. Kaneko, it's all right if you tell the police about me. I won't be defeated," Mr. K said. That night the two of us drank sake to our heart's content.

About ten days before the bombing, a formation of twenty-one to twenty-five American airplanes invaded from Hiroshima Bay. They did not bomb, but passed over Ujina and the Mitsubishi Shipbuilding Factory at Enami and went toward Itsukaichi. Anti-aircraft guns of the shipping corps of Ujina and others shot at them many times and brought down one airplane.

The aircraft crashed in a farm in Itsukaichi, and when the two American soldiers parachuted toward the Mitsubishi Shipbuilding Factory, the parachutes caught on the building, and they became captives. I was in the process of transporting goods to the Shipbuilding Factory. The conscripted Mitsubishi workers shouted that they would beat them to death. Military police came right away, blindfolded the two American soldiers, and took them to the Fifth Division. Seeing the young American soldiers, I thought, "They are going to be killed." Since it was rare that American airplanes flew over Hiroshima, I also thought that this might be a bad omen.

In those days I also witnessed Chinese people put to work at Ujina beach carrying dirt for construction of harbor facilities. I learned that they had been captured in Singapore and brought to the Fifth Division. About ten people were carrying heavy dirt under strict supervision every day from early in the morning. It is possible that other people were put to work in Hiroshima. At the time of the bombing, they would all have died if they had stayed at the barracks of the division, which was near the target area; but if they had been at work in Ujina, ironically they might have been lucky enough to be safe. I was not able to find out about the safety of those people who, like us, had been brought from a foreign country and experienced the bombing. However, it is clear that the Japanese and Koreans were not the only people who experienced the bombing.

There were many shooting stars on the night of August 5. I remember hearing voices from the neighborhood, "Another shooting star." I went to bed saying to my wife, "This is an eerie night."

The Whole Family Around the Table

On the sixth, there was a siren in the morning, but it stopped, and the whole family started to eat breakfast together at around 7:50. Besides my wife and myself, Kinue (oldest daughter), Shizue (second daughter), Matsue (third daughter), and Hiroaki (first son), we had as our guests that morning my uncle and his wife who lived in Ikuno, Tosei-ku, Osaka, and my younger brother who had been drafted for work and his wife and children—eleven of us surrounded the table.

I finished eating first, went to the living room, and pulled a cigarette from the drawer of a chest. At that instant, the electric wires that ran through the living room and the bath at the other end of the living room shone as though throwing out a bundle of fire. I cannot forget seeing clearly beyond the light the face of five-year-old Matsue, who was just coming out of the bathroom on the side of the bath.

When I came to, it was too dark to see anything. The wind started to blow, and finally I could see a little. I thought it strange because distant mountains that should not be in sight were in sight, as well as the Chugoku Shinbun as far as one kilometer away.

Having crawled out on their own through slits in the crushed roof, my children stood in the street. My wife was all bloody, her chin cut by a falling board from the roof. My uncle's head and arms were also covered with blood. My feet were pressed under a beam or something, but I mustered all my strength and finally was able to pull them out. "Big brother!" someone called, and, on turning back, I found my younger brother's wife unable to move, her feet caught. I moved slates and pieces of wood to save her. Then my wife said, "Matsue isn't here." All of us called her name, but there was no answer.

Then a fire started from somewhere, and flames spread toward us. I heard a voice calling me somewhere: "Dad." It sounded like Matsue. "Dad, I'm hot," she screamed. I ran toward the place where I was stuck until a while ago and desperately called Matsue through the smoke.

Again I heard a voice, "Hot," and, on looking at the opening out of which I had come, found Matsue. The opening was small, however, and she could only move about in vain. The fire was coming close. Flurried, I felt as if my chest was pressed tight. Thinking that I would rather take care of her with my hands than let my own child burn, with all my might I pulled her legs, which I saw on the other side of the opening. Then luckily her body slipped out through the opening.

The fire rapidly spread. After all I could not save our son Hiroaki. I had my family run for safety toward the Meiji Bridge. On the way, following them, I saved a woman and her child who called for help under a house.

When I went to the place where my family was supposed to be, there was no sign of them. Since the rain was black, some said it was oil. But it was rain. Perhaps the rain grew black mixed with dust since houses in Hiroshima City collapsed all at once.

Avoiding inhaling bad air, I tried to walk into the wind as much as possible.

Although I made the rounds of all the first aid places in the city, I could not find my family that day. Exhausted, I dropped asleep.

I went round the first aid posts again early the following morning. The Japan Bank of Fukuro-machi was also turned into a first aid post. There for the first time I learned that it was an atomic bomb. But I did not know why it was called that.

From the first aid post of Ujina, I went to the Army Medical Inspection Office of Ninoshima. In the infirmary I found my wife, her face swollen. "Because I fell with bad bleeding while running, a driver from somewhere carried me to Ujina, and from there I struggled to this place," she said. We were reunited after six days. But where were our children? I took my wife to her parents in Koi and started to look for our children the following day.

I found my uncle and his wife in a school on the way to Enami. My brother found us on his own after a week. We were happy for each other, as though the dead had come to life.

I found the children on the twelfth day at the first aid post in Saka-machi, Aki. Finding them there, I called, "Shizue." I still remember that they looked at me, ran to me saying "Dad," and shed tears. About two hundred injured people filled the place. On entering, I found my younger brother's wife and her children. Matsue had a burn on her belly. My brother's wife was crying with bruises and a headache. We were so happy to be reunited that we wept. All the surviving family members having come together, I finally felt relieved.

Daughters Die

Early next morning I went to a temple in Koi, interred the bones of Hiroaki, who had died, and prayed that he would rest in peace.

When two weeks or so passed, foam-like bumps appeared all over my body and I was terribly itchy. At the hospital they said, "Probably it's food poisoning," hardly giving me any medicine. I went to an acquaintance who lived along the upper part of the Ota River and recuperated for a while. I felt helpless since my health only declined.

The news came that our second daughter Shizue, who was staying with my younger sister in Osaka, was in critical condition. As though running after it, on August 27 the news arrived that she had died. Worried about the rest of the family, I went back to my wife and the surviving children. Flies gathered around the mouths of both my wife and children, and the smell was bad. The day after I arrived, our youngest daughter Matsue also died.

This won't do, I thought, and on consulting my sister in Osaka I put my brother and his wife, my wife and oldest daughter, my uncle and his daughter—the six of them—in the Red Cross Hospital in Momoya, Osaka. Although they experienced the atomic bomb in the same location, everyone had different symptoms. Kinue, too, died on September 18. Again I took her bones to the Koi temple.

I myself was in pain, my entire body swollen, and although I stayed at an acquaintance's house, I could not even sleep nights. When I could not sleep I thought of many things. How can it be that the great Hiroshima was destroyed, people and buildings, all by just one bomb? How can it be that the big city was buried under human bodies and corpses of horses and cows?

I did go to the hospital despite the pain, but I obtained no special medicine. Since some people had died in two or three days just from inhaling the gas, I felt anxious thinking that I would probably die, having been directly exposed to the bomb. Wishing somehow to get rid of the gas that was in my body, I went to a drug store to buy blister plasters and pasted them on the worst places to see what would happen. After a few days, juice the color of egg yolk started to come out, and after a week, yellow ooze sticky like honey kept coming out for about five days. Around then the swelling began to decrease little by little.

Around November 10, all the family members hospitalized in Osaka came back. The topic came up of going home for now and taking ginseng and Chinese medicine to get better, and our trip home was set.

I decided to consult my wife's younger brother who worked at Takehara Station. On a day of heavy rain, I arrived at the Isobe Hotel, where he was staying, around seven o'clock in the evening. While I was talking with my brother-in-law, two American military policemen came over. Since my brother-in-law was in charge of the warehouse of Takehara Station, they seemed to have come to investigate something about materials. They wore pistols on their waists. I felt a chill at heart, because I did not understand their language.

Soon an interpreter came. She was a young Japanese woman who had returned from Hawaii and was fluent in American English. After talking about this and that with my brother-in-law, one of the military policemen said, "My younger brother was killed by the Japanese army in Singapore. I had meant to kill Japanese to get revenge when I came to Japan, but when I actually came here, I realized that we are all the same human beings. We citizens are not enemies of one another. As a human being, I can no longer kill." He said, "From now on let's be friends," and shook hands with us. We drank and parted with smiles for each other.

Homeland and the Death of Parents

In mid-December we took a train from Koi Station to Shimonoseki. I cried in the train, thinking of my dead children and my health.

We arrived at Shimonoseki the following morning, but there was no Shimonoseki-Pusan ferry, so we had to wait more than ten days in the waiting room in the cold. We got on the ferry around the 27th and arrived at Pusan on the night of the 30th. We were able to exchange the money we had brought back from Japan at the bank at the pier in Pusan.

The Pusan we saw after eight years had completely changed: Japanese had disappeared and instead Americans overflowed. Through the introduction of an acquaintance I obtained a house at Tong Daesin-dong, where my parents, my wife and I, and my younger sister lived together to recover from our illnesses.

My father, who had back pains in addition to keloid scars, tried various Chinese drugs, but he did not easily recover. My mother had back pains and headaches, and she had a poor stomach, but she seemed to get better little by little. My wife's complexion was poor, perhaps because she had bled so much. After spending a few years getting treatment for the family, all the money we had brought from Japan went, and at last we had to sell our house. Despite the treatment, however, in 1948 my father died, complaining of excruciating pain.

Soon there was the June 25 disturbance in Korea.*

Since rumor had it around the time of the bombing that no plants would grow in Hiroshima for seventy-five years, I thought human beings would not of course have babies. But my wife had a baby again. I was worried and wished that the baby would not be crippled. Fortunately the child born was healthy. Having heard of those exposed to the bombing who had children who were not good, I had felt uneasy, though I kept it from my wife.

After returning, my wife complained about a pain in the right arm, but no cause was found even though she visited the hospital. Around 1949 she had an operation at the hospital because her right arm was swollen as if with a broken bone, though without pain. Many slivers of glass came out. After they were taken out, her pain seemed to have gone.

In 1958 my mother also died at sixty-three.

While in Japan, my family and I did our very best for the sake of Japan's war. For that reason, four children died, and those who survived are still unhealthy. Due to the atomic bomb we lost our life insurance and postal savings which we had kept in Japan, documents and all.

Didn't peace come to Japan and the world because we were hit by the atomic bomb? I would like Japanese people to ponder this well and tell the Japanese government on our behalf not to abandon Korean victims of the atomic bomb. It is the way of human beings for the Japanese government, no matter what happens, to treat us equally as Japanese people.

---

*The outbreak of the Korean War.

PICTURES BY ATOMIC BOMB SURVIVORS

The girl was bleeding, with many wounds on her chest. Walking barefooted, we avoided stepping on all the scattered fragments on the road. We were tottering, yet our minds were lucid as we headed single-mindedly for our homes where our families awaited us.

Past Matoba, I think it was around Akebono, Kojin-machi, there was a shrine on each side of the street, and the whole place was a sea of flames. Only the street was unburnt. There was no longer any other path. Our jackets, which we had dipped in water a while ago, were already completely dry, as if ready to catch fire.

There was no time to lose. I soaked my jacket with the water in a tank on the side of the road and ran desperately. I was hot; I was scared. Was this the end? Oh God. I prayed and prayed along the way. On finally reaching our destination and looking back, I was shocked anew by the horrible sight of this world. Dead bodies lay in shelters and under fallen trees. By the time I delivered the girl to her home in Nakayama, the summer night was all dark. [Michitsuji Yoshiko, age fifty-one]

白島町 縮景園の裏門に通りかかった
時一人の男の幼児が門にすがって泣いて
いた。声をかけてさわって見ると彼は
死んでいた。吾ガ子と思えば胸がつまる。

When I was walking by the back gate of Shukkei-en Garden, Hakushima-cho, I saw a young boy clinging to the gate, crying. I called to him, and touched him, and found him dead. To think that he might have been my own child—my heart ached.
[Name unknown]

August 7, around 8 a.m. on the road in front of the old Hiroshima Broadcasting Station.

Since I had gone to school in Ujina, I met the bombing separately from my parents. At 7 o'clock on August 7 I went from Ujina to Hijiyama, heading for the ruins of my house in Nobori-cho. I saw few people in the vast scorched field. For the first time I saw charred bodies, one on top of another, in the water tank by the side of the old broadcasting station. On the road forty or fifty meters from Shukkei-en Garden, I was shocked to see something unusual. I went close and realized that it was the corpse of one who looked like a woman, charred black with one foot off the ground in a running position, a baby clutched in her arms. Who on earth was this person? The cruel sight remains clear in my mind.
[Yamagata Yasuko, age forty-nine]

八月八日昼前焼跡に帰って来た時の様子
向ふ左一軒おいて私の家でした

Before noon on August 8, when I returned to the ruins. My house was the second from the left.

An old neighbor who was bed-ridden with palsy was unable to flee and was burnt to death. Only her belly remained unburnt, smoldering.

A woman couldn't find her older boy and fled with her younger child. The following day, removing roof tiles, she found the white bones of the boy under the house, face down.

The Kan'on Bridge fell in the middle. (upper)
Kan'on, Honmachi, August 8, 1945. (upper right)
Water tank: one with his face dipped in the water. (middle)
She was dead, leaning on the bridge. (right)
[Motooka Shigeko, age sixty-four]

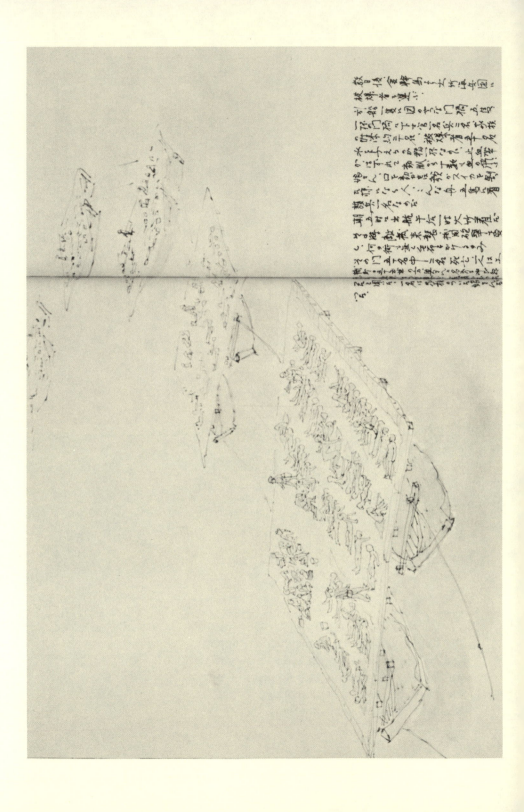

Several days later, we carried the injured from Kanawa Island to the Otake Marine Base.

A boat pulled five rafts like the ones in this painting. On each crowded raft were one noncommissioned officer, two soldiers, about twenty family members accompanying the injured, and fifty injured people. The best that could be done was to give them water. A girl spurted blood from an artery when her bandage came loose, and another person's face looked like a split watermelon when she moved her lips. There was only one medical orderly for every five boats.

The boats left at five in the morning to arrive at Otake at one in the afternoon. At that moment an enemy plane appeared and fired on us with machine guns. We could do nothing but put blankets over the injured.

Two out of the fifty on the rafts died. One was a man from Kami-Noboricho. He got up, calling his wife, walked several steps, then died. I learned later that his wife went to another unit and also died. The other victim was a girl with her family tending her.
[Hara Yoshimi, age fifty-eight]

August 9, coming down to the Enko River, a girl breathed her last, with no one to help her.
[Yamashita Masato, age fifty-two]

Pointing at heaven, a black charred boy, age four or five, on the bank of the West Parade Ground.
[Yamashita Masao, age fifty-two]

CHILDREN'S VOICES

CHILDREN'S VOICES

Tsujimoto Fujio (**5 at the time of bombing**)

When the atomic bomb fell, I was safe, being in the air raid shelter dug into a slope in a corner of the Yamazato Elementary School playground. I am afraid that grandmother, my friend Naoshi Tagawa, and I were the only ones spared among those who were at the school at that time.

If any survived, that must be just a few. For everybody is now dead. . . .

As the alarm sounded, old folks and children in Ueno-machi all escaped to the shelter as we were supposed to. Since there was a civilian guards headquarters and a first aid post at school, guards, doctors, and many other adults were there. School teachers were also at work there.

Since no airplanes came, the alarm was cancelled. Everyone went outside the shelter. Many children were loudly playing all over the playground.

Adults and teachers also came out to the playground to relax. The playground was full of people and noise.

I heard a sound.

Other children were making so much noise that they didn't seem to hear it.

Grabbing my grandmother's hand, I ran toward the shelter.

"Enemy plane," the watchguard on the school roof shouted, hitting the bell.

All the people on the playground rushed to the shelter.

I was the very first to run into the shelter, all the way to the back.

Already there had been a flash. And I was hurled against the wall by a strong wind.

. . . .

As I looked out after a while—all across the playground were human beings, as though blown over.

So many lay there that the dirt of the playgound could hardly be seen. Most were dead and immobile.

However, here and there some kicked their legs or raised their hands. Those who could move crawled into the shelter. So the shelter was full of injured people.

My big brother and little sisters, who had also been slow in running into the shelter, were crying with burns. Grandmother had taken out her rosary and was praying. I sat at the shelter entrance waiting for my mother and father.

As much as thirty minutes later, mother finally came. She was covered with blood.

She had been hit when she was preparing lunch at home. I cannot forget my joy when I clung to her.

Although we waited and waited, my father never appeared.

He had gone out in the morning to work as a civilian guard.

Those alive died in pain one by one. My little sisters died the day after.

As for mother, she, too, died the following day.

Then big brother died. I thought I would die, too. For everyone who slept side by side in the shelter was dying.

But grandmother and I survived, perhaps because we didn't get radiated as we were all the way back in the shelter.

Grandmother and I went around every day after that examining the faces of the dead. It was to look for father. But, whether alive or burnt to death, father was nowhere to be found.

Those who survived collected wood in the playground and burned many corpses there.

My big brother was also burnt. Mother too became bones before my eyes, and fell crumbling between the embers. I gazed at this, crying.

Grandmother watched it saying the rosary prayers.

If you go to heaven, you can see your mother, grandmother says. Grandmother is already old, so maybe she can go to heaven soon, but since I'm still a child, it'll be tens of years before I can see my gentle mother, play with my big brother, or talk with my lovely sisters.

I entered Yamazato Elementary School. I'm a fourth grader now. The playgound is all cleared, and many friends are happily at play. Those friends don't know that many children died and were burnt here.

I, too, cheerfully play, running around the playground when I'm with my friends. But sometimes I remember that day.

And, crouching where mother was burnt, I touch the dirt with my fingers.

When I poke deeply with a bamboo stick, pieces of black coal come out. When I stare at the spot, mother's face dimly appears in the earth.

When I see other children walk on that place, stepping with their feet, I get mad.

Each time I go out to the playground, I remember that day. The playground is sweet. And it is sad.

I will attend this school four or five more years.
I wonder if I will feel like this every day during that time.

Grandmother and I held a funeral for my mother, big brother, and little sisters, and buried their bones under the tomb. But, although father's cross stands there, his bones are not underneath.

Father, father, where are your bones?

Where are you sleeping, father? You left that morning in good health.

Grandmother and I now live alone in a shack we built on the ruins of our house. Although she is over sixty, she goes to hunt for baby clams in the lower reaches of the Urakami River, because we can't eat unless she works. In the evening she comes home soaking wet.

By selling those baby clams, we two are living.

In the old days, we had a store. We sold soy sauce, salt, soy bean paste, sweets, and even toys. Moreover, father was a master of well digging and made good money. We dressed well.

I want us to be back in the old days once again. I want my mother, I want my father, I want my big brother, and I want my little sisters.

If everyone were alive, we'd be able to live in a house where the rain doesn't leak in. Grandmother wouldn't have to work so hard, and I could study more happily.

I wouldn't have to lose in fights with other children. Grandmother goes to the cathedral to attend mass every morning. She also recites the prayer of the rosary. Then she says to me, "Everything is God's providence. It's all right, it's all right."

I wish I could have her clean heart.

Nagai Kayano (5 at the time of bombing)

My brother and I were in the mountain house in Koba. My mother came from Nagasaki with clothes.

"Mom, did you bring Kaya-chan's, too?" I asked right away. My mother said, "Yes, I brought lots of Kaya-chan's clothes, too," and stroked my head.

This was the last time that she stroked me.

My mother said, "When there's no air raid next, come down to Nagasaki again, okay?" And she left right away in a great hurry.

After the bomb had fallen, it was my father who came to the mountain house in Koba. Father's ears and head were wrapped in bandages.

After father's wounds had healed, we went down to Nagasaki, all of us together.

My house had been a big one, and my mother had been there . . . but when we came back, nothing was left but ashes.

We built a house of zinc sheets on the ruins. Later we put in two glass panes to make it brighter. We slept there, but it was tight, and what was troublesome was that my brother's legs kicked me.

Though the house was built, mother didn't come no matter how long we waited.

Now father is always in bed. His hands can move, but his body can't move. When he goes out, he is put on a stretcher.

I wish father could walk soon.

Then, I'd like to go to the mountains holding hands with him, and draw pictures.

Kawasaki Sakue **(11 at the time of bombing)**

As a lot of bombs fell on Uragami on August 1, we all hid in the big air raid shelter in Aburagi Valley. Since there were air raids every day after that, we just stayed there. On the 8th we went home for the first time. And everyone in the family ate together. It was really after a long time that the whole family gathered.

My mother said, "It's hard to tell when we can be together again, so tonight let's have a regular Neighborhood Unit meeting."

The meeting was held at our place. My mother said to neighbors, "When we die, let's die together holding hands."

Everybody laughed aloud together. My mother, too, laughed cheerfully.

The following day—

Somehow we didn't feel much like leaving mother. Although the air raid alarm sounded, we kept on playing inside instead of running to the shelter. My mother said over and over, "I feel as though it may be dangerous today, so take shelter quick."

Still we dilly-dallied. Finally my mother pressed our lunch to us and made us go to the shelter, as though chasing us out. My mother alone remained in the house and worked busily, pumping water and taking off rain doors to prepare for air raids.

We were playing in the big shelter which all the people in town had dug together at the foot of the mountain.

It flashed—I remember that, if nothing else. Did I lose my senses when I was blown over by the wind from the explosion? When I came to, people were squeezed tightly in the big shelter. Where on earth had this many people come from? I could hardly tell how many hundreds were there. Moreover, through the entrance of the shelter more people continued to enter. Swollen like pumpkins, they tottered in, crying and shouting. Most people were naked, stripped of their clothes.

More and more squeezed in, and soon I couldn't even move. Even so, feeling paralyzed from staying still too long, I tried to move a little. Each time I did, people near me screamed in pain. They all had bad burns and injuries.

What kind of big air raid had happened? It must have been something unusual, I thought. No matter whom I asked, the only answer I got back was "totaled," and no one knew the truth.

Parents' voices calling their children, children's crying voices wanting their parents—many voices crossed one another in disorder, hit against the mud walls and echoed back, merely sounding wharr wharr wharr like groaning.

I started to worry about my mother. Was my father safe? And my big brother?

Although time passed, none of my family appeared at the entrance to the shelter. I was too terrified to go out. The noise of an airplane, probably flying low, was constantly heard.

The air in the shelter gradually grew foul. I thought I was going to choke. I started to feel sick.

About five o'clock my father came, looking healthy. We were so very, very happy that we cried aloud together.

Immediately my father held me up and took me out of the shelter, slipping between and straddling over many people. How good the outside air tasted!

I came to know the air for the first time then.

I suddenly pepped up. And I started to care for the injured. Care—well, since I didn't know what to do, I asked them, "What would you like?'' Everyone equally answered, ''Water!'' I searched around in the neighborhood, but clear water was nowhere to be found. Although there was a little pool of water in front of the shelter, that water was muddy and I couldn't let the injured drink it. As I remained at a loss, an injured person crawled out of the shelter, and I am sure he badly, badly craved water, for he put his mouth to the water by himself and gulped the muddy water as if it tasted good. Then, satisfied, he tried to crawl away, but before one minute passed, he dropped to the ground and no longer moved. When I went near him, he was already dead.

One by one, injured crawled out, drank from this muddy water, and, soon after finishing drinking, died without exception. Seeing this, I sank in a thought:

''How poor human beings are. They die from a single mouthful of water.''

A woman came to look for her child. She called the child's name in a loud voice, but no answer came from anywhere. The woman went around taking a look one by one at those who died after drinking water. Suddenly she clung to one. This was the child she was looking for. The mother lifted up the boy's corpse, called his name loudly with her mouth pressed to his ear, beat his chest, patted his fingers, trying everything she could. Gradually she seemed to go insane.

The mother resembled my mother in age and appearance. The boy, her child, looked very much like my big brother. I thought of my mother and big brother. Neither had come back. My big sister didn't show up either.

Suddenly, the mother let go of the body of her child and stood. She ran to those who were caring for the injured and grabbed both hands of one of them.

''Why didn't you save my child?'' the poor mother cried hysterically.

I almost thought that the mother might now pummel and kill me.

A student came reeling, supporting himself on someone else's shoulder. On looking carefully, it was my big brother who was in medical school. We ran to meet him. He was breathing with difficulty.

On the way back to the shelter supporting my brother, as we approached the side-hole, we saw a young man lying there. It was a neighbor. Glancing at him, I was shocked. His belly was torn open, and the intestines had come out. Perhaps hearing our footsteps, he shouted in a loud voice, ''Bring something . . . can't you see what pain I'm in? . . . do something! . . . kill me! . . . come on . . . bring me something sharp! . . . oh what pain! . . . come o-on . . . who? . . . who's there? . . . come o-on. . . .''

He was no longer conscious. Before our eyes, he dropped dead. I was so terrified that I went this way and that in a fluster. My body shakes even now when I recall this.

That night we spent looking after my brother, quite beside ourselves. Since a lady from the same neighborhood unit was alone with massive injuries, we also cared for her. Since my mother never appeared after all our waiting, I cared for this lady with all my heart, pretending that she was my mother. However, this lady breathed her last before dawn. I started to worry seriously about my mother now.

Since there was no doctor there, when the day dawned we took my badly injured brother to the university hospital. Of the two remaining smoke stacks of the hospital, one was bent in the middle. Under it a temporary first aid post was open, professors and nurses of the university who had survived busily working. If my brother had been healthy, he would have been helping them.

A doctor gave my brother many shots. Watching this, I was very happy. I felt certain that he would get better.

But after all it was no good. On the fourth evening he called me and said in a faint voice, ''Goodbye. We must part. Sakue, carry on with my dream. Study hard, and achieve what I was always saying I would do.''

He seemed to speak more, but I only saw his lips move and heard no words. Then he died.

What he was always saying was this: ''I will study hard, become a worthy person, become a fine doctor, and let the world know my name.''

These words now became my duty. In my head these words are always alive.

After that we returned to our old home again. The house was crushed, half burnt. Sitting in front of it, we waited for our mother to appear. Feeling that she might turn up unexpectedly, we waited vacantly, unable to work at all.

Many, many people passed before us, looking for corpses.

In time, we started to feel that my mother and big sister might have been under the house. So we decided to dig under the crushed house. We dug and dug but we couldn't find them. Even then, we kept on digging as though drawn by something.

After digging all day, finally we came across something black. Encouraged, we dug on, and as expected we found it to be a corpse. Was it my mother? My sister? Or a stranger? We dug around it to expose the entire body. The body was burnt black. Now we were to unearth the head.

The head—strangely, it was whole, unburnt. It was my sister.

It was my sister who I had wanted to see so badly every day. Imagine my joy when I saw her face . . . I smiled despite myself.

Then, I suddenly became sad and cried.

Now it was just my mother. The following day, and the day after, we patiently looked around for her. Maybe it was due to our efforts, or maybe my mother's soul pulled us: finally her corpse was found at a close neighbor's place. She was dead, facing the lady of the house. Probably they were talking about something.

Surrounding my mother's body, we cried and at once felt relieved.

However, since we did not know what to do with the bodies, we just left them as they were. There was not even one green leaf as far as we could see, let alone flowers for offerings.

There were many chores to which we survivors had to attend. We could not afford to stay with my mother and sister.

After a week, everybody started to incinerate corpses. It seemed that rigid rules had already disappeared. Survivors burnt close relatives one by one. Unidentified bodies were piled together and burned.

On the burnt fields of Urakami, which now were in clear view, flames burning people were red here and there.

My mother burnt red.

My sister, too, burnt red.

And they became a few bones.

Picking up those bones, we put them in the fireplace. Since this was such poor treatment, I was afraid that my mother and sister might resent us.

Since this ended it, it was decided that we would retire to the country. When preparing for the move, from somewhere, we don't know where, a girl of about three appeared in front of us, and seeing me, she said "big sister" and clung to me.

Surprised, I looked at her, but I didn't recognize her at all. I asked her name, but she didn't answer. We had no idea whose child she was.

"I'm not your big sister," I said again and again, but she said, "Yes, big sister, my big sister," and just clung to me, smiling.

I was sure that this child survived alone, and that she had a big sister who looked like me. She was a really lovely girl. We decided to raise her until some relative appeared. The girl became used to us right away. Lonesome as we were, having lost three members of the family, we started to laugh again, welcoming her as a new family member. Induced to laugh by the lovely little child, we summoned new courage and worked busily preparing to leave Nagasaki.

After three days, when we were just about to leave, the girl disappeared. All of us searched in separate directions, but we could not find the lovely girl.

We left for the country, giving up our search. What on earth was that little angel girl?

Sakaki Chizuyo (4 at the time of bombing)

As the air raid alarm went, everyone went into the shelter. We took the rice still in the pot in which it had been cooked. Since the alarm was canceled, we ate together in the shelter. Grandma, father, mother, big sister, little brother Kah-boh, and I were all there.

Dad said, "Shall we go out and see?"

So we went out. The sky was all blue.

Mom said, "I'm going home and see. I'll be right back."

Dad and mom went home.

After that, someone came running screaming, "A bomb's falling—!"

Grandma and we three children were so surprised that we ran into the shelter and stayed still, pressing ourselves to the wall all the way in back.

After a long while, when we went outside, still scared, every house, every one of them, was flat.

Then dad and mom came running hard.

We ate the rice from the pot. Since we had to leave some for tomorrow, we ate one bowl each. We slept just like that in the shelter.

The following day, dad and mom went to Koba and built a hut. We moved into this hut.

Soon after that, dad and mom started to have pains. And, very much in pain, they died of atomic disease.

So, grandma went to the rice refining place. Big sister was taken to a relative's house. Kah-boh was taken to a Tomachi family.

I was taken to Aunt Yaeko's.

Aunt Yaeko married. She took me with her to this house we live in now. And Yamazaki Chizuyo, I am told, changed to Sakaki Chizuyo, which is now my name.

At the Sakaki's there is a big sister who goes to a girls' school. When I'm bad, she scolds me, "Chizuyo!"

Usually, she is nice and calls me "Chizu-chan."

My dad now is also a kind dad.

By now, I call Aunt Yaeko "mom." Mom sometimes scolds me out of respect for dad and big sister.

When I'm sad, I think of my old mom.

Kataoka Yasuo (10 at the time of bombing)

That day I was babysitting since the morning.

The air raid alarm was canceled, so I took the baby to mother for nursing. Mother was working in the field. Even while the baby was nursing, I was restless because I thought an air raid might come again at any moment.

When the baby had as much milk as he wanted, I went home with him. Then I sat at home, but I couldn't keep my mind off air raids, and I could settle neither on babysitting, study, nor play.

So I held my baby brother and sat on the verandah where we could see mother in the field.—At that moment, a white light pierced my eyes.

Still holding my little brother, without thinking I went flat on my tummy. Something like dust filled the whole place, choking us. Finally, I could no longer breathe.

When I came to, the baby I thought I still held was not there any more. Frantic, I tried to look for him. However, my body did not move. I writhed with all my might, but still I could not move. And it was all dark around me.

Before I knew it, I was voicing a prayer over and over again: "Oh merciful Lord, deliver us."

. . . .

When I opened my eyes unthinkingly, I saw a long, narrow white thing before my eyes. When I stared at it, it was something like a cloud. After I thought about it for a while, I realized that it was the outside light peeking through pillars of the crushed house.—I was under the house.

Now with a really desperate effort, I tried to move my body, mustering all my strength. This time I was able to pull my hands and legs through big pieces of wood, and I could move my body. I tried hard to get out, aiming toward the long strip of sky between pillars. And I just barely managed to climb out. At the same time my big sister also crawled out. The baby had been blown off.

Although I thought only our house had been hit, as I looked around, every house was totally shattered. What kind of big bomb fell, and where, I wondered and wondered. Terrified, I ran into the shelter in the mountain, holding the baby. There were two people who had bad burns. When I found them to be mother and little brother, I was startled. It was really strange that people in the field could have burns.

I ran to my mother right away and clung to her.

"Cheer up, cheer up," I said, but at heart I worried and worried that mother might die soon. So, I prayed to the Lord with all my heart.

Mother said to my little brother, who was in pain by her side, "Pray to the Lord. Ask Virgin Mary to pray for you."

Without resisting, my little brother started to recite "Ave Maria." Hearing his voice of prayer under his painful breath, I couldn't believe that the little brother whom I had played with until this morning was really going to die, and I was so sad that I wanted to tear my heart. Mother, too, looked in pain, reciting a prayer.

Father, whom we had waited and waited for, finally showed up in the late afternoon, looking unhurt. I was so happy that my nerves relaxed despite myself.

My brother continued to pray "Ave Maria" all this while, but after dark he suddenly became silent. Feeling him with my hand, I knew that he died then.

Since then there has been no day that I don't think of my little brother.

Mother, who I thought might die, survived. However, her scars from the burns are stiff, so she is restricted. Even so, she cheers herself up and works in the field every day. Thanks to that I can go to school.

Mother has big keloid scars from the burns. But I don't think them ugly.

Sakamoto Suguru (5 at the time of bombing)

My house was on the mountain in back of the cathedral.

At that time mother was working in the paddies down below. Big sister and I were inside.—The engine noise of the airplane was heard.

Flash, it went. Boom, a big sound was heard, and the house crashed.

I was under a pillar. I rose by myself and came out.

Big sister was under a wall. She, too, rose by herself and came out.

Both of us went to the shelter.

Mother had come up from the paddies to the foot of the shelter.

She was sleeping there silently. Her hair was burning.

Three strangers came and carried my mother sleeping into the shelter.

Since there was dirt on her face, I washed it with water.

After that, big sister and I went inside and sat beside our mother.

Then a stranger put his hand on mother and said to my big sister, "This person's dead."

Then he brought a straw mat, wrapped mother in it, dug the earth in front of the trench, and buried her.

I always go there with my sister to weed.

While weeding, I think of mother who is sleeping underneath.

Mine Noriko (6 at the time of bombing)

Mother took me to the shelter and said, "Airplanes'll come, so don't go out, stay still—"

Putting her basket on her shoulders, she went to get grass for the goats.

Inside the shelter were also strangers. Since the flame of the lamp mother had lighted was small, I tried to pull the wick to make the flame bigger—at that moment, flash! it went in front of my eyes.

I thought the lamp had fallen. But the lamp had not fallen. Boom, boom. . . .

Scared, a cry broke out of my mouth.

Inside the trench it shook, and dirt fell here and there. I shouted, "A bomb. . . ."

In a while, many people came into the shelter.

I was really worried because mother didn't come. I looked at the faces of people coming in one by one, but still mother didn't come.

Those who came in were all pale, their hair in disarray and blood streaming from their heads, hands, and faces. They talked fast, stammeringly, "Wh—what . . . was that? . . ."

"Overwhelming, indeed. . . ."

"It dropped behind my house I'm sure."

"No, I'm sure on the armory."

"How many did they drop? . . ."

"Quite a lot, I'd say."

Since an adult mentioned the armory, for the first time I remembered my big brother. My big brother had not returned since he had gone to the factory yesterday.

Thinking that my big brother might die, I couldn't help going thump, thump, feeling scared.

Then mother came running, panting.

There was dirt on her face. When it flashed, she jumped into the potato field, she told us. Still grasping the cord of the empty basket, she repeated many times, "Noriko, Noriko, how did you do? . . . How did you do?"

Big brother who worked at the armory came back after about an hour, with a wound in the side of his belly. Blood was streaming down his clothes.

I followed mother to see our house. We found that our house and our neighbors' houses had all burned down.

When we went to the storehouse, we found that a lot of rice, wheat, and potatoes were burnt.

Mother and I wrapped as many burnt potatoes as her kimono could hold.

I thought that our goats must have died, but they were bleating as usual.

I gave grass to the goats. And we went back to the shelter and gave burnt potatoes to the neighbors.

Everyone was glad, thanked mother, and ate them with pleasure, skin and all.

REIKO

Shoda Shinoe

1 Reiko's mother died instantly by the atomic bomb together with two little children who were Reiko's younger brothers.

After finishing the funeral of the three, Reiko's father became ill with the atomic bomb disease and died in the house where the author of this story was taking shelter.

It was late August of 1945. Before taking his last breath, Reiko's father repeated, ''Reiko's on my mind, Reiko's on my mind.''

''I know Reiko is on your mind, but please don't worry. I'll think of her as much as possible, and do as much as possible for her,'' I said.

''Please be good to her,'' he said, and passed away.

Since I was unhealthy myself and also poor, days went by even though I often recalled this and thought of Reiko.

One of her relatives was rich, and since she seemed to be staying at his house I refrained from visiting and inquiring.

One day in 1952, however, Reiko came to see me, looking lost and lonely.

''How have you been, Reiko? How are you doing now?'' I asked.

''I don't know where to live and what to do now, and I feel torn,'' she said.

''What do you want to do most?'' I asked Reiko.

''I want to get a job somewhere and live on my own,'' she said.

"Then let's try to find a job," I said.

I handed Reiko's resumé to someone kind and asked him to find her a job.

In a month or so, Reiko's job was set.

She went to work from my house, while helping me with the housework in the morning and at night. I wished so much that she would stay, but my family then ran a hotel and the environment was poor.

Thinking of what place would suit her best, I finally decided that she should stay at the home of her remote relative who was a salary man.

2 Reiko worked at a middle school, first helping in the office, and after a while as the head of the student store. She was so busy that she rarely visited me.

One day Reiko's relative with whom she was staying came over.

"Is Reiko well? I am so concerned about her," I said.

"Reiko's so perverse that she's scary and I don't like her," she said.

"How perverse?" I asked.

She said that Reiko had muttered: "I wish they'd drop another bomb so that everyone surviving now would lose both parents as I did, get terrible keloid scars, and be as poor as I am."

"So is that why you say Reiko is scary and perverse?" I asked.

"Not only that," she said, and complained about this and that.

She raised her voice and said, "As the saying goes, 'Stay away from problems, you get no troubles.' I can't take care of a girl like Reiko."

I said nothing, but/deep down I thought, "I hope I can kindly care for those who are cared for by no one in the world."

3 Four years passed.

I had heard from no particular source that Reiko had moved into the quiet house of a widow who lived alone and, while working hard at her job, was also learning flower arrangement and tea ceremony from this landlady.

One day Reiko came to see me. "I feel like marrying a kind

person. Please arrange something for me," she mumbled.

The moment I heard her words I thought of a young man.

His parents, too, died instantly by the atomic bomb, and his three big brothers had gone to the front. Wondering about how he was doing, I visited his older sister's house.

After going this way and that many times, I was finally able to arrange a meeting between Reiko and the young man.

Both were working, so they came over to my house after work.

It was a moonlit night. The river below the verandah where they sat was glittering.

Having known well both Reiko's parents and the young man's parents, I could not refrain from praying that the two would be able to be blessed with true happiness.

They found each other agreeable. However, Reiko's rich relative was opposed.

The reason was that the young man's salary was small.

I heard through a third person that they blamed me for having introduced them to each other.

I said to Reiko, "Your rich relative who's opposed feels that way because she loves you, so you shouldn't be angry."

After a long period of tangles, Reiko finally said, "If we can't make a living, so what; we'll die together."

It was as if those opposed were defeated by Reiko, who was burning with eager love, and the wedding was set.

It was decided that the ceremony should take place at my house.

4 The rich relative, too, came to Reiko's wedding. For the party afterward, all the relatives gathered and kindly looked after Reiko and her things.

One day after a while, I met the person who had found Reiko's job.

"How has Reiko been?" I asked.

"Reiko has become alive and pretty, eyes shining. I am really glad for her," he said and added, "Heartfelt congratulations!" Hearing this, tears of joy filled my eyes.

It was August 1960.

The Sixth International Rally to Ban Atomic and Hydrogen

Bombs was held in Hiroshima.

Heading for Hiroshima, multitudes joined in a great march of 6,400 kilometers in total.

This was an expression of mankind's dream for peace.

I asked Reiko, who visited me after a long time, "Did you go to the Peace Rally?"

"No, I don't go to such a thing. I hate that kind of fuss. On such an occasion I want to slip quietly out of Hiroshima, go into the mountains, and cry to my heart's content," she muttered. Then, lowering her voice, she whispered, "Though I didn't attend the Peace Rally, I made sushi and took it to the memorial tower after dark. The two of us ate the sushi on the lawn of the Peace Square, then came home."

5 Eight years elapsed after Reiko married. It is a long, long time, but to us who are poor and busy, it is a short time.

To me Reiko's wedding feels like just a little while ago.

One day Reiko came to see me.

I muttered, "You have no kids. Are you trying not to have any?"

"Even though both of us work, making a living is quite tough, and besides we hear that bomb victims give birth to cripples. So we are not having kids," Reiko whispered in a small voice.

One day after this, Reiko's husband came by motorbike.

"How is Reiko? I've been thinking of her," I said.

"She is working hard. But every day on coming home, she complains about her work for at least one hour. It's her character. I think it my discipline to listen to her," he muttered.

I felt grateful from the bottom of my heart to Reiko's husband for being patient, thinking it his discipline.

"Please care for her," I said, feeling like bowing my head sincerely toward him.

6 Reiko has a good sense of color.

Today, too, she wore a dress with a youthful, quiet design, though with subdued dignity, and carried a handbag containing a half-finished lace doily so as not to waste time. Moving her hand to tat, she said, "We are finally settled, so to speak. Now we can live on my husband's salary alone. So, I think I will quit my job. I feel like having a baby. We said to each other that we will raise the baby with love even if we have a cripple." Tears filled my eyes.

After that Reiko did not show up. Worried, I went to visit her.

She told me that she had worked until a convenient time for the employer and quit after her successor had become familiar with the job.

Right now she was going to the hospital every day with a bad case of morning sickness.

Their one-room apartment was kept neat, and lace work beautifully decorated the tops of the radio and mirror stand.

I put in a vase the pink, white, and cream tulips, the best of the tulips I grew.

"We wanted a chest of drawers, so we had chest-of-drawers savings, but they all went into my hospital fees," Reiko muttered.

"Let's start the chest-of-drawers savings all over again when you are better. Let this be the first installment." I gave her a small amount of money, and we smiled at each other.

Reiko and I went to the hospital together.

I met her doctor.

The doctor said, "She should stay in the hospital and take precautions until her morning sickness is under control."

Reiko was admitted to the hospital. After much suffering, she finally gave birth to a girl baby, as I learned by a phone call.

The person who called was her rich relative.

7 Through the glass door of the hospital I stared at the premature baby in the incubator. Then I approached Reiko's bed. She had experienced a difficult birth.

"What bliss," I whispered.

"For the first time after birth I had a chance to know others' compassion. My baby would have died had they not pitied us. So, I thought and thought about her birth as a grace and decided to name her Megumi (Grace)," Reiko muttered thoughtfully.

"I'm really glad, Reiko," I said, feeling hot behind my eyelids.

Sometime later I went to see Reiko, who had been released from the hospital.

It was a cold February day. The room was kept warm with steam heat.

In a little, lovely bed was a pretty comforter covered with a snow white sheet, and near Megumi's pillow was a thermometer for checking the room temperature.

Clean diapers, sunned and looking as if still retaining the sun's smell, had been brought in, a heap of several dozen filling the room.

Folding the diapers, Reiko enjoyed telling me about childcare.

Meticulously clean, Reiko sterilized everything before storing it. She was so thorough that it was as if nothing more could be expected in the human world.

If Megumi cried a little so that she turned red around the corners of the eyes, it called for a visit to the doctor's.

"I'm so busy," Reiko smiled.

8 In August 1962, NHK reporters visited me.

"We are in charge of the program 'Profiles of Japan,'" they said. "Are there any cheerful topics about people who are now happy after post-atomic bomb struggles?"

Sympathizing with the reporters who had come all the way from Tokyo with a camera, I happened to think of Reiko.

I recalled that some time ago Reiko had quietly said, "If I had not met the atomic bomb, still had both parents, lived in wealth without any inconveniences, had no keloid marks like these, and had been a beautiful girl, I wouldn't have been able to experience the happiness of the truthful human heart as I do now."

Thinking of introducing Reiko to them, I got in the NHK car with the three people, and the four of us visited Reiko's place.

Reiko then rented the upstairs room of the house of her husband's older brother and his wife. Having the three people wait in the yard where clean snow-white diapers were drying dancing in the wind, I went up to her room and explained the reason for our visit.

Reiko was resolute, unlike her usual self.

"I am really sorry on your account, but I decline. I will never see them. I had a really bad experience in being written up in the newspaper. Please decline for me," she said firmly.

Lowering my head repeatedly, I apologized to the NHK people: "I am sorry. She seems to have had a very bad experience before and will not consent," I said and asked them to leave.

9 I told my younger brother, who works at the University of Kyushu, about the resolute Reiko.

"Reiko's great. You're dumb. You meet reporters and chat and chat, so you get written up. From now on, always behave like Reiko," he said.

I sobbed. My younger brother always scolds me and makes me cry. Each time I cry I feel miserable.

I want kindhearted people. Those who live comfortably dream of peace, engage in movements, and say "Long live the future." But I only wish to think of the feelings in the depths of the heart of Reiko and others.

I could not refrain from thinking about what I could do to help erase her thought when she says "I wish they dropped another atomic bomb, so that everyone surviving will lose both parents as I did. . . ."

Those sad and disheartened with the same struggle and agony as Reiko's can be found everywhere in Hiroshima, no, everywhere in Japan.

World peace is born out of each family's peace, and family peace sprouts from the peace in each individual's heart, I think.

10 Reiko came to see me with her only child, Megumi, when I was ill. It was a cold day in January 1964.

I learned that Megumi was now three. She was growing steadily and looked tall and intelligent.

Megumi wore lovely clothing: white dotted slacks and a dark grey jacket with small, genteel embroidery.

Her somewhat brownish hair was light and glossy. Her face was small, but her head looked big.

Reiko was plump, almost bursting. She was full of smiles, looking very happy, as if unable to contain her love for Megumi.

"How is your health, Reiko?" I could not refrain from asking.

"When I overdo it, I become short of breath, as might be expected. I get freckles, too. Isn't that awful?" said Reiko, smiling.

"Megumi may become an only child," I said.

"Yes, when I think of how painful it was, my hair almost stands on end. If I have another child, I'll die," Reiko laughed.

"You're the only mother of Megumi. Please take good care of yourself so you'll live long. I hear that the Buddha said that having no parents is the worst poverty, and I think it's really so," I said.

"It is," Reiko nodded deeply, her eyes moistening.

"For Megumi, who has no siblings, cousins are the closest. So provide opportunities for her to see her cousins and let them learn to be good to each other and care for each other. Human beings are really lonely," I said.

"Indeed, I have also been thinking the same way lately," Reiko said.

"Every day my husband rides around on his motorbike on the job. So I am really worried that he might be in a traffic accident. On Sunday when he took Megumi to the Tenmaya Department Store to have fun, I was so worried that I thought I would try calling Tenmaya to find out if they had gotten there safely, and I went to the greengrocer's shop. But I thought about it and realized how embarrassing it was, so I didn't call. I tend to be a little hysterical," Reiko smiled.

11 Reiko, who had lived in the misery caused by the atomic bomb, came to know joy through her husband's love.

Watched by the kindness of human beings, she gave birth to Megumi, experienced maternal love, and felt the precious value of life. Praying that no accident would befall her husband and that Megumi would not get hurt, she is doing her best in housework and childraising.

Now Reiko would not say "I wish that they would drop another atomic bomb so that everyone would lose both parents as I did. . . ." However, the paper, radio, and television are full of ominous news.

''Reiko, nothing is dependable,'' I thought deep down in my heart.

Silently watching with tearful eyes the pity and sadness of human beings who make great efforts depending on what is undependable, I whispered alone as in a prayer:

''Reiko, please become aware that you are protected by what is invisible to human eyes, by what is not human. And plant that feeling deep inside lovely Megumi, too.''

BIBLIOGRAPHY OF ATOMIC BOMB LITERATURE

Novels

Agawa Hiroyuki. *The Devil's Heritage*. Translated by John Maki. Tokyo: Hoku-
seido, 1957.

Chinook, Frank. *Nagasaki: The Forgotten Bomb*. New York: New American
Library, 1969.

Hersey, John. *Hiroshima*. New York: Knopf, 1964. (1985 edition adds a final
chapter written forty years after the bomb.)

Ibuse Masuji. *Black Rain*. Translated by John Bester. Tokyo: Kodansha International, 1966.

Stroup, Dorothy. *In the Autumn Wind*. New York: Charles Scribner's Sons, 1987.

Short Stories and Collections

Ariyoshi Sawako. "Prayer." *Japan Quarterly* 7, 4 (1960).

Hayashi Kyoko. "Ritual of Death." Translated by Kyoko Selden. *Japan Interpreter* (Winter 1978).

Minear, Richard, ed. and trans. *Hiroshima: Three Witnesses*. Princeton: Princeton
University Press, forthcoming 1989.

Oe Kenzaburo, ed. *The Crazy Iris and Other Stories of the Atomic Aftermath*. New
York: Grove Press, 1985. (Includes Ibuse Masuji, "The Crazy Iris"; Hara
Tamiki, "Summer Flower" and "The Land of Heart's Desire"; Oda Katsuzo,
"Human Ashes"; Ota Yoko, "Fireflies"; Sata Ineko, "The Colorless
Paintings"; Hayashi Kyoko, "The Empty Can"; Inoue Mitsuharu, "The
House of Hands"; and Takenishi Hiroko, "The Rite.")

Saeki Shoichi, ed. *The Catch and Other War Stories*. Tokyo: Kodansha International, 1981. (Includes Oe Kenzaburo, "The Catch"; Umezaki Haruo, "Sakura-
jima"; Hara, Tamiki, "Summer Flower"; and Hayashi Fumiko, "Bones.")

Memoirs

Akizuki, Tatsuichiro. *Nagasaki 1945. The First Full-length Eyewitness Account of the Atomic Bomb Attack on Nagasaki*. Translated by Nagata Keiichi. Edited by Gordon Honeycombe. London: Quartet Books, 1981.

Barker, Rodney. *The Hiroshima Maidens*. New York: Penguin, 1985.

Chujo Kazuo. *Nuclear Holocaust: A Personal Account*. Translated by Asahi Evening News. Tokyo: Asahi Shimbun, 1983.

A Citizens' Group to Convey Testimonies of Hiroshima and Nagasaki. *Give Me Water. Testimonies of Hiroshima and Nagasaki*. Tokyo, 1973.

Coerr, Eleanor. *Sadako and the Thousand Paper Cranes*. New York: Avon, 1971.

English Department, Hiroshima Jogakuin High School, ed. *Summer Cloud, A-Bomb Experience of a Girls' School in Hiroshima*. Tokyo: Sanyusha, n.d.

Hachiya Michihiko. *Hiroshima Diary: The Journal of a Japanese Physician, August 6–September 30, 1945*. Translated and edited by Warner Wells. Chapel Hill: University of North Carolina, 1955.

Hibakusha. Survivors of Hiroshima and Nagasaki. Translated by Gaynor Sekimori. Tokyo: Kosei, 1986.

McCormack, Gavan, ed. *Twice Victims: Koreans at Hiroshima*. Translated by Ok Su Kang. Tokyo: Korean Peace Committee in Japan, n.d.

Nagai Takashi. *The Bells of Nagasaki*. Translated by William Johnston. Tokyo: Kodansha International, 1984.

————. *We of Nagasaki: The Story of Survivors in an Atomic Wasteland*. Translated by Ichiro Shirato and Herbert Silverman. New York: Duell, Sloan and Pearce, 1951.

Oe Kenzaburo. *Hiroshima Notes*. Edited by David Swain. Translated by Toshi Yonezawa. Tokyo: YMCA Press, 1981.

Osada Arata, ed. *Children of the A-Bomb: The Testament of the Boys and Girls of Hiroshima*. Translated by Jean Dan and Ruth Sieben-Morgen. New York: G. P. Putnam's Sons, 1963. (Harper & Row paperback, 1982.)

Shiotsuki Masao. *Doctor at Nagasaki*. Tokyo: Kosei, 1987.

Testimonies of the Atomic Bomb Survivors. City of Nagasaki, 1985.

Trumball, Robert. *Nine Who Survived Hiroshima and Nagasaki*. New York: Dutton, 1957.

Poems

Kurihara Sadako. "Four Poems." Translated by Richard Minear. *Bulletin of Concerned Asian Scholars* 21, 1 (1989).

Toge Sankichi. *Hiroshima Poems*. Translated by R. Jackman, D. Logan, and Shioda Tsutomu. Tokyo: Sanyusha, 1981.

Plays

Goodman, David, ed. and trans. *After Apocalypse: Four Japanese Plays of Hiroshima and Nagasaki*. New York: Columbia University Press, 1985.

Children's Stories and Comic Books

Association of Hibakusha Teachers. *In the Sky Over Nagasaki: An A-Bomb Reader for Children*. Wilmington, Ohio: Wilmington College Peace Resource Center, 1977.

Kinoshita Renzo and Sayako. *Pikadon*.

Nakazawa Keiji. *Barefoot Gen: A Cartoon Story of Hiroshima*. 2 vols. Santa Cruz, Calif.: New Society Publishers, 1985, 1988.

Nasu Masamoto. *Children of the Paper Crane. The Story of Sadako Sasaki, Her Classmates, and Their Struggle with the A-bomb Disease*. Translated by Transnet. Armonk N.Y.: M. E. Sharpe, forthcoming.

Maruki Toshi. *Hiroshima no Pika*. New York: Lothrop, Lee and Shepard, 1980.

Art, Photography, and Film

Dower, John, and John Junkerman, eds. *The Hiroshima Murals: The Art of Iri Maruki and Toshi Maruki*. New York: Kodansha International, 1985.

————. *Hellfire: A Journey from Hiroshima*. A film on the Hiroshima Murals. 16 mm. and video. Distributed by First Run Features.

Hiroshima and Nagasaki: The Harvest of Nuclear War. 16 mm. Available from Peace Resource Center, Wilmington College, Wilmington, Ohio.

The Meaning of Survival. Hiroshima's 36 Year Commitment to Peace. Photographs and text edited and published by the Chugoku Shimbun and the Hiroshima International Cultural Foundation. Hiroshima, 1983.

Japan Broadcasting Corporation (NHK), World Friendship Center in Hiroshima. *Unforgettable Fire: Pictures Drawn by Atomic Bomb Survivors*. Supervised by Howard Schonberger. Translated by Leona Row. New York: Pantheon, 1977.

Selected Studies

Alperovitz, Gar. *Atomic Diplomacy: Hiroshima and Potsdam*. New York: Simon and Schuster, 1965. (1985 edition with a new introduction.)

Braw, Monica. *The Atomic Bomb Suppressed. American Censorship in Japan 1945-1949*. Lund Studies in International History 23. Lund, Sweden: University of Lund.

Burchett, Wilfred. *Shadows of Hiroshima*. London: Verso, 1983.

Committee for the Compilation of Materials on Damage Caused by the Atomic Bombs in Hiroshima and Nagasaki. *Hiroshima and Nagasaki. The Physical, Medical, and Social Effects of the Atomic Bombings*. Translated by Ishikawa Eisei and David Swain. New York: Basic Books, 1981. (An updated and abridged edition of this work is *The Impact of the A-Bomb. Hiroshima and Nagasaki, 1945-1985*. Tokyo: Iwanami Shoten, 1985.)

Daniels, Gordon. "The Great Tokyo Air Raid, 9-10 March 1945." In *Modern Japan. Aspects of History, Literature and Society*. Edited by W. G. Beasley. London: George Allen & Unwin, 1975.

Dower, John. *War Without Mercy. Race and Power in the Pacific War.* New York: Pantheon, 1986.

Guillain, Robert. *I Saw Tokyo Burning. An Eyewitness Narrative from Pearl Harbor to Hiroshima.* Translated by William Byron. Garden City, N.Y.: Doubleday, 1981.

Lifton, Robert. *Death in Life. Survivors of Hiroshima.* New York: Random House, 1967.

Rhodes, Robert. *The Making of the Atomic Bomb.* New York: Simon and Schuster, 1986.

Schaffer, Ronald. *Wings of Judgment. American Bombing in World War II.* New York: Oxford University Press, 1985.

Sherry, Michael. *The Rise of American Air Power. The Creation of Armageddon.* New Haven: Yale University Press, 1987.

Sherwin, Martin. *A World Destroyed.* New York: Knopf, 1975.

U.S. Strategic Bomb Survey Reports, Pacific War. No. 3, *The Effects of Atomic Bombs on Hiroshima and Nagasaki*; no. 13, *The Effects of Atomic Bombs on Health and Medical Services in Hiroshima and Nagasaki*; no. 60, *The Effects of Air Attack on the City of Hiroshima*; no. 93, *The Effects of the Atomic Bomb on Hiroshima, Japan.* Washington, D.C.: Government Printing Office, 1945–1947.

Wyden, Peter. *Day One. Before Hiroshima and After.* New York: Simon and Schuster, 1984.

Libraries, Collections, and the Japanese Literature

Nihon no genbaku bungaku (Japan's atomic bomb literature). 15 vols. Tokyo: Harupu Shuppansha, 1983. The most extensive Japanese language collection of atomic bomb literature.

Wilmington College Hiroshima/Nagasaki Memorial Collection. Wilmington, Ohio. The preeminent collection of atomic bomb related materials in English and Japanese.

THE AUTHORS, PHOTOGRAPHERS, ARTISTS, AND THEIR WORK

Agawa Hiroyuki, "August 6" (Hachigatsu muika), 1947, in *Agawa Hiroyuki jisen sakuhin* (Agawa Hiroyuki: Self-selected works II). 10 vols. Tokyo: Shinchosha, 1977.

Agawa Hiroyuki was born in 1920 in Hiroshima. On graduating from Tokyo University in 1942, he was trained in the Naval Air Corps in Taiwan and worked in communications and intelligence in China. He returned to Hiroshima, where his parents had experienced the atomic bomb, in March 1946. Their reunion is recounted in his earliest work, "Nennen saisai" (Years and ages, 1946). "August 6," as Agawa notes in a postscript, combines the stories of friends and acquaintances who had experienced the bombing into the testimony of one family. Occupation censorship at the time was strict, but the story passed because, the author later observed, "it made no reference to the problems of aftereffect and contained no overt criticism of the U.S."

Ma no isan (Devil's Heritage, 1953), a documentary novel, is a fuller account of the bombing through the eyes of a young Tokyo reporter, handling, among other topics, the death of his Hiroshima nephew and survivors' reactions to the Atomic Bomb Casualty Commission, the U.S. agency that conducted research on atomic victims. It was translated into English in 1957 by John F. Maki, as well as into Chinese. Agawa wrote about his experiences as a student soldier in *Haru no shiro* (Spring castle, 1952, Yomiuri Literary Prize) and *Kurai hato* (Dark waves, 1974). His other major works include *Kumo no bohyo* (Grave markers in the clouds, 1955), *Gunkan Nagato no shogai* (The life of the warship *Nagato*, 1975), and three biographical novels, *Yamamoto Isoroku* (1965), *Yonai Mitsumasa* (1978), and *Inoue Seibi* (1986). Agawa has also written many travelogues.

Hayashi Kyoko, "Two Gravemarkers" (Futari no bohyo), in *Matsuri no ba* (Ritual of death). Tokyo: Kodansha, 1976.

Hayashi Kyoko was born in Nagasaki in 1930 and spent most of her childhood in Shanghai. She returned to Nagasaki in March 1945 and enrolled in Nagasaki Girls' High School. She experienced the bomb at a munitions plant in Nagasaki where students were mobilized to work. Seriously ill for two months, she subsequently suffered from fragile health. Hayashi attended the nursing section of the Welfare Faculty for Women affiliated with Nagasaki Medical School, but she left before graduation. She started to write in 1962. In 1975 her autobiographical story about her experience of the bombing, "Ritual of Death" (Matsuri no ba, *Gunzo*, June 1975; translated by Kyoko Selden in *Japan Interpreter*, 1978; *Nuke Rebuke*, 1984), received Bungei Shunju's Akutagawa Prize. "Futari no bohyo" ("Two Grave Markers," *Bulletin of Concerned Asian Scholars*, vol. 18, 1986) appeared in the same year. Hayashi's works in the seventies include a short story, "Nanjamonja no men" (Mask of whatchamacallit, *Gunzo*, February 1976), and a sequence of twelve short stories titled *Gyaman bidoro* (Cut glass, blown glass, 1978). All but the fifth story in that collection, "Kosa" ("Yellow Sand," translated in *Stories by Contemporary Japanese Women Writers*, edited and translated by Noriko Mizuta Lippit and Kyoko Selden, 1982), which handles the author's experience in Shanghai, are related to the bombing. One story, "The Empty Can," was translated by Margaret Mitsutani in *The Crazy Iris and Other Stories of the Atomic Aftermath* (edited by Oe Kenzaburo, 1985).

Hayashi's first full-length novel, *Naki ga gotoki* (As if nothing had happened, 1981) introduces a survivor who was brought up in China and who wishes to become a "chronicler of August 9." Her wartime Shanghai and Nagasaki experiences are the primary sources of her writing.

Missheru no kuchibeni (The Michelle lipstick, 1980) is a collection of short stories about wartime Shanghai, and *Shanghai* (1983, Women Writers' Award) is a travelogue based on her return to Shanghai after forty years. The Nagasaki theme continues in her two most recent collections, the Kawabata Prize-winning *Sangai no ie* (Home in the three worlds, 1984) and *Michi* (The path, 1985). Hayashi lived near Washington, D.C., from 1985 to 1988, and her *Tanima* (The valley, 1988) includes stories written during her stay in the United States.

Ota Yoko, "Residues of Squalor" (Zanshu tenten, 1947), in *Nihon gendai bungaku* (Modern Japanese literature). Vol. 2. Tokyo: Kodansha, 1969.

Ota Yoko (1906–1963) was born as Fukuda Hatsuko in Hiroshima City. Her parents divorced when she was seven, and she was adopted by the Fukuda family. Three years later her mother remarried, taking her to a new home. Ota early developed an interest in literature. After graduating from a girls' school, she taught sewing at an elementary school and took various secretarial jobs, moving frequently among Tokyo, Osaka, and Hiroshima. She started to write serious fiction around 1929. After experiencing the bomb in Hiroshima, she concentrated on writing about the bombing. In the fall of 1945 she wrote *Shikabane no machi* (The town of corpses, translated by Richard Minear, 1989). The novel was censored and finally published three years later with portions deleted. This was followed by *Ningen ranru* (Human tatters, 1951, Female Authors' Prize) and *Yunagi no machi to hito* (The city of the evening calm and its people, 1954). "Han-ningen" (Half human, 1954, Peace Culture Award) portrays the struggle with mental illness of an author threatened by radiation disease and fears of an impending world war. The four-volume *Ota Yoko shu* (Collected works of Ota Yoko), edited by Sata Ineko et al., was published posthumously in 1981. Her *Ruri no kishi* (The shore of a wandering journey) was made into a movie in 1956.

Nakayama Shiro, "Stone's Sleep" (Ishi no nemuri), in *Shi no kage* (Shadow of death). Tokyo: Nanbokusha, 1968.

Nakayama Shiro was born in Hiroshima in 1926 and experienced the bombing as a third-year student in the Hiroshima First Middle School. In 1953 he graduated from the Russian literature department of Waseda University. "Stone's Sleep" is from his first anthology of short stories. All the stories in this and two other collections, *Shomuto* (Fog light, 1974) and *Ujina sanbashi* (Ujina pier, 1975), are related to the Hiroshima bombing. *Ten no hitsuji* (Heavenly sheep, 1982) is a documentary on Syed Omar, a Malaysian student who was attending Hiroshima University of Science and Technology at the time of the bombing and who died in Kyoto in early September of 1945. This is the first atomic bomb story focusing on the eight Southeast Asian students studying in Hiroshima at the time of the bombing. They were among some two hundred "special overseas students from the south" who came to Japan between 1943 and 1944.

Poems by Atomic Bomb Survivors: Selections from *Nihon genbaku shishu* (Anthology of Japanese atomic bomb poems). Tokyo: Taihei Shuppansha, 1970; tenth printing, 1978.

This anthology contains 219 pieces edited with commentaries by Professor Ohara Miyao, playwright Kinoshita Junji, and novelist Hotta Yoshie. The selections represent "poems of atomic bomb victims, including elementary school children and wives who live quietly in corners of the city without raising their voices, along with works by some professional poets." The anthology claims to be the first to bring together poems from both Hiroshima and Nagasaki. It is divided thematically into four parts: "The Flash of Light," "Requiem," "Rivers of Hiroshima; the Sky Over Urakami," and "The

Nuclear Era: Future Landscapes.'' The pieces translated here are chosen on the basis of poetic eloquence and poignance rather than balance in themes, authors, or areas. Written over a dozen years between 1952 and 1966, they depict moments of fortitude, compassion, acceptance, protest, and, in particular, wails for lost children.

Tanka and Haiku

Tanka and haiku are traditional short poems, usually in one line and without punctuation. In principle tanka have thirty-one syllables in 5/7/5/7/7 units, and haiku have seventeen syllables in 5/7/5 units. The translation does not follow the syllable count. Wherever possible it does honor the original punctuation and line division, occasionally adding commas and extra spaces for clarity. Haiku are translated in one line; tanka are rendered in two lines, breaking the line at a light caesura which normally occurs after the first twelve or seventeen syllables. A few selections are preceded by a title or brief introduction, such as ''A-bomb anniversary lantern floating,'' a common practice in Japanese poetic tradition. These are omitted in the translation except in the separate free verse haiku sequence by Matsuo Atsuyuki.

The poems were selected from major anthologies contained in the fifteen-volume *Nippon no genbaku bungaku* (Japan's atomic bomb literature, vol. 13, 1983), and from Matsuo Atsuyuki's *Genbaku kusho* (Selections of haiku on the atomic bomb, 1975).

Genbaku kashu Hiroshima (Hiroshima atomic bomb tanka anthology, 1954) is a compilation of tanka chosen in a public competition by fifteen Hiroshima poets. Two hundred and seven people submitted some 6,500 poems, of which 1,753 poems by 220 mostly anonymous poets were chosen.

Genbaku kashu Nagasaki (Nagasaki atomic bomb tanka anthology) was edited by Okamoto Yoshiro and published with the assistance of the Nagasaki Tanka Poets' Association in 1967.

Kushu Hiroshima (Hiroshima haiku anthology, edited by the Hiroshima Haiku Association, 1969) collects 2,657 haiku edited by Toyonaga Keizaburo, a member of The Citizens' Association for Helping Korean A-Bomb Survivors. Another Hiroshima anthology represented here is *Kinoko-gumo* (Mushroom cloud, 1956), edited by Moriwaki Yukari and others. This collects *senryu*, vernacular haiku that emphasize wit and satire. Two selections from this anthology are placed at the end of "Haiku from Hiroshima."

Kushu Nagasaki (Nagasaki haiku anthology) was published in 1955. It collects 2,200 poems by 725 people, arranged according to three categories: "Before the War," "At the Time of the Bombing," and "After the War." The Nagasaki Atomic Bomb Anniversary Haiku Competition is annually sponsored by the Nagasaki Haiku Association. The selections included here are from Nippon no genbaku bungaku (Japan's atomic bomb literature). They are dated 1954–1980.

From Matsuo Atsuyuki's Genbaku kusho (Selections from haiku on the atomic bomb, 1975), the entire sequence under "1945" is translated here. Two of the author's children, age four and one, died of the bombing, followed by his first-born son, a first-year middle school student. His wife died soon afterward, and he was left with his first daughter, who was ill for many years. Matsuo's haiku, censored during the occupation, were first published in 1955.

Many of these brief poems are about fire, burns, keloids, charred bodies of the dead, loss of close relatives (especially of children), bonfires for burning the bodies, orphans, or radiation illness. A tanka introduces a mother who daily sets the table including a place for her lost child. After a month she still hopes for his return and, pretending that he is still alive, follows the custom of providing food for a family member who is away so that he won't be hungry. In one haiku a mother momentarily mistakes another child for her dead daughter. This daughter had composed a haiku in which she misses a dead boy, perhaps her little brother, who used to catch cicadas.

One key theme is the heat. Survivors recall the scorching sun on burns and the craving of wounded and dying people for water. When the atomic bomb anniversary approaches, one poet fills a container with water so that returning souls of the dead will not thirst. Another refers to the fully sprinkled Urakami streets near the great cathedral of Nagasaki for people to walk on. Traditionally in midsummer water is poured for coolness over the yard, near the gate, and on alleys. Amply watered on the A-bomb anniversary, the cool streets are ready for passers by or for the thirsting souls of the dead.

A Hiroshima haiku tells of an American jeep from the Atomic Bomb Casualty Commission coming to ask for the body for autopsy the moment a family member died. Readers of such memoirs as those by Tada Makiko and Ishii Ichiro (included in this volume) as well as of Agawa Hiroyuki's *Devil's Heritage* will recall citizens' diverse reactions to the ABCC.

Christianity was brought to Nagasaki by the Portuguese in the late sixteenth century. It was soon banned by the Edo Shogunate, but, despite persecution, many Nagasaki Christians preserved their faith underground until the ban was lifted in the Meiji period. Many Nagasaki poems, including a haiku that refers to this tradition of secret faith, present Christian themes, as do some of the children's stories from an Urakami elementary school (selections contained in this volume).

One last thing to note is the use of insect images. The dead are associated with flies, fireflies, cicadas, and dragonflies. In addition to the nightmare memory of flies swarming on the dying and the dead, those insects have seasonal associations with the bombing that took place in the summer. The whispering sound of flies' wings, the lights of fireflies, the cries of cicadas, and swarming dragonflies all suggest the ghosts of the dead. Behind these poetic images is the Buddhist belief in reincarnation. Because of the metamorphosis they go through, insects have traditionally suggested rebirth. Thus, a haiku hears dead children's sobs in cicadas' cries. In one haiku dragonflies also suggest Japan, whose poetic name, Akizu-shima, according to tradition meant "the land of dragonflies."

The short poems chosen here represent the voices of citizens, including some who had never previously composed poems, rather than the works of professional poets.

Domon Ken, "The Boy Who Was a Fetus: The Death of Kajiyama Kenji," in *Hiroshima*. Tokyo: Asahi Shinbunsha, 1958.

Domon Ken was born in Yamagata prefecture in 1909. He entered the law department of Nihon University in 1929 but quit before graduation. After working briefly in various photographic ateliers, in 1935 he went to work for the English-language photo magazine *Nippon*. In 1939 he became a photographer for the Society for the Promotion of International Cultural Relations (Kokusai Bunka Shinkokai). His work then focused on traditional arts. Domon photographed Muroo-ji, a Nara temple, then turned his attention to the bunraku puppet theatre. This work bore fruition after the war in the form of *Muroo-ji* (1954, Mainichi Shuppan Bunka Prize) and *Bunraku* (1972). His interest in traditional art culminated in Koji junrei (Pilgrimage to old temples, 5 series, 1963–1975, 1971 Kikuchi Kan Award).

In approaching contemporary subjects, Domon applied techniques of socialist realism to photography. His 1958 photo essay *Hiroshima* (Mainichi Photography Award, Association of Japanese Photographic Critics Award) stirred much response. In 1960 he criticized the situation in Japan's declining coal industry with a hundred-yen album printed on coarse paper, *Chikuho no kodomotachi* (Children of Chikuho mining town), the recipient of the Mainichi Art Award.

He is also a celebrated essayist. A two-volume work, *Shinu koto to ikiru koto* (Dying and living), was published in 1973. *Domon Ken zenshu* (Complete works of Domon Ken, 10 vols.) was published in 1985.

When Domon first went to Hiroshima in July 1957 to photograph for *Shincho Weekly*, he had no deeper interest than as a journalist. He returned to Hiroshima many times, however, "driven by something like a mission for a man who handled a camera." Domon came to the realization that Hiroshima, which he had thought of as a tragedy out of the past, lived on in the form of keloids, leukemia, brain injury, blindness, emotional scars, and death. Besides "The Boy Who Was a Fetus," *Hiroshima* includes realistic photographs of patients at the Hiroshima Atomic Bomb Hospital, some undergoing operations; brain-injured and blind children; people bed-ridden for thirteen years; and a happily married couple, both survivors with keloids, with a healthy toddler. Each set of photographs is accompanied by a documentary essay.

Citizens' Memoirs from *Genbaku ni ikiru* (Living with the atomic bomb), edited by the Atomic Bomb Memoirs Editing Committee. Tokyo: San'ichi Shobo, 1953, an anthology of twenty-seven stories by survivors, and from *Hibaku Kankokujin* (Korean hibakusha), edited by Pak Subok, Shing Yoongsu, and Kwak Kwaihun. Tokyo: Asahi Shinbunsha, 1975.

Among those exposed to the bombing were Koreans, Chinese, students from Southeast Asia, Americans of Japanese descent who returned to Japan for their education prior to the war, and American, British, Australian, Dutch and Indonesian POWs. These accounts detail the postbomb experiences of Japanese and Korean victims.

Children's Voices from Nagai Takashi, ed., *Genshigumo no shita ni ikite* (Living under the atomic cloud). Tokyo: Sanko Shuppansha, 1949.

The seven accounts of the Nagasaki atomic bombing have been selected from compositions by Yamazato Elementary and Junior High School students. The authors of these selections, written a few years after the war, were between four and ten years old at the time of the bombing.

Nagai Takashi (1908–1951), the editor, was a Catholic scientist and author. He was born in Matsue, Shimane prefecture, the son of a doctor. In 1928 Nagai entered the Nagasaki Medical College (now Nagasaki University), where he later taught radiology.

The city of Nagasaki is the historical center of Catholicism in Japan. In the late sixteenth and early seventeenth centuries, half of Japan's early Christians lived here, with Urakami as the center of Catholic life. When the Tokugawa government banned and persecuted Christianity, many Christians went underground. In Nagasaki, the faith survived these trials. At the time of the bombing, some ten thousand Catholics were said to be living in Urakami.

Nagai Takashi was baptized in 1934 prior to his marriage to a woman from a Catholic family. She was killed and their home was destroyed by the bombing. A number of Yamazato school children were also Catholics, as exemplified by the first and fourth accounts included here.

Nagai had contracted leukemia in the radiology laboratory before the bombing, but injuries from the bomb aggravated his condition. From his sickbed he directed rescue operations of the University Hospital, studied the effects of the bomb, and wrote several books. Among his best-known works are *Nagasaki no kane* (The Bells of Nagasaki, translated by William Johnston, 1984) and *Kono ko wo nokoshite* (Leaving these children). The former describes the Nagasaki atomic bombing as experienced by the author and his colleagues at the Nagasaki Medical College. The latter is a testament expressing his feelings for his two children, Makoto and Kayano, whom he knew he was to leave soon. Kayano is the author of the second memoir in these selections.

We of Nagasaki: The Story of Survivors in an Atomic Wasteland, written for English publication and translated by Ichiro Shirato and Hubert B. L. Silverman, 1951, contains the memoirs of five adults and three children, relatives and neighbors of the author, including his two children. Nagai's more technical writings, *Nagasaki Idai genshi bakudan kyugo hokoku* (Report of Nagasaki Medical College atomic bomb relief activities), were discovered in 1970. All these works are included in the *Nagai Takashi zenshu* (Complete works of Nagai Takashi, 1971).

Shoda Shinoe, "Reiko," in *Pikakko-chan*, edited by Kurihara Sadako and Koura Chihoko, illustrated by Nakano Hirotaka. Tokyo: Taihei Shuppansha, 1977.

Shoda Shinoe was born in Hiroshima in 1910. She graduated from Aki Girls' High School in 1928. In 1947, evading Occupation censorship, she secretly published *Sange* (Penitence), a tanka anthology. She continued to write poems, memoirs, and children's tales until her death from cancer in 1965. "Reiko," along with "Chanchako bachan" (Old woman in chanchako), was posthumously published in *Dokyumento Ninhonjin* (Document of the Japanese), vol. 8, edited by Tsurumi Shunsuke et al., 1969. *Pikakko-chan* contains seven stories, including "Reiko" and "Chanchako bachan."